"Too many of us have been taught that spirit is good. I am grateful for McBride... bring together both the spirit and the bo... her personal experience to show us how... teacher. *The Wisdom of Your Body* deftly draws from ancient and contemporary sources to emphasize that if we are connected to our bodies, we are connected not only to community but also to the Divine."

—**Richard Rohr, OFM**, Center for Action and Contemplation

"If you have ever felt disconnected from your body and wanted to find the way home to yourself, please read this book. McBride's insights are a gift to us—through tender stories and valuable expertise, we learn the importance of embodiment and what it means to be human. I believe this book can lead us all toward healing."

—**Kaitlin Curtice**, author of *Native: Identity, Belonging, and Rediscovering God*

"This book is a gift. A gift filled with wisdom and sound research all eloquently threaded together. This book is also a key for unlocking the unacknowledged mysteries and marvels of the human body and how it connects to everything. This will be a book you can't put down and one you come back to year after year as you relearn the wisdom of your body as it continues to change and grow."

—**Arielle Estoria**, poet, author, artist

"An essential read for any on the journey of spiritual, mental, or physical wellness. McBride's teaching and invitation to connect with the wisdom of our bodies changed my life."

—**Scott Erickson**, author of *Say Yes: Discover the Surprising Life beyond the Death of a Dream*

"Everyone who knows Hillary McBride falls in love with her. She has this magic in her personal life and clinical work that disarms you and suddenly, you're in love. But the deeper thing is that she gives you insights, keys, and practices to fall in love with yourself. And this is what she does in *The Wisdom of Your Body*. This book and its practices are what our society desperately needs because it creates lasting change at the heart of who we are."

—**Lisa Gungor**, musician, author, and co-conspirator of Sacred Feminine

"McBride holds the reader close with the fierce gentleness of a mother, just as she holds herself. All the while, her words wink at and dare each of us to say a resounding and resonant yes to our bodies—to their sacredness and to their salty, earthy goodness. I believe this work, this vulnerably and brilliantly written book, will create healing ripples in the world for years to come."

—**Audrey Assad**, artist, author, mother

"McBride has changed my life through her combination of powerful intelligence and extraordinary tenderness. This masterpiece will awaken us individually to reclaim the wonder, delight, and beauty of our bodies, and collectively to dismantle the systems that have told us otherwise. McBride presents hard science and mind-blowing facts in a compassionate voice that results in a can't-put-it-down companion for all who are seeking the confidence and self-love we know we're capable of. What a treasure!"

—**Mari Andrew**, author of *Am I There Yet?*

"McBride has written us a road map back home. Back into our bodies, which are our true home and our gateway to healing. Reading her words feels like a mixture of the most attentive, attuned doctor sharing deep wisdom and science, a parent expressing loving tenderness and care, and a treasured friend offering camaraderie and communion. McBride's words are a gift to the world."

—**Ruthie Lindsey**, speaker and author of *There I Am*

"No single leader has impacted my concept of healthy embodiment more than McBride. Her work fundamentally changed the way I talk about, think about, treat, and cherish my own body. Perhaps the best endorsement I can offer is that I gave a copy to each of my daughters. We will be talking about McBride's work for decades."

—**Jen Hatmaker**, *New York Times* bestselling author of *Fierce, Free, and Full of Fire* and *Of Mess and Moxie*; host of the *For the Love* podcast

"Wise, political, powerful, and deeply healing. Hillary is such a worthy guide, the kind you can trust in the most dangerous wildernesses of your body and soul and mind. I could not be more grateful for this book."

—**Sarah Bessey**, author of *Jesus Feminist*, editor of the *New York Times* bestseller *A Rhythm of Prayer*

"As a gay man raised evangelical, I was quick to despise my body and learned to float above it. This book is the indispensable tool I've been looking for. My soul and my body shout: Required reading!"

—**Jedidiah Jenkins**, *New York Times* bestselling author of *Like Streams to the Ocean* and *To Shake the Sleeping Self*

THE WISDOM OF YOUR BODY

Finding HEALING, WHOLENESS, *and* CONNECTION *through* EMBODIED LIVING

HILLARY L. McBRIDE, PhD

Brazos Press

a division of Baker Publishing Group
Grand Rapids, Michigan

Published by Brazos Press
a division of Baker Publishing Group
PO Box 6287, Grand Rapids, MI 49516-6287
www.brazospress.com

Printed in the United States of America

Library of Congress Cataloging-in-Publication Data
Names: McBride, Hillary L., author.
Title: The wisdom of your body : finding healing, wholeness, and connection through embodied living / Hillary L. McBride, PhD.
Description: Grand Rapids, Michigan : Brazos Press, a division of Baker Publishing Group, 2021.
Identifiers: LCCN 2021006695 | ISBN 9781587435522 (paperback) | ISBN 9781587435539 (casebound) | ISBN 9781493433896 (ebook)
Subjects: LCSH: Health. | Mind and body therapies. | Medicine, Preventive.
Classification: LCC RA776 .M1168 2021 | DDC 613—dc23

LC record available at https://lccn.loc.gov/2021006695

Author is represented by The Christopher Ferebee Agency, www.christopherferebee .com.

Some names and details have been changed to protect the privacy of the individuals involved.

Baker Publishing Group publications use paper produced from sustainable forestry practices and post-consumer waste whenever possible.

23   24   25   26   27   7   6   5   4

For anyone who was ever told, shown, or made to believe
that your body is anything other than sacred and wise

Contents

An Invitation to Begin

I have a childhood memory that shimmers. It is late summer, and I am out riding bikes with my best friend. We are pedaling as fast as we can down a long stretch of even pavement with ditches on either side that separate the road from the surrounding farmland. To our right, a heron. It stands there immobile and patient, the picture of waiting. To our left, rows of raspberry bushes go on and on until they dissolve into the horizon. The sun is sinking and, as instructed, we will soon be home for dinner—something cooking on the grill, new potato salad, and the front door open to keep the air moving through the house. But until then, we rule the road: sweat and summer sun on sticky necks, part laughing, part squealing with delight, panting breaths as we pedal hard and fast. In this moment, with my bodily senses turned all the way up, I am totally alive.

When I think about being human, the fragile, precious, and mysterious journey we each take from birth to death, I think about the body. The body is the place where all of this happens. We know that when we are young. As babies, we reach out to touch our own feet or stare at the face of a parent, and we know how to take it all in. We learn to walk, and then to run, realizing

1

our bodies can take us somewhere fast—and create an instant game of chase with someone who loves us. We learn to use one part of our body to care for another part of our body: a hand holds a toothbrush to clean our mouths, wields a hairbrush to arrange the hair on our head, or rubs soap into our skin under running water. We learn our bodies can shape the world around us as we jump in puddles and feel we are all-powerful. The delight of it all moves up and out through our lips as we giggle and laugh, telling the world around us through waves of sound that our body knows joy. All of that happens through the mystery of being a body.

Yet so many of us have forgotten about this mystery. For some of us, that forgetting is intentional and swift. We notice things that feel distracting, overwhelming, or inconvenient, and we want them to stop; or someone else tells us that the knowing knot of fear in the pit of our stomach is wrong and we need to make it go away. For others, the forgetting happens slowly over time. It accumulates in receiving disapproving looks from others, sitting still in long work or school meetings, being told to put "mind over matter," or pushing the novelty and mystery of physical sensation into the furthest corners of our awareness. Or we have a defining experience where the bottom drops out and the voices in our head make pronouncements: *Your body is bad*, or *Your body made this happen*, or *You cannot trust yourself*. So we make silent vows to lock away the dangerous parts of us and label them "not me."

No matter how or why we get there, no matter how well it may have served us, forgetting the body also costs us something—individually and collectively. We lose the fundamental building blocks of human thriving, connection to ourselves and others, and the fullness of pleasure, wisdom, empathy, and justice. Connection to our bodily selves allows us to internalize a sense of safety and connection that tells us who we are, what we long for, and how to be most fully alive. If each one of us is a body, then the body is the constant invitation to see ourselves as connected to each other. The person you come to see as your hero or your enemy took a breath right now, just as you did. Regardless of our circumstances or what we have been told about bodies, remembering and reuniting with our bodily selves is a radical act to undo our need to earn our worth, helping us wake up to the fact that there is something sacred right here, in this moment, always present and always available. That connection to our bodily selves is available to us in every moment. We have always been embodied, but sometimes we need a gentle invitation to remember that. We need to encounter our physicality and to know that this breath, these hands, these lungs and eyes and cerebrospinal fluid, this body is good. Consider this your invitation.

Some of what you read on these pages might feel familiar in a bodily way, as if I am putting words to things you already know. Or it might seem disorienting or incongruent with ideas you have held or have been instructed to hold. As you read, I invite you to be curious, to see every reaction as a doorway to knowing yourself better. Know that your body will be communicating, sending messages, like a quickened heartbeat, a jolt of tension, a long exhale. Please listen—these sensations are initiating a conversation with your thinking brain. Allow yourself to be curious about what that communication might mean for you or what it tells you about your past. This thoughtful engagement with bodily sensation is a form of integration essential for wholeness and healing.

Then keep the conversation going by talking to others. The end of each chapter includes some things to think about and some things to try. Use these prompts to take the content off the page and put it into conversational spaces. Whether you have a formal discussion in a book club or a casual one with a friend, please talk with people in your life about what you are reading (making the choice to share more vulnerable things with the trustworthy people). Just by doing so, you are inviting the people around you into more awareness, integrating your own learning more deeply, and changing how we talk about bodies culturally. As you will learn throughout the book, doing so is good for our individual well-being and the health of our community.

A note on the stories in this book. All the stories are real, but sometimes the names have been changed at the request of the person whose story is being told. When using an alias, I also changed or left out details to protect anonymity. I have also honored each person's choice of personal pronouns, which includes using the pronouns "they," "he," and/or "she." All stories are used with permission.

This book speaks to issues predominant in a Western culture, a context that in different ways and at different times has both afforded me social power and restricted it because of my body. I am in an ongoing process of trying to better see the harmful ways I have been shaped by and perpetuated the dominant culture's problematic stories about bodies. Although the writing of a book must end, my personal learning will not, and for that I am grateful.

I also anticipate that our collective thinking about the body from a biological, philosophical, and sociopolitical perspective will continue to develop. In the future we will know more than we do now. I hope that knowing more will help us create a more just and loving world. In whatever ways you can, please take these ideas as a jumping-off point for you to keep learning, thinking, and experiencing yourself as a body in new, more connected, free, and compassionate ways.

Theresa Silow, a professor of somatic psychology, has said, "The body is not a thing we have, but an experience we are."[1] May this book be an invitation into an even deeper experience of who you are, and may you encounter that experience as sacred, connected, and loved.

1

Fully Alive

Exploring and Understanding Embodiment

I was thirteen the first time I threw up on purpose. I hid in the back of a dark bathroom, just beyond the reach of a buzzing fluorescent light that hung above and to the left of the bathroom stall. I was there with my eating disorder, and together we were beginning what would be a very quick descent into an even darker place—the complete eradication of myself through the disappearance of my body. Physically, parts of my body would shrink away as I became small. My freedom to think about the world outside the narrow container of my fragile mind would evaporate. My voice, both my inner knowing and the vocal sound a body makes, and my ability to want or desire anything would vanish. Soon, I would chip away the parts of myself I knew, like picking flecks of blistered paint off a wall, revealing what had once been there only by its absence.

The room began to swirl as stars shot like fireworks across my vision. I slid down against the bathroom stall until I was half lying and half sitting. I tried to catch my breath as beads of moisture formed in protest across the back of my neck, the sensation a voice begging me to stop. My body softly whispered the objection: *Why would you hurt me like this?*

Choosing to Be Fully Alive

That dark moment in a bathroom stall happened almost twenty years ago. Today, I am someone people consider an expert about how we relate to our bodies and what gets in the way of that. Although I have been doing this work for some time—through the academic perils of a master's degree, a PhD, and ongoing clinical training and research projects—I am far from having all the answers, as if that were a thing that could happen. But I am fascinated by the questions, struggles, and delights of what it means to be human—to *be* a body in this time and place. The deeper I dive, the clearer it becomes: being fully connected to the body is about being fully alive.

For some of us, the complexity and richness of being fully alive is difficult and we struggle to consent to all it holds: loss, grief, pain, aloneness, illness, the pangs of hunger or fullness, the grip of fear, and the finality of death. In fact, we may even be trying to avoid feeling these things at all costs. But in the process, we also lose access to the beautiful things that come with being fully alive in our bodies: pleasure, joy, energy, connection, sensuality, self-expression, creativity, being held, and savoring the sun's warmth. We can't avoid the painful things we experience through our bodies without sacrificing the good, the beautiful, the rich.

But we did not find our way to a disembodied existence on our own: we had centuries of help. Western philosophical influences like Gnosticism, the Greek thinker Plato, and later Descartes (whose theories influenced the development of the Enlightenment) all had a significant influence on widespread religious, philosophical, and cultural thought. They influenced a popular line of thinking that went something like this: the soul and the mind are distinct from the body. Although the church originally condemned Gnosticism as a heresy, the church was not (and still is not) immune to a Gnostic worldview, which at its worst suggested that matter was evil, the spirit and body were distinct, and we needed to escape this world to find salvation. Plato, Descartes, and Gnosticism suggested that the body has needs and limitations but that truth exists in the mind. The goal is to leave the body, rising above it to find that our being now exists in a space not weighed down by the realness of flesh and blood and pain and death and desire.

You might have even heard this idea as an encouragement from someone: mind over body or as it's often said, "Mind over matter." Over time, this line of thinking became the foundation of our common discourse. Through our language and thought, we have carried on this disconnection. We say, "My body won't let me . . ." or "I can't believe *it* won't . . ." without realizing our language tells on us, revealing a problematic narrative woven into our cultural fabric. Still, none of it fully removes us from this essential truth: we *are* our bodies.

The body is central to our experiences, to our sense of ourselves, to our autobiographical narratives. The body is the only way we have to move through life. Yet research about body dissatisfaction and body hatred shows us that the majority of us—up to 90 percent of those of us in Western culture and in communities touched by globalization, inclusive of women and men—loathe our bodies.[1] Numbers this high and this pervasive among both men and women have led researchers to characterize the Western relationship with the body as "normative discontent," so normal we can forget there is any other way to relate to our bodies individually and culturally.[2] We've been taught to see our bodies as objects, as appearances to evaluate. And we get frustrated that our bodies are different from what

7

we've been told they should be: not white enough, able enough, straight enough, male enough, old enough, young enough, thin enough, muscular enough, not ever quite enough. The list of not-enoughs is endless—and costly. It's a form of hand-me-down shame that robs us of time, money, opportunity, and energy. But ultimately what body hatred costs us—individually and collectively—is the fullness of life. We lose out on the goodness that comes through our body. And if we are our body, we miss out on experiencing our own goodness and the presence and wisdom that comes from deep connection to ourselves. We also lose out on connection with others: the quality of touch offered to soothe a wound, kissing someone who makes our body feel electric, or celebrating how breasts can nourish and nurture a baby. There is so much goodness within and between us because of our bodies, the bodies we spend so much time trying to get away from, control, or blame.

Becoming Embodied

By the time I started seeing Liz, my therapist, I had been sick for a long time. She was my last-ditch effort for recovery from an eating disorder that was stubborn, life-threatening, and eroding all the most beautiful parts of my life. The experts had given all sorts of names to my behavior and the way I was feeling: bulimia nervosa, anorexia nervosa, OCD, depression, and anxiety to start. Those names quickly became my names, indistinguishable from my sense of self.

It was several years after the first time I purged, and my family had tried everything they could to help me get well. But I wasn't really "there" for most of it. I was riding a pain-escape merry-go-round and not reflecting much on it. Thinking back now, it seemed as though *I* did not exist anymore; in my place was a desperate, defensive, and hollow version of me—half a life.

8

I believed that Liz really saw me. Unlike the medical experts, who saw a set of symptoms or an eroding body, Liz saw *me*. She saw me as separate from the pathology of the eating disorder—that "I" was not "it"—in a way that I was not able to do for myself. She never once asked me what I weighed. We talked about the forces that shape how so many people feel about their bodies—existentialism, feminism, colonization, the sociocultural framework, and more. We drummed together. She described the joy she felt in her short, soft, and round body as she was aging, and sometimes we watched TED Talks on her small office computer. She called me a "philosopher queen," and when she looked me in the eye, her gaze said, "I know there is more to you than this."

She cupped her hands around the remnant flame of spirit inside me, protecting the flickering light until it grew stronger, and then placed my own hands around the flame and made me the protector of this growing force. Unlike the early stages of the eating disorder—which felt like a toxic love affair with a violent and abusive lover who also sometimes brought me security and generous gifts—therapy felt like a slow climb out of a hellish pit of madness and darkness so vast it was impossible to imagine any other way of being.

I had been seeing Liz for about three years and had just returned from my first trip to Europe. I felt a rush of excitement as I sat down in the corner chair—I couldn't wait to tell her about climbing a volcano in Greece, jumping off the front of a huge ship into the Mediterranean, and an adventurous train ride through Bavaria. I expected her to ask me more questions about my trip and about how my eating had been while I was away, but she didn't say much at all. When the conversation paused, she smiled, her eyes alive with spark and spice. "Do you notice how you're sitting in the chair today?" she asked.

Silence.

Once more, "Do you notice how you're sitting in the chair today?"

Silence, again. Her words reached my ears but didn't mean anything. I was unsure how to answer because until this point in my adult life, I had never actually been aware of my body from the inside. I was a floating head. Most of the time, it seemed like nothing existed from my jawline down. If something bodily did exist, I only knew how to scrutinize it as if detached, and from the outside.

"Do you know how you used to sit when we first met?" she asked.

I slowly shook my head. "How did I sit when we first met?"

"You used to sit like this," she said, and pulled her knees up to her chest, wrapped her arms around her legs, and rested her head on her knees with her gaze turned away. I saw her curled up in a ball and for the first time saw myself from the outside. Seeing this normally unapologetic and fierce woman looking so small in the chair shifted something in me. I felt grief and compassion for the version of me who had to be so tucked away, who had tried so hard to disappear that she had literally taken up as little space as possible.

"It is so good to see you taking up more space," she said. "I can see from how you are sitting that your relationship with your body is healing. You're not hiding as much. What you do with your body says so much about what is happening inside of you, and how it is to be you."

This conversation felt like a flipped switch—an epiphany. The only way to describe it is that my consciousness, my sense of myself as a person, was stuffed into my skull, like a balloon pinched at my neck. The fingers of patriarchy, pain, avoidance, sorrow, and objectification were firm around my neck, the base of the balloon. Liz's question pried the fingers off the balloon, and my sense of self started flowing into all the parts of me. The awareness was sudden and all-encompassing: it moved down my neck and shoulders, into my arms and out to my fingertips. It filled my torso and pelvis and sit bones, and it poured down into my legs and ankles and feet. I became aware of how I was filling the chair—sitting cross-legged, palms open and resting on the arms of the chair, my chest open, and my face up and looking squarely at her. For the first time in years, I was fully present—body and mind together in a lingering awareness that spread throughout my form.

I also noticed something else: this awareness and presence felt *right. It was rich and safe.*

How did I arrive here? I thought, full of wonder. All this happened in real time, in what for her was a few moments of silence but for me felt eternal, as if I'd lived all the lifetimes ever lived in a single moment.

Does my left foot always feel like it's going to fall asleep when it's tucked under the back of my right leg?

Have I ever felt myself while sitting in a chair before, filling the chair, arms and fingers even draped over the sides?

How is Liz sitting? Plump body also filling the chair, but differently—her knees bent with feet on the floor, shorter, and sitting back—less upright than myself, more relaxed. Her demeanor is gentle but direct, like she's commanding a ship. And I got all of that just by looking at how she was sitting.

The ways I had been protecting myself from pain were starting to fall away. I didn't need them anymore. I began to realize that I would always be my body, but the way I experienced my body could evolve—and that evolution could be deeply good.

We all have moments in our lives when we realize how much has changed. We see a current photo next to a childhood photo and are struck by the transformation. This experience was like that. And it woke me up to a whole new dimension of existence. Suddenly, I was more in the room, more of myself than maybe I'd ever been, fully present with myself and with Liz.

I left her office that day a different person. However, it wasn't until several years later that I found the name for what had happened that day: *embodiment.*

Understanding Embodiment

There is no unified definition of embodiment, but we often hear of it when people are talking about a quality or idea being lived out. Someone will say that a leader embodies the style of leadership that they talk about. But here I'm using the word to describe something broader than that: the experience of being a body in a social context.

I began learning about embodiment through my research and clinical work with body image. I focused on eating-disorder prevention, specifically what it looks like when women love their bodies. A big chunk of eating-disorder prevention and body-love work centers on body image: the idea that we hold in our minds an image of what our body looks like. And generally, we have feelings about that image. We evaluate our body based on what we've been told is good, or not so good, when it comes to that image. It's great to have a positive mental representation of the body, but this is not the same thing as embodiment. It's like finding a beautifully wrapped present on the table at a birthday celebration but never opening the box to experience the wonderful something inside waiting to be enjoyed, received.

I have sat with women, men, and nonbinary folks who thought that changing their body image—specifically, their thoughts about their body—would help them have a healthier relationship with their body. So they tried to beat a new perspective into their perception. It often sounded like this: "If I just notice hurtful thoughts about my body and change them, then I'll feel better about myself." Or, "Every time I think, 'I hate the way I look,' I'll try to substitute it quickly with a positive thought. Then, over time, that will become my new thought, right?"

Inevitably, they end up tired and frustrated. We might want our negative thoughts to disappear, but we can't get rid of them with thought substitution alone. After all, that does not identify where those thoughts come from in the first place. As proverbial wisdom reminds us, we cannot solve a problem with the same level of consciousness that created it. Thoughts are like blossoms on a flower—there's a stem and then a whole root system beneath them. Thought substitution alone is like plucking off a dandelion bloom, glue-gunning a daffodil blossom on the stem, and expecting daffodils to keep blooming. In this case, lasting change requires digging up the roots of one flower and planting a new bulb to grow the other. These new bulbs are embodied experiences; the soil is the context that supports our blooming.

The neuroscience of healing has proven to be true time and time again. Change does not happen through trying to trick ourselves out of a story we have been groomed to rehearse through our developing years. Rather, transformation happens from the ground up: when we have a new experience of ourselves and hold our attention on it long enough for it to sink in.

Learning embodiment—how to be in our bodies in a way that protects us from body shame—requires more than just thinking differently about our appearance. It requires curiosity, attention, sensation, and acceptance, which then allows us to develop a healthier and more stable relationship with our body as a whole. This relationship with our body includes our appearance but also requires relearning how to experience the body from the inside out. Being in our body gives us access to all the wisdom that our bodies hold. This allows us to know ourselves more fully, experiencing ourselves as good and sacred, and hold safety within ourselves no matter what happens around us.

Embodiment is a way to heal the mind-body divide we experience within ourselves and, more systemically, within Western cultures. To do so we need to understand the self *as a body*. Our body and our personhood are so intimately connected that they can never be separated. We are not just

13

a mind, or brain, carried around by a meat-puppet of flesh and bones. Embodiment is a kind of re-membering of who we really are, because what we picked up along the way was *dis*embodiment. But disembodiment is not how we come into the world. It can be unlearned, while embodiment, our birthright, can be remembered. So embodiment is a coming home, a remembering of our wholeness, and a reunion with the fullness of ourselves.

Embodiment coach and author Philip Shepherd says it like this: "If you are divided from your body, you are also divided from the body of the world—which then appears to be other than you, or separate from you, rather than the living continuum to which you belong."[3] Experiencing this connection between our mind and body has profoundly significant political, relational, philosophical, ecological, and spiritual implications. It changes everything about how we experience ourselves and others, drawing us into deeper wisdom and often providing us with insight that a fragmented way of being could not produce.

Two Ways of Thinking about the Body

In Western cultures, we're taught to think about the body through the lens of possession: *having a body*. This suggests that your body belongs to you in the same way your phone or your car belongs to you. We hear this way of thinking in our speech: "I just can't get my body to do what I want it to," "My body isn't cooperating with me," or after achieving something, "My body really showed up for me today." The assumption is that I, or the self, is distinct from yet contained within the body—and maybe even unwillingly trapped there. As the thinking goes, if only we could be free of this physical form, then we could truly be free. It's the belief that there is a self that has a will and that the body may or may not choose to cooperate with that will. *It* may have an agenda or way of being of its own. A philosopher named Maurice Merleau-Ponty gave us the paradigm for this way of thinking: *body as object.* The body is a thing.

But there is another way of thinking about the body. In this way of thinking, the body is not something you have but something you are: you *are* your body. Although we have all experienced being a body at some point, for many adults it can feel foreign or even impossible. Try repeating after me: I am my body. How does it feel to say it that way? Your body is alive, conscious, and indistinguishable from your *self*—the two cannot be disentangled. From this perspective, the mind is the body and the body is the mind. Merleau-Ponty refers to this perspective as *body as subject.* The body is a being, conscious, and the place where our sense of "I" exists and engages with the world. Merleau-Ponty's original French can also be translated as *body-for-self,* as if to say the body is not against the self but *for* life and the self, the soil within which the mind and personhood emerges.[4] This nondual perspective of the self invites us to consider the ways in which believing the self to be divided—the mind as separate from the body—has been both damaging and neuroscientifically incorrect.[5]

Being a body, seeing the self as inextricable from our physicality and our physicality as the expression of our personhood, invites us into wholeness. But when the self has been shattered and fragmented—as it has been for many of us—collecting the fragments, believing they belong to us, and naming them as good is a politically rebellious, spiritually powerful, and biomedically healing practice.

While disembodiment on an individual level represents the fragmentation of the self, disembodiment on a cultural level is diagnostic of a cultural pathology. Tada Hozumi, cultural-somatics practitioner and activist, has identified this as the effect of historical traumas from inter-European imperialism.

15

Such historical trauma is passed down epigenetically and inter-personally through descendants of light-skinned Europeans and is revealed in the fabric of Western, largely white culture.[6] In this culture, it seems we have started to recognize this unease and fragmentation. In our desire to experience wholeness again and remedy the poverty within our context, we have looked to other cultures and traditions, typically those of people of color, for their wisdom, embodiment practices, and insights (for example, yoga, Tai Chi, martial arts, and breath work). We must speak about embodiment while acknowledging that these are not new conversations or practices; otherwise, we rehearse the systemic wounds that divided us from ourselves and each other. Our individual healing can't happen without addressing our need for collective healing, culturally and as a collective human body.

Where there has been dissociation, we want association, weaving back together parts that were never meant to be sepa-rate. With this level of fragmentation, viewing the body as an object—a thing, but a precious thing—is an entry point for healing. Perhaps it is even the first and most important step of remembering our wholeness and ultimately affirming our bodies as the place of our being-ness.

Sometimes I imagine this process as collecting the shattered pieces of a family heirloom. To put it back together, we have to search for all the fragments, even the ones that scattered under the fridge, as if to say, "This, yes, this part is also essential for being whole again." We need to reclaim every shattered frag-ment of our body to experience wholeness. Healing happens as we invite our bodies back into the narratives of our lives. Even if our body still feels somewhat separated from the self, this invitation can be the first act of acceptance and arrival to learn to say to ourselves, "This is my body." Because every mo-ment comes with an invitation, I invite you to pause and say to yourself in this moment, "This is my body."

Practicing Embodiment

You might be familiar with the adage about fish in water. In a 2005 commencement speech, David Foster Wallace describes two young fish swimming along when an older fish swims by and says something like, "Morning, boys, how's the water?" Once alone, the two younger fish look at each other and wonder, "What the hell is water?" Wallace goes on to say that "the most obvious, important realities are often the ones that are the hardest to see and talk about."[7]

Embodiment is the water in which we swim. We have never known any reality outside of our bodies. And yet, it is precisely because we are so immersed in being bodies—and because our collective thinking has been shaped by a particular cultural framework of post-Enlightenment, settler colonialism; heterosexism; supremacy of white bodies; and patriarchy—that we often forget that the body is the very center of our existence. It doesn't help that even writing and reading about embodiment is an abstraction of the real thing. So, to take embodiment off the page and into real life, try this experiment. It's an exercise designed to help you experience how the two ways of thinking about the body—body as object and body as subject—are both related and distinct.

Use your dominant hand to hold the forearm of the opposite hand in front of you. Imagine your dangling arm and hand as an object. You might use your dominant hand to jostle your nondominant arm and hand around and see how your fingers move, flopping about. Do your best to mentally categorize your arm and hand as a thing. Notice how they hang there, limp and motionless. Then set your nondominant hand onto your lap, as if it were part of a machine being operated from the outside. Try to notice how this makes you feel. What would happen if you really started to think about your arm and hand this way?

Now, imagine your arm as yourself—alive and conscious. You can decide how you would like to move your hand and arm.

You might wiggle your fingers, but this time it is you who does the wiggling—the movement comes from the inside out. You might reach out to touch something and experience yourself extending into the world. Perhaps you decide to move an object and realize that you are enacting that choice through your own movement. If you moved something, try holding in your mind that the object was displaced by you—you as a body made an imprint on the world. You also might want to try moving your hand in a manner more expressive of who you are. If you were in fact your hand, how would you reveal yourself as a hand? What motion would you make? Would you point? Move your fingers and hand up and down? Clasp your other hand? Do nothing at all? Is this the first moment in the day when you felt free to make a conscious choice about the way your body moves in the world?

Whenever I do these exercises, I notice an uneasiness when thinking about my arm as a series of parts that function as a flesh-machine. But when I practice moving my hand freely, this little experiment of choosing movement reminds me of my capacity for agency and the pleasure of making choices about my own body.

The Story of Who You Are

The way we are in our bodies tells the story of who we have been up to this point in our lives. It reveals what we have been told by others about ourselves, how we self-identify, and what we believe about the world and our place in it. For this reason, our embodiment may be our most comprehensive nonlinguistic form of autobiography. Embodiment is the self in motion, the living, breathing story of who you are and the culture and people you have come from.

Perhaps the simplest way to describe the experience of embodiment is this: the *way* that you *are*. Merleau-Ponty defines embodiment as the "perceptual experience of engagement of the body in the world."[8] Embodiment is the conscious knowing of and living as a body, not as a thing distinct from the self or the mind. It is the how, what, why, where, and who of existence—the ground zero of consciousness, of present-moment living. It is to be present to yourself and your experience from the inside out.

Experiences are hard to describe because they happen outside of language. Simply thinking about how to describe our body, or our experience of our body, takes us out of the sensory and into the abstractions of language: categories, constructs, and symbols we use to build bridges between our experiential knowing and others' experiences.

To truly experience embodiment—and not just think about it—try noticing what you're sensing as a body right now. How is your body positioned? Where are your limbs? How are you holding yourself? Are you fidgeting? Lying down? Is a particular sensation making it difficult to take in this information? Are you feeling comfortable? Contorted? Are you trying to take up as little space as possible, or are you stretched out—arms and legs flopping down where you feel most at ease? Are you trying to avoid something sensory, such as fatigue, hunger, or pain?

The way you are in this moment says something about you, and it might reveal something about your internal state—for example, that you are tense because you are stressed or that you are fidgety because you are anxious. It might reveal the social messages you have received: perhaps you are closed in on yourself because you have been shamed for taking up space, or perhaps you are sitting up straight because you've been told you should have a strong, confident posture. What might your posture right now have to say about your family of origin, your sense of security in your environment, your inner emotional state?

Your embodiment is always telling a story.

Learning to listen to, interpret, and work with this story is central to connecting to wisdom, an integration of what we sense and how to make sense of it.

Exploring embodiment can sometimes be overwhelming and at other times feel like a treasure hunt of self-discovery. Either way, these questions are helpful only if they're engaged with compassion and curiosity. Come back to them again, perhaps at a different time, and see how your emotional state, environment, or social context changes your answers—exploring whatever you find with gentleness.

The Pain Point

I am sitting across from a fifty-something man wearing a sharply pressed suit; he has come for a session on the way home from work. He lays his suit jacket neatly beside him on the couch. When sitting, his pant legs rise up to reveal colorful striped socks that don't quite match his "I'm-someone-important-at-work" look. I raise my eyebrows and glance at the socks. He catches the nonverbal cue and smiles. "A gift from my daughter," he says, eyes gleaming.

He knows I have some background information because I have already spoken with his cardiologist, who regularly refers clients to me. These days, most of the referrals seem to be for midlife, workaholic men doing their best to be successful and stoic. My client tells me he has never been to therapy before and is confused about why his biomedically focused heart doctor sent him to a "feelings and talking doctor," which is how he describes my line of work. He says he has been having some medical problems and that he is coming to me to comply with doctor's orders but doesn't think he needs to be here. The message I hear is, "Don't get too excited; there's nothing to see here—this is just an issue of the heart," a double entendre in this case. I wonder to myself, *What is the organ of his heart saying about what it has been carrying for so long? What would it say if it could use words instead of sensation to communicate?*

I know better than to disclose my flicker of excitement about all the vibrancy and ease on the other side of our work together. In time, he will come to be someone I adore, and his wife will send me notes once in a while to thank me for helping her husband come back to life. But first, we have to get to the heart issues he so wants to avoid.

In another time and place, I am sitting in silence with a nonbinary teen who is staring at the ground, both focused and far off. It's hard to tell if they are bored, gathering courage, or deep in thought. Eventually I will ask, "What happened inside? Where did you go?" But first we will sit quietly together, week after week, making friends with the silence. Some things are better felt than said, and so we drop into the living moment to be with *what is* without rushing to describe it.

This young person evokes such a sting in me, my sadness overflowing out of my chest into my throat as I recall our work together. They, too, have been referred by a doctor; their physician giving them my name after a long list of medications failed to curb the exhausting panic that was spilling into their life. This tender human had survived an act of sexual violence, which had left their body wrought with fear. It had made certain places terrifying, as if another act of violence were always just about to happen. We will do trauma work for longer than we were both expecting, because more traumas will happen. We will be crushed and resilient, together. But these moments of silence that run like a meandering stream through our connection will set the foundation for their body to feel at rest again—a home no one can take from them.

We may think of these two people as being from very different worlds. We have learned to focus first on the differences between us—our clothing, skin color, body shape, posture, and patterns of movement. We forget that the body is a great unifier—a thread that weaves all humanity together.

What unifies these two people and their stories is the experience of a pain point—bodies crying out to tell stories that have been disregarded or dishonored. Most people forget about the body until pain, aging, illness, trauma, incarceration, or impending death brings it to the fore. These experiences are a frustrating reminder that we can never truly put mind over matter and overcome our physicality. The body tells the truth— the painful parts, the joyful parts, and everything in between.

The mind-body divide undergirds mainstream thinking, but our collective tension is visible. When we are hurting psycho-socially—our pain revealing itself in our emotions, thoughts, behaviors, and relationships—most of us don't seek help until suffering shows up in our bodies, as if the emotional suffering is not reason enough to ask for support. One of the underlying messages here is that the body needs to be paid attention to only when there is a problem. The body becomes the scapegoat and, as a result, we often miss the more subtle bodily messages that come before the alarm bells. And there are messages before the alarm bells sound, believe me.

While learning how to have an attuned and compassionate relationship with the body was central to my research on em-bodiment, my curiosity accelerated when referrals from physicians and other health care professionals started pouring in to my clinical practice. A gastroenterologist sent patients with irritable bowel syndrome to learn about stress regulation; a cardiologist sent patients suffering from chronic anxiety; an allergist sent patients who had reactions despite the absence of allergens. A gynecologist referred patients whose sexual trauma resurfaced during vaginal exams; a chiropractor referred patients who had debilitating back pain despite clean MRIs; and a urologist referred patients who had erectile dysfunction as a result of emotional and relational stressors. In each narrative it was impossible for me to ignore the mind-body connection. Our bodies are telling the stories we have avoided or forgotten how to hear—and sometimes our inability to feel our feelings (the messages that precede the alarm bells) means our bodies have to scream in order to get some attention.

Bodies and Society

We have a subjective experience of ourselves as bodies, but that exists in a social and cultural context. Your way of being as a body does not occur in isolation. How and why you are the way you are has a lot to do with where you're located, with whom you self-identify, who has called you an outsider or insider, and what has hurt you. This may be a painful realization if we think of ourselves as independent of the world around us.

As much as we think of ourselves as individuals, we are located in social, historical, environmental, political, and spiritual contexts. We must look at the larger social and political ideologies that shape us, including our collective disembodiment, to understanding how we became so disembodied. This could mean, for example, realizing that our mind-over-matter mentality isn't something we came up with so we could play a football game with a sore ankle but that it comes from the influence of Greek thought and Enlightenment ideology woven into our social fabric. It also means grasping that our cultural views of land as an object to be used, conquered, or stolen are relics of settler-colonialist ideologies—as is the belief that we are hyper-rational individuals who can exist and thrive outside of community. These cultural views have cut off the deep knowing of our interconnectedness to our bodily selves, each other, and the earth.

Together, these influences create the proverbial water in which we swim. They dictate the scripts we are handed about gender, religion, family of origin, ethnicity, and socioeconomic status. So embodiment is the way you are in the world, but that embodiment is influenced by who you have been allowed to be—through what has been discouraged and encouraged—and your sense of safety and agency in it all.

For some, especially those for whom being in the body feels unsafe, disconnecting from the body can be an unconscious survival tactic. For others, disconnecting may feel like a moral choice, especially if we have been taught that our body is inherently evil or that it caused the hurt or violation done to us by others. In these contexts, we might even feel morally superior for being able to disconnect from the body. If so, an invitation to reconnect to the body can feel terrifying or dangerous, as if being embodied requires embracing the very things we have been trying so hard to flee.

While for some of us it may take an event—a serious illness or a trauma—to remember that we are bodies, many people do not have to wait for a specific event to remember the centrality of their body. That's because their body is placed outside the cultural hierarchy of the "ideal body," and so they learn early on that their body makes them "other." Most forms of oppression are directed against the body as "isms": racism, sexism, ableism, heterosexism, ageism, sizeism, and so on. The message underneath these isms is this: *You are less valuable in this society because of your body*. This exemplifies the body-as-object narrative mentioned above: people are reduced to body-objects, not empowered as body-subjects. Because of their inability to leave or transcend or conquer their unruly body, the social context suggests to some that they are nothing more than a body, less-than in a world that does not value the inherent goodness of bodies. This creates a trap: their body becomes central to their identity while also being something they are unable to conquer in a social context that privileges the conquered body.

Acknowledging the social landscape that our embodiment exists within is complex. For some, embodiment is a valuable foray into personal growth and self-connection; for others, it is like stepping back into the scene of a crime. Embodiment comes with a particular kind of ache, liberation, or both, depending on whether the person experienced body violation, illness, or pain. To say that you are your body is not to further overidentify each of us with the ways our bodies have been made objects, but rather to remind us that our personhood is inextricable from our physicality. This is meant to rehumanize us all and to distance us from the paradigms that separated us from our bodies in the first place, as if any of us could ever transcend our bodies.

The body is where life happens—both the beautiful and the painful, our individuality and our relationships, the now and the past—but many of us have forgotten ourselves as bodies. We did so in order to survive the pain or to be compliant, but in the process we left behind so much of the beautiful. We cannot leave one without leaving the other. At best, most of us have a conflicted relationship with our bodies, forgetting there is more to being a body than our appearance, or tolerating that appearance. At worst, the stories we tell ourselves are ones of shame, hatred, frustration, confusion, or indifference. But there is another way.

Remembering

It has been years now since that moment in therapy with Liz when I remembered myself as a body, but I am still learning what it means to be embodied. I research the relationships we have with our bodies, specialize in this work in my therapy practice, and write and speak about it, but all of these activities are relatively disembodied. The irony is not lost on me. I can sit all day reading about neuroanatomical structures responsible for how we sense emotion as a bodily process, only to realize hours later that I have forgotten to eat a meal or that my leg is numb. To do what I ask people to do—to live embodiment and not just think about it—I have been looking for ways to weave myself back into wholeness, for thread to stitch back together the fabric of my life into something greater than the individual parts. And so, on Wednesday nights, I clear my schedule, drive to a dimly lit community center on Vancouver's West Side, and gather with strangers for several hours of movement and music to practice coming back into my body.

This particular evening, it is cool outside as the sun sinks away from the darkening blue sky. I have to pull hard on the door of the studio to get it open. I almost walk away, but the door opens on the fourth yank. Nervous, expectant, I climb the long flight of stairs up to the second floor where the air is thick with heat and I can feel the vibrating drumbeat in my bones. I am here to move; I am here to dance into my muscles the reminder that being a body is good, that I am free, that I no longer need to disappear.

The long, open room is filling quickly with all sorts of people, and I'm trying not to think about what anyone else is doing or thinking. I'm there to remember myself. The volume and tempo of the music increases, and Bettina, the woman facilitating the evening, invites us to drop down into our bodies—to allow our bodies to speak, to respond, to sense, to move. "Between our heads and our toes, there are a million miles of unexplored wilderness," she says. And with that, I imagine removing the part of my brain that censors and judges the way I take up space. I put it in a jar near the door where my shoes sit, and I give myself over to the music, letting my body lead the way, telling the stories of all I have known and felt, each story held within this body.

Remembering our embodiment, actually practicing the goodness of being a body, is something like putting together a puzzle one piece at a time. Together, we will start with the edges and work our way in. If you do puzzles, you know to start by fitting together the smooth outside edges to set the frame within which the rest of the picture can take shape. I am still learning to do this, and you will too—we will do it together.

━━━ ♥ ━━━

To help you process and practice what you read, every chapter concludes with something to think about and something to try. My hope is that this book serves you well by helping you go beyond a set of disembodied ideas and into an experience of being fully present and connected with yourself and with those around you.

SOME THINGS TO THINK ABOUT

- How and why is my body positioned the way it is right now?
- What stories have I been told that might make me feel like this is the best or only way to be in my body right now?
- What if the stories were different?
- How might I be differently, as a body, if I were in another setting?

SOME THINGS TO TRY

Here's an exercise to get you out of your thoughts and into your senses. Start to tune into yourself and notice: What are you touching right now? What is your skin in contact with? What is the temperature of your body? What about the temperature of the air around you? What parts of you feel tight? What do you smell? What emotions do you notice emerging in your body? Take a deep breath in, and let it slowly out. Thank yourself for taking a moment to slow down and pay attention.

2

How We Become Disembodied

Lies about Our Bodies and Finding Our Way Home

When I was growing up, my parents often took me to a museum called Science World. Inside were exhibits with live bees in a beehive and installations demonstrating how sound waves work and what happens to different materials undergoing temperature change. Many installations rotated in and out, but a favorite permanent exhibit was located just past the entrance—a series of tall mirrors, each distorting the reflection in one way or another. I could stand in front of one and see how I would look if I were double my size, twice as tall, or had a head three times the size of my body.

I knew what I looked like because I'd seen consistent images of myself in mirror after mirror and photo after photo. So, when I went to Science World, I could laugh at what I saw in these mirrors because I knew they were distortions. But what if

I had grown up only ever seeing myself in distorted mirrors? It would make sense that I would believe what I saw there because it would be all I knew.

Mirrors can reflect or distort reality, so mirrors are a great metaphor for our societal and cultural context. The images our contexts reflect back to us, both literal and figurative, over the course of our lives shape how our brains develop structurally, which then shapes how we feel about ourselves and the meaning-making we do to pull it all together.[1] The cultural mirrors all around us are constantly telling us, in both obvious and covert ways, that there is a right way to have a body—and it is something other than yours. Like the mirrors at Science World, this is a distortion. But when all we've seen are distortions, it's hard to distinguish the truth from the untruth, much less to deeply believe the truth. Distorted messages about bodies are so ubiquitous that we rarely notice them. That is the power of our sociocultural context: we are the proverbial fish who are unaware of water, even when the water is polluted.

Naming the Untruths

As long as the pervasive distortion stories of our culture feel normal, they go unnamed. But once the stories are named, we can begin to assess how they shape us. Then we can write true stories—embodied stories—that give us more space to live within. And we can use our elbows to press out the stories until they are deep and wide enough to include each and every one of us.

To get us started in the process of naming untruths about bodies, I've compiled a list of what I've heard from listening to people's stories and exploring what research says about what causes people pain.

You are not your body. Some of us might have been told outright that we are not our bodies, but that, at our essence,

30

we are our souls or our thoughts. For the rest of us, this is an unspoken but insidious message that undergirds disembodiment. Talking about a body as separate from the person, as if the *self* lives elsewhere, has allowed us to distance ourselves from the lived realities of our bodies. We do this because it helps us cope with pain, fear of death and disease, and the reality of incarcerated or policed bodies, and it helps us disconnect from the site of oppression and trauma. It helps us push through. We can work longer hours, dismiss our hunger, and protect ourselves from being judged as weak for honoring our bodily cues. After all, most of us have been sold a story that bodies have limitations that need to be overcome. But this myth has made us silent about body hierarchies that value some bodies more than others. It has disconnected us from the present, from our pain but also our joy, and from whatever else is right here. When we buy into the distortion that a person is not their body, we collude with oppressive systems that devalue certain bodies, and we perpetuate the negative impact these systems have.[2]

You need to subdue and control your body because it is dangerous. Often when we peek under the hood of control, we find fear. So it is with the body. Because we have learned to fear the body, we have tried to control it.

Somatophobia—fear of the body—is reinforced through long-standing and pervasive cultural, philosophical, religious, and existential ideologies. Among the many things we fear about the body are death, animal and instinctual impulses, pain and illness, and devaluation based on appearance, trauma, and injustice. Although most of us have at some point experienced our bodies as scary places to be, there isn't anything problematic about bodies in general. In other words, bodies are good in the same way that nature is good. What's problematic, and deeply so, are the cultural stories we are told about bodies that have us devalue ourselves and others and that teach us to treat our bodies as things we need to overcome. Along with these disembodying cultural narratives comes our inability to understand bodies as good when we experience things like trauma, illness, and death. These stories and their accompanying fears have created a confirmation-bias cycle in which our devaluing, misunderstanding, and scapegoating of our bodies is considered proof that our bodies deserve that devaluation in the first place.

Think about someone who scares you. How likely would you be to walk up to that person and say, "I find you terrifying. Let's explore that." Probably not very likely. Similarly, if our only way of interacting with our body is through a fear-based paradigm, we are unlikely to even try to understand our bodily selves. Yet our devaluation of bodies leads to psychosomatic disorders and prevents us from honoring the bodily cues we have learned to ignore, messages telling us that something is not right, that we need medical attention, or that it's time to rest or receive care. If we cannot listen to these messages, we cannot begin to live lives of peace (because we are at war with ourselves), presence (because we are not in the here and now), and pleasure (because we are disconnected from our own sensations).[3]

Some bodies are better than others. No one body is more valuable than another body, but body hierarchies are pervasive and are typically reinforced by those who have a body placed higher on the socially constructed value scale. Body hierarchies shape what we believe and how we behave, and they have been used to justify horrific abuse. For example, the devaluation of Black people by white people has been used to justify slavery, murder, rape, incarceration, police brutality, voter suppression, and countless other ongoing atrocities. The devaluation of women by men has been used to discount the experience, expertise, and perspectives of women and to justify barring women from leadership positions, denying women the right to vote, and legislating against women's reproductive rights. The devaluation of people with physical disabilities by those who are not living with a physical disability has helped create a civil infrastructure that prevents those with physical disabilities from changing the systems that oppress them. And so on. If people are not their bodies, then this does not matter. But if people are their bodies, and if we value people, then we are required to dismantle these hierarchies.[4]

Bodies must present within rigid binaries of gender. Assuming a direct relationship between reproductive anatomy and rigid gender roles shapes the gender-based projections spoken over our lives before we are even born. Babies seen to have female genitalia on an ultrasound machine are expected to be sweet and kind, playful and cute, while babies with male genitalia are expected to be tough and sporty, aggressive and self-confident. These expectations shape everything from the toys kids are given and the clothing they wear to what they're told about how they can physically move through the world. In this narrative, there are only two acceptable ways of being in the world—one for males and one for females. Boys can spread their legs wide on the bus, take up both armrests on an airplane, and engage in locker room talk; girls must keep their legs crossed, take up as little space as possible, and be kind and polite.

Of course, the gender scripts themselves have changed considerably over time and differ from culture to culture. Most of us tend to adhere to the script we're given because fitting within a societal groove minimizes the discomfort or even violence we are likely to experience if we step outside that groove. But in adhering to a binary gender script, we restrict our access to the full range of human experience. This inhibits men from connecting to characteristics labeled feminine and women from what has been deemed masculine, and it excludes those in our communities who don't identify with either label.[5]

Ideal women have sexual, young, thin, and fertile bodies. Most of us learn early on that women's bodies are most desirable when they are thin, sexualized, and youthful. This devalues women's needs, skills, ideas, and complexity. It privileges women who meet these criteria but also undermines them by attributing their worth to their appearance or what their bodies can do for others. It teaches younger women that aging women, women who are not mothers, or women without reproductive organs are less desirable or valuable. It creates psychological distress, instills weight bias, and leads to an obsessive focus on appearance. To state it clearly: appearance is not what matters most about women, or any of us for that matter. All women are valuable as people, equal and powerful regardless of appearance or what their bodies can do for others.[6]

Bodies are impure, and pleasure is sinful. Sex, sexuality, desire, arousal, eroticism, orgasm—all of it happens in and through the body. Whether the context is religious or secular, wherever there is a paradigm of sexual control, bodies will be perceived as a problem, which results in a host of distorted stories. For example, when sexual activity is seen as impure, sexual purity becomes synonymous with moral or spiritual purity, and women are expected to be sexual objects for others' pleasure. A belief in the impurity of sexuality is also linked with blaming and shaming women as the cause of impurity in men (an assumption of heteronormative sexuality) and with an overall culture of body shaming. Denying the goodness of pleasure and bodies has left individuals and communities without the skills and understanding necessary to negotiate what constitutes safe, mutually enjoyable, consenting, and pleasurable sexual activity. Further, it creates the illusion that sexuality and spirituality are fundamentally distinct from each other, and it prevents people from experiencing their sexuality as good or even as an expression of Divine indwelling.[7]

Appearance is all that matters about your body. If our bodies are a gift, we have learned to focus on the wrapping and have forgotten how to enjoy the gift itself, not to mention the

34

deeper meaning and significance of the gift. As a result, we often become adept at the game of appearance comparison and control. It doesn't help that other people tend to celebrate this about us, celebrating when we change our bodies to look more like the ideal. But body-image research shows that the closer we get to achieving our ideal appearance, the more conditional our sense of worth becomes, and the more we fear what it will cost us when our appearance inevitably changes. When we conflate appearance with the body—and if we have struggled to appreciate our appearance—it makes sense that we might try to get as far away as possible from our body. That, of course, is only a defensive strategy, because we can never actually leave our body, and even frustration and shame about our appearance are experienced in our body as emotions.[8]

You should change your body. The diet and weight-loss industry is a multibillion dollar juggernaut driven by the false promise that we will be happier, healthier, and more desirable to others if we change our body in one way or another. But the data about diets shows that they are not effective for weight loss, with most people regaining more weight than they originally lost, and in many cases diets not improve biomarkers traditionally thought to measure health.[9] The belief that we have to change our body to be happy creates conditional self-worth, which means we can be happy and valuable only if our body never changes back. It leads to an unhealthy preoccupation that increases the likelihood of disordered eating, food and exercise compulsions, anxiety, and depression related to rigid thinking and undernutrition. And it promotes the false belief that it's better if there is less of us. Instead of changing our body, what we need to change is how we think about, talk about, and care for our body. Becoming more connected to our body, seeing our bodily self as inherently worthy, good, and lovable, means we can pay more attention to our unique bodily needs, which might include intuitive eating, healthy forms of movement, self-care, and a balanced lifestyle that includes rest and routine care.[10]

Fat bodies are unhealthy. Fear of fat often begins for us when "fat" is an insult hurled at us on the playground. But before it filters down to taunts among children, the bias against fat and the preference for thin masquerades as a health concern for those with bodies higher on the weight spectrum. Everything from New Year's resolution weight-loss campaigns to parental concern at the dinner table to before-and-after images on social media has convinced us that fat is both morally problematic and unhealthy. The weight-biased culture has construed fatness as synonymous with laziness and gluttony; in some faith communities, being fat is even identified as a sin. Although many of us assume such health claims are based on science, we might not know that weight bias and thin preference emerged about a hundred years before the medical establishment became concerned with fat as a health issue.[11] In fact, it was the preference for thin that ultimately drove the research to prove that fat was bad and thin was good. In *Fearing the Black Body: The Racial Origins of Fat Phobia*, Dr. Sabrina Strings demonstrates how fear of fat is inextricably linked with racism, the American slave trade, classism, and European migration in the nineteenth century. The most recent scientific research reveals that what constitutes health is much more complex than weight alone.[12] Health is composed of several highly individualized factors impacted by environmental, psychological, economic, and genetic history, as well as current and future needs. Health also includes mental well-being, relationship satisfaction, and community belonging and safety.[13]

Others get to decide what is best for your body. If you were ever told as a child to give Aunt Grace or Uncle Bill a hug, even when you didn't want to, then you've experienced what it's like to have someone else decide what's best for your body. And it doesn't end in childhood. Doctors, partners, and political and religious leaders (and their corresponding structures) all have power to take away your right to choose what's best for you— particularly as it relates to size, appearance, health, gender, sex, and power. Because we exist in social contexts in which people in power make choices about our bodies, we can know two things: (1) ultimately, our body is our own, and (2) we can advocate for the fair treatment of all bodies, and we can advocate that those in power protect our right to choose what is best for our bodies. Given how early the body-for-others paradigm begins, we could all benefit from making a regular practice of acknowledging that we do in fact have ownership over ourselves. To say "this is my body" is to state that this body belongs to no one else; it is not an object anyone else gets to own or control. In so doing, we reclaim the body-for-self paradigm.[14]

Bodies get in the way of what really matters: theology and intellect. Theology and intellect aren't superior to the physical aspect of human experience, but we have a history of using them as a way to escape, or bypass, the difficult realities of our bodily existence. But prioritizing theology and intellect over other forms of wisdom, knowing, and spirituality is in many cases a by-product of privilege. Who has the luxury of being able to identify more with thinking than with bodily existence? Traditionally, it was men of high status who could spend their time in the academy or seminary rather than engaging in physical labor or caring for children. Others with less privilege or status could not escape the needs and demands of their bodily existence, especially since social status related to the amount of physical labor a person did. Historically, those with the least social status have been people of color, women, and those with physical disabilities. The paradox here is that the individuals who had more social power because of their bodies did not experience themselves as defined by their bodies, but they made choices that affected the day-to-day bodily realities of others. Obvious examples of this include men determining the reproductive rights of women, or people without disabilities designing buildings that restrict building access for those with disabilities.

While thinking, theology, and philosophizing in and of themselves are not bad, we miss out on the full picture of being human when we use these things to get away from the life lived as bodies. And we miss out on the ways in which rooting these practices in our bodily experiences creates even more grounded, complex, nonhierarchical practices that lead to integration and the honoring of lived experience.[15]

This list of distorted stories is a lot to take in, isn't it? I confess I didn't enjoy writing it. Still, it is important to name the insidious narratives that shape our perspectives, slip into our conversations, and influence our thoughts about others. Naming them allows us to notice them in action, to see the polluted water we have been swimming in, and to craft a new set of ideas that help us move forward. In order to begin moving forward, we need to understand how the ideas we choose to believe work their way into our everyday lives.

How We Become Embodied and Disembodied

While researching body image early on in my graduate studies, I came across the work of Dr. Niva Piran, a scholar who spent three decades researching embodiment and how it can help prevent and treat eating disorders. Her research has heavily influenced my own clinical and academic work.

Piran describes embodiment as feeling a sense of positive connection or being at one with our body.[16] We feel power and agency in our physicality, and we sense that we are not just observing our bodies from the outside but living through them from the inside out. When we feel embodied, we can take up space, move freely in public and private, and challenge external appearance standards. We can connect to the needs and rights of others while simultaneously experiencing and expressing our individuality. We can experience emotion as anchored in the body, care for and protect our body, and use our body as a source of wisdom when interacting with the world. This matters for our health as a whole person and for our individuality as well as our interconnectedness.

Piran describes disembodiment, or disrupted embodiment, as an experience of disconnection from our body.[17] When this happens, our body is the place where we feel disempowered and constricted as well as lacking in competence, safety, and presence. Disembodiment leads us to harshly criticize our body based on sociocultural appearance standards, and it negatively shapes our body-based behaviors, such as how we exercise, rest, feed ourselves, and care for ourselves when ill. How we treat our body is based not on what we need but on what others tell us to do. This makes it difficult to identify our needs, express them in the world, and trust our body as a source of valuable information. Behaviors characteristic of disembodiment include self-harm, forgetting or disregarding bodily needs, trying to make our body disappear or conform, following diets instead of hunger cues, and pushing our body to the limits even when doing so causes us pain or injury.

Through extensive research, Piran has identified three domains or pathways through which we develop embodiment or disembodiment: the *mental domain*, the *physical domain*, and the *social domain*.[18] Depending on what happens in each of these domains, we can move toward either a more unified sense of self or a more fragmented sense of self. What we experience shapes the kind of relationship we have with ourselves as a body—including our ability or inability to believe we are our body at all.

Three Domains of Disembodiment

Disembodiment happens in the *mental domain* when we experience "mental corseting," or when we buy into constraining social ideals. This happens when cultural distortions become so integrated into our thoughts that we lose our ability to challenge them. As a result, we might self-silence by rarely expressing our needs and emotions—a phenomenon associated with depression—or we might see our body as an object. This often happens early in development, especially to girls. When their bodies change and their social interactions change as a result, they learn that their bodies exist in the "public domain."[19] Mental corseting can also include holding to narrow definitions of gender.

In the *physical domain*, we experience disembodiment as "physical corseting." We are physically corseted when the body is unsafe, neglected, or violated. As a result, we might live with limited freedom and movement or with externally imposed restrictions on desire, appetite, and comfort. This often happens as a result of sex-based discrimination or gender scripts, such as being told, based on your sex, that you should or should not move in certain ways. Girls are often told to keep their legs together when sitting, to be quiet, and to play politely. "Do not climb that tree in your pretty clothes!" Boys are often shamed for any movement or expression considered feminine and are encouraged toward more masculine forms of play. "Go throw a football around." Another example of physical corseting is the expectation that as we age, we become more "mature," which is often code for physically restricted and sedentary.

Disembodiment happens in the *social domain* when we experience social disempowerment. We are socially disempowered when we are treated with prejudice or are objectified and when we sense that we need to use our appearance to maintain or reclaim that social status. In Piran's research, girls with less social privilege wanted to change their appearance to gain more social status; girls with more social privilege were more afraid than their peers of losing social power if their appearance changed. Because social power is identified through appearance and ability, those whose bodies are subject to oppression or marginalization, or those who fall lower on the made-up body hierarchy, are likely to experience disempowerment. The body becomes a place that is unsafe, is treated as a scapegoat for a person's suffering, or is changed to accrue more social power.

While each domain can be a pathway to disembodiment, each can also offer us a pathway to embodiment.

Three Domains of Embodiment

We are more likely to experience embodiment in the *mental domain* when we have mental freedom. Mental freedom shows up in three ways: (1) the ability to challenge societal ideas about the body, (2) the ability to challenge rigid gender stereotypes, and (3) the ability to freely express ourselves. Mental freedom also includes the ability to passionately engage with parts of the self that have nothing to do with appearance. Some of us had mental freedom growing up, and others of us did not. But all of us can experience it now by challenging the restrictive labels society puts on us. Though we are handed ideas about our body and about others' bodies that often hurt us more than we know, once we're aware of the distortions, we can tell new stories that help us feel free and authentically ourselves.

We are more likely to experience embodiment in the *physical domain* when we have physical freedom. Physical freedom includes physical safety, care, respect, rest, movement, and competence, as well as the freedom to accept without shame our physical desires, appetites, and developmental changes. Our social context shapes how much freedom we have; some

41

contexts make it more or less safe for a person with intersecting marginalized identities (like race, level of ability, gender, and size) to have access to physical freedom. Some of us were told we could be free in our bodies but only until a certain age when we then had to behave ourselves.

Finding physical freedom as an adult means engaging in movement that feels comfortable and playful, allowing us to be how we want to be. For me, that has included dancing, often wildly and with abandon. I've danced in group classes with strangers who were using mobility aids, naked and alone in my home, and in a moonlit desert with other women also seeking whole-person freedom. We experience physical freedom when we pay attention to our desires and needs, and when we are willing to challenge any social, familial, or religious beliefs that conflict with those desires and needs. For many of us, full physical freedom means reassessing what we learned growing up—through friends, the media, or parents—about everything from how much food we can put on our plate to what kind of activity we're allowed to do for fun.

To increase our physical freedom, Piran suggests (1) engaging in physical activity that feels free, expansive, and unrestricted by appearance standards; (2) existing in spaces where our bodies are safe; (3) tuning in to ourselves and providing self-care; and (4) connecting pleasurably to our desires. Because we are all connected to each other and my physical freedom is bound with yours, we need to be creating communities where all of us can experience physical freedom.

Piran's research has showed that, when it comes to the *social domain*, we are more likely to be embodied when we have social power. This means having the freedom to be outside the role of "other" and feeling empowered to stand up to inequity. Embodiment in the social domain also requires addressing the sociopolitical context that marginalizes certain bodies. If you have social power, you have a responsibility to both acknowledge

42

your privilege—the social stories and systems from which you have benefited—and widen those stories and systems to make them inclusive for everyone.

If you have not had access to social power everywhere, it is essential to find spaces where you can experience power, access your resilience, and be free from the discrimination that makes you feel unsafe or othered (because of gender, race, ethnicity, weight, social class, sexual orientation, abilities, etc.). Even if the dominant cultural script has suggested otherwise, you can build social power by investing in validating relationships with those who share similar identities and experiences.

Those of us in leadership positions also must create spaces where all bodies are valued. That includes empowering and supporting people who have been marginalized or othered to speak up about what makes them feel valued, and modeling that it will indeed be valued when they are courageous enough to speak up.

Becoming, Again, the Bodily Self

While most of us think that change happens because we learn new ideas—and, yes, that is part of it—the deepest and most lasting change happens when we have new experiences and then integrate them into the larger story of our lives, and our collective story.[20] Embodied experience is undeniably the most powerful channel of change. Ultimately, remembering our bodily selves, becoming embodied again, is slow work—it is compassionate instead of perfectionistic, communal instead of individualistic, process oriented instead of achievement oriented, and mutual instead of hierarchical. We cannot arrive there through the same mechanisms that pulled us out of our bodies in the first place. When we have embodied experiences little by little, and go about this in a new way, we are able to craft a new story and enter into a new experience of ourselves.

Then we wake up one day and realize the world has become a better home for all of us to be in our bodies.

We've already covered a long list of lies and distortions that lead to disembodiment, so here is something more hopeful—a list of truths you can use to begin walking the path of embodiment. Think of them as invitations to remember what you once knew about your body before you unlearned it. These are not items on a checklist or things to achieve, as if you could arrive at embodiment and stay there forever. They're more like suggested directions to a new home; once you've practiced the route often enough, any time you leave you can find the way back by heart.

This is my body. After leaving your body, intentionally or unknowingly, the first step back to embodiment is reminding yourself, "This is my body." Simply acknowledging that you have a body can be a revolutionary act; it can also be a painful one if it requires acknowledging the reasons, individual and collective, that you left your body in the first place. This might highlight your need and your right to take care of your body— learning to pay attention to what your body needs, such as food, sleep, safety, care, play, movement, pleasure, boundaries, and comfortable clothing (or non-oppressive pants, as my friend Madison calls them). If you've lived disembodied for a long time, you might need to get to know your body again: what was true about your body the last time you were aware of your body may no longer be true now. Allow yourself to be curious, to update your narratives, and to need new or different things. You might also be surprised by the wisdom there, gems for the journey inward.

My body and my mind can be friends. Integration of the fragmented parts of us is integral to our experience of wholeness. One way to generate integration is to think of your mind and your body as friends. Doing this allows us to take a thing you know how to do in your outer landscape (friendship) and use it to map out a new way forward for your inner landscape (mind-body connection). You can't expect your inner world to feel like kinship if you don't treat yourself with the same kindness and respect you offer to others. For example, how you talk to your best friend on your worst day is surely nothing like how you talk to your body on your worst day. If you wouldn't talk to your friend or child or partner the way you talk to your body, then it's time to flip that around—borrow what you know about talking to others and use the same kindness and care when talking to your body.

This is one way to move from treating the body as an object (a thing) to treating the body as a subject (a person). Most of us think about and treat an "it" with less care and attunement than we treat a "someone." So try that. Think about and treat your body as a friend you want to know better. And feel free to use a pronoun to help humanize your physicality. Calling your body "she," "he," "they," or "you" can cue your brain to remember the "personhood" of your body. When my stomach makes an audible growl in a meeting, I might say, "Oh, she's telling me I'm hungry, and I'm learning to listen to her, so let's take a break for lunch." Or when I'm alone and feel a tightness in my chest, I might ask, "What are you trying to say?" Then, like I do with any of my other friends, I listen to see what happens next. In deep friendship, we often say we are sorry, so as you build friendship between your mind and your body, at times it may be appropriate to say "I'm sorry I left you" or "I am sorry I believed you were against me. You never have been, and I am learning that now."

My body is a resource. Our bodies are constantly speaking up, telling us who we are and what it is like to be us. These signals tell us what feels good, when we feel alive, when to eat and sleep and cry, what is unsafe (or what has felt scary in the past), what matters to us, and how we are different from or similar to the person next to us. All of these messages are resources, giving us what we need to get through the day and the journey of life.

If you're willing to pay attention to and dialogue with what's happening inside of you, you'll find that your body already knows the answers about how to live a full, present, connected, and healthy life. Even a trauma response is a resource, helping you to get ready just in case and to stay safe after things have been very unsafe. If you notice a sensory cue, even as simple as hunger, fatigue, or the tingling of a foot about to fall asleep, try thanking yourself for providing the information about what was needed.

If it is hard to understand the body as a resource (because you are used to thinking of it as a liability), try this instead. Identify a *context* in which you have felt a lack of freedom—where it would have cost you something to listen to your body. For example, perhaps you felt shame or insecurity noticing how your belly spilled over the top of your jeans. Once you have that context in mind, instead of being critical of your body, be critical of the context—specifically, the ways in which it limited your freedom. In the example above, this could mean being critical of the body stories you learned through images and advertisements that made you feel shame about a body that did nothing wrong.

My body is a resistance. Bodies are political, meaning they wield power in the public sphere—and some are granted more power than others. Having power can mean feeling safe within a physical space or having access to certain kinds of spaces, such as boardrooms, an elected office, and leadership positions. Likewise, how we engage our bodies is political. How we are as bodies in space is a form of voice or an expression of ourselves. If we enter spaces where bodies like ours have been invisible or rejected, our mere presence is beneficially disruptive—challenging the political narrative about who gets access to what kind of space—and paves the way for bodies like ours to enter that space again. Additionally, if we have a body that society deems valuable, and if we stand with other bodies that our dominant culture marginalizes, we are using our body to break down the barriers that enforce body hierarchies.

We can also use our bodies to resist problematic systems. I have learned from scholars and theologians Robyn Henderson-Espinoza and Tricia Hersey that in a culture that has been oriented toward consumerism, profit, and achievement, it is a form of resistance to listen, rest, and be present. This could mean intentionally practicing rest or stillness to untangle ourselves from the drive to perform or achieve. Because of how much our heads are down, looking at our phones, it can even be an act of resistance to put down our devices and look up and around in the world, keeping our hands, eyes, and minds free from constant stimulation and the ensuing anxiety or numbness. While there are many forms of resistance (some forms are more or less accessible or poignant for each of us), we can be thoughtful about how we use our body to resist injustice and oppressive systems by paving a way for a future where all bodies can simply be as they are.[21]

My body is a sanctuary. A sanctuary is a sacred space—a place we go to encounter the Holy and sacred. But then we leave that place and come back to our regular lives, where we have been led to believe that things are ordinary and unsacred. I used to think that the sacred place where I met the Divine was always somewhere else, somewhere that was not "here" in the rhythms of my daily life. But now I see that the Holy is very much here—my body is a sanctuary, a mobile home of the Divine.

Ask yourself, "What do I miss out on if I believe the Divine is out there but not here? How does that change how I treat myself? How I treat others?" Believing that your body is a sanctuary provides helpful reminders and invitations that can lead you back to embodiment. For example, if the body is sacred, do you treat your body as such? This could mean being gentler, being more nourishing, or choosing to listen to your sensory cues instead of ignoring them, understanding we are not just form or function but being itself. Historically, labeling the body as the dwelling of the Divine has been harmful for many people's bodies, resulting in bodily control, food restriction, and all-or-nothing practices of sexual purity. Instead of using this paradigm to move into more rigidity and guilt, we can remember that the sacred is already here just as we are, in us from the get-go, which invites us to know that we do not have to change to be loved or valuable. And sometimes in knowing that, we are inspired to treat others' bodies and our own from a place of love, care, and connection.

If your body is the place where the Divine dwells, then you always have direct and immanent access to the Divine. That is sometimes comforting, sometimes healing, and sometimes a reminder that you do not have to keep trying to earn love—you can access it, always. And if the body is sacred without condition—meaning that not just male bodies, white bodies, nondisabled bodies, or thin bodies are sacred, although those are sacred too—then your body and the body of your neighbor deserve to be treated as sacred as well. When you know this deep down in your bones, you're also more likely to challenge any social structure, idea, behavior, or system that tries to tell you otherwise.

Choosing Mirrors

All of us heard stories spoken about our bodies that we had no say over. Some of them were true; some pressured us to fit in; others were damaging and hurt us in ways we may still be discovering. Most of us were handed distorted mirrors on a larger scale too, mirrors that reflected culturally distorted stories about bodies—and most of the time, we didn't even know it was happening. But everything we've experienced has also brought us here as we are in this moment, with questions or longings for something new. We have the ability to change and to choose. It is never too late to create new experiences of ourselves as a body, to tell new stories, and to join the long line of people who have been doing this work and walking the path of embodiment long before we came around. We can always pick better mirrors on purpose.

SOME THINGS TO THINK ABOUT

- In what ways was your body restricted when you were younger? In what ways was your body allowed to be free?
- What early messages did you learn about bodies?
- If you could go back and tell your younger self something loving about your body, what age would you go back to? What would you say?
- What kind of friend are you on your most loving days? What would it be like to treat yourself the same way? What love languages would you use (for example, words of affirmation, quality time, giving gifts, acts of service, physical touch)?
- What social or cultural messages shaped how you experience your bodily self?
- When have you felt the most social power? How was that experience related to your body?

SOME THINGS TO TRY

- Put your hands anywhere on your body and say, "This is my body" or "Here I am." Try doing this several times, letting your hands rest somewhere different each time.

- Place a hand on your chest or belly first thing in the morning and feel yourself breathing. Say to yourself, "Good morning. I'm glad we get to spend the day together."
- Notice the media you consume and take note of what it makes you think or feel about your body or the bodies of others.
- Find a physical activity that makes you feel good, and go do it. Maybe it's jumping in a lake, sitting in a sauna, or dancing. If you're not sure what it could be, start paying attention to experiences that help you realize you are a body, and do those activities more often.

3

The Body Overwhelmed

Healing the Body from Stress and Trauma

This chapter is about trauma and stress. Trauma responses are unique to each of us—what is benign to one can feel overwhelming to another. If you have some responses to your own trauma or mine while reading, this chapter will help you understand those responses by explaining how traumatic memory works. On the pages that follow, I discuss some details of my own car accident trauma, but other mentions of physical, sexual, and emotional trauma and abuse are presented without detailed examples. If you have trauma, know that this chapter might be useful to read, challenging to read, or both. You are not required to read it, now or ever. If you have concerns, you could choose to read it more slowly or to read it in the presence of someone or something comforting.

I was lying on my massage therapist's table, face in the padded hole, and Chopin was playing softly in the background. As

51

the therapist worked her strong but kind hands across my back and down my left side, her oiled fingertips tried to assure my shoulder, "You don't need to hold on so tight. Let me help you let go of whatever you are holding on to." My body had been lying there long enough that I had started to sink into that delicious, heavy place of full relaxation. Then: a striking pang, and a scream was spilling out of me, half pleading, half commanding, "DON'T HIT ME!" Instantly, I was sitting in my car watching a truck swerve across the center lane and speed toward me.

Then, as quickly as the flashback came, it was gone. But my heart was beating furiously, and any semblance of relaxation I had felt had turned to high alert.

We both got very quiet. She knew about the car accidents; it was the reason I was seeing her. She bent down and whispered, "Are you okay?" Panting and feeling as embarrassed as I was scared, I hesitantly offered, "Yeah. I think . . . I just got so scared. I thought the truck was going to hit me again. Right when you pressed into that spot, I was back there." We both held the silence for what felt like longer than it probably was.

"I'm so sorry," I said. "I know you were not going to hit me; you have never hurt me. I think I was just remembering what happened, like it was somehow stuck in my body."

A flashback. A memory emerging like a ghost out my shoulder, taking over my mind, my whole body, and throwing me back into the scariest moment of my life.

We paused again. I started to settle enough that I could once again hear my favorite nocturne playing in the background. Still crouched next to me, she put her hand on my back and said, "I know. Are you okay to keep going, or do you want to stop for today?"

Another long pause. "I'm okay," I said.

"Only when you're ready," she replied.

I was seeing the massage therapist as part of a comprehensive treatment regimen suggested by my doctor following two car accidents that had happened only two months apart. By this point, I clearly met the diagnostic criteria for post-traumatic stress disorder (PTSD).

The first crash had happened on a December morning four months earlier as I was driving to work on the highway. As traffic in front of me hit a natural lull and I started to slow down, the driver of the car behind me, distracted, continued at highway speeds. I saw him coming in the rearview mirror and watched him plow into the back of my car. Then everything went black.

I came back to consciousness like a computer rebooting, the progress bar showing I was only partway there. According to the clock, it had been only a minute since the crash, but it was eerily calm for a highway during rush hour, and my neck and head were already pulsing. I could see people scrambling out of their cars and coming toward me, and I could hear the familiar sounds of West Coast December rain rhythmically hitting my windshield.

My physical rehab was coming along, for the most part. Nearly two months later, in early February, I was able to resume running for a medium-length distance without suffering a headache or back or neck pain. I was by no means recovered, but I was making progress.

Two days after that run, an unusually large snowstorm hit the Pacific Northwest. Although roads in some areas of our city were perilous and residents were warned to stay at home, everyone at my workplace was expected to come in—if the buses could make it to the university campus, we should too.

That afternoon, the weather conditions worsened. With the December collision at the front of my mind at 1:47 p.m., I informed my supervisor that I had rebooked all my afternoon clients and was leaving early. At 2:08, I sent a text to a friend at work to let her know I was going home and would see her later that week. At 2:12, my car had been hit head-on by a truck that had swerved into my lane. The impact sent my car spinning, tossing my body like a rag doll. The car came to a rest only when it slammed driver's side first into cars parked along the side of the snowy street.

When I opened my eyes, all I could see was shattered glass and the powdery airbag smoke. The smell of my burning clothing in the air, and I couldn't catch my breath. I couldn't speak. I couldn't figure out what had just happened. My body shook uncontrollably as I coughed and gasped for air.

This time, there was no post-accident calm. Because it was early afternoon, families were outside enjoying the snow and several people witnessed the accident. Through ringing ears, I could hear people shouting. One voice rose above the rest: "Call the ambulance! I think someone died, someone is dead in there—call 911." I couldn't see outside the car. I couldn't find my voice to clarify that I was very much alive. But I also remember wondering in that moment whether the voice might be right. *Had I died?* I was still shaking, more violently now. My body was moving out of control, as if trying to thrash its way out of this smoky, ice-cold trap.

So many parts of this experience were unimaginably awful. Seeing the truck coming and having certainty in that moment that I would die. Being hit, and then having a second collision when I slammed into the parked cars. Not being sure if I was alive, dead, or somewhere in between. The catastrophic rush of pain that hit my body when the shock seemed to wear off—pain that was quite specifically everywhere.

Then the ambulance arrived—and it was driving straight toward me. As I saw the headlights appear through the dust and smoke, a very small part of me knew the ambulance was approaching slowly, but the rest of me thought it was coming at me just as the truck had done—head-on and fast. I squeaked as I tried to scream, my voice finding its way out of my throat again, "No, no, no! Stop! Don't hit me!" I said it over and over again as the ambulance crept its way carefully toward my car.

In my mind, in my body, I was about to be hit again. I had no concept of time. Context was irrelevant. The only thing I knew was that a second set of headlights was now crossing the same part of my visual field exactly like the first set of headlights, and I was stuck there, trapped in the car with my clothing on fire.

A team of first responders rushed to help me get out of the car, weaving my body out of the crumpled metal like thread through the eye of a needle. They were supporting my fragile body in specific ways under the assumption that my neck, pelvis, knee, arm, and back were broken.

Once I was finally in the ambulance, a tidal wave of tears came cascading out of me. Combined with involuntary shaking, the tears made for a particular sensory duet. I got a very strange look from the paramedic who was in the midst of comforting me when I suggested that my body was likely discharging a sympathetic stress-mobilization response that had been impaired when I felt trapped in my car. It was a strange moment for my prized knowledge about the neurophysiology of traumatic stress to make an appearance between jolts and tearful gasps. One part of my mind was narrating with exquisite accuracy the phylogenic hierarchy of the stress response, while the other part of my mind was still trying to figure out if I was actually alive. All the while, I continued shaking violently and gasping for air.

When Information Helps

Although part of me was terrified, another part of me knew that everything I was experiencing made sense. The shaking, the crying, the memory fragmentation, the thinking it was happening all over again when the ambulance approached my car—all of it was important and part of the holy survival mechanisms embedded in human biology over hundreds of thousands of years of evolution. And survival mechanisms are good, for exactly these moments.

Knowing this meant two things. First, I did not have to rush through any of the processes to make them go away. I could advocate for myself and for the space I needed to begin to process the trauma, even while at the scene of the accident. Second, I did not judge or shame myself for what I was experiencing. When we have nearly died—or encountered anything overwhelmingly scary or stressful—the last thing we need is to feel as if there is something weak or morally wrong about our reactions. At best, such judgments may temporarily diminish the reactions only to drive them deeper inside the body and compound the trauma.

What we need when we are hurting is patient understanding that proves to our whole brain-body system that we are safe. This shows us that whatever we went through is in the past—it is not happening again in this moment as we try to make sense of it all. This kind of compassionate response—generated internally or from others—begins the process of healing the stress and trauma, even within moments after it occurs.

So what do we need to understand about the systems that help us survive during stress and trauma? Here are five true things about the whole brain-body system that most people never learn in school.

1. The brain and body are not separate but intimately connected and in constant dialogue (no matter what we might do to silence that dialogue).
2. Our brain-body system is wired primarily for two things: survival and social connection. Survival and social connection are so closely connected that they are interdependent.

3. Stress and trauma responses are not inherently bad. In fact, they are necessary adaptive responses to things that threaten our survival/relationship drive.

4. If we stay in survival responses too long and without receiving help, our brains and bodies adapt, making it easier to remain in survival responses than to get out of them.

5. We can heal. Our brain-body system is adaptive, and we can use safety cues and relationships to return to a state of rest. This takes time, but it is never too late. And because social connections are central to our survival, we can get back to safety more quickly when we engage the healing process in the context of relationship.

On the following pages, we'll sort through what this means. But for now, take a moment to notice what happened in your body as you read each of the statements above. Did anything make your body tighten and feel hot, or soften and relax? Did anything evoke compassion for something for yourself or someone else? If you reacted to something, be curious about what you felt. You might even choose to say, "This list makes sense, even if I don't understand it fully right now."

Onward, to the Nervous System

The nervous system is a complex information highway that uses nerves and neurons to send messages from the very bottom of your feet to the top of your skull and throughout all your organs, muscles, and cranial tissue. The nervous system has two distinct but connected components: the central nervous system (brain and spinal cord) and the peripheral nervous system (everything outside the brain and spinal cord). A basic understanding of the nervous system reveals that who we are as human beings is so much more than just our ability to think or plan or do abstract reasoning—it is our whole self.

While some branches of our nervous system are responsible for our conscious action in the world—such as reaching for a glass of water when thirsty—most of our nervous system operates unconsciously, either because it is pre-programmed into our wiring thanks to evolution or because of what our body has experienced regarding what is safe or unsafe for us.

We call this unconscious operator the autonomic nervous system (ANS). It is doing things all the time to help us stay alive: triggering the release of hormones we need to dodge a moving car, coordinating digestion and sleep-wake cycles, and letting us know when it's time to go to the bathroom. We don't even think about the ANS most of the time because it does its work in the background. But sometimes our ANS does something that is impossible for us to ignore—it triggers an unexpected and confusing response to stress and trauma.

Defining Stress and Trauma

I use the words *stress* and *trauma* together because they are lesser and greater degrees of the same thing rather than two totally different things. Stress is an activation of the mind-body system in response to experiencing *a stressor*—illness, traffic, death, important events, big life changes, natural disaster, or even the anticipation of those things—together with *the perception of threat posed by that stressor*.

Whether or not we perceive a stressor as threatening is unique to each of us, usually determined by a combination of past experiences, genetics, and the meaning we give to something. In other words, the same event might create stress in one person but not another. For example, although running a marathon is a huge physiological stressor, it's unlikely you'd perceive it as a threat if you signed up for it, trained for it, and had friends cheering you on. Because you have control, you would perceive the experience as meaningful rather than threatening. You can imagine it would feel very different for a person forced to run a marathon against their will.

The stress response is good! We need it for survival; it is a helpful and necessary response to what is happening around us or within us. However, this good thing can be damaging when we experience it for too long or too frequently, or when we have learned to be afraid of it. You may have heard stress described as the "silent killer." When we fear stress itself, we might feel afraid or shame ourselves for having a stress response. We get stressed about stress, and all it does is overload our nervous systems. How we *perceive* stress determines whether the effect on our physiology and even our cognitive performance is positive or negative.[1]

A stressful event becomes a trauma when we feel overwhelmed and powerless. *Trauma* is a Greek word that means "wound." In the therapy community, trauma is defined by how a person experiences an event, not by the event itself. Dr. Rick Bradshaw has offered this helpful definition: trauma occurs when something *negative* and *unexpected* happens, and it leaves us feeling *confused*, *overwhelmed*, and *powerless*.[2]

Not all of us have experienced the big traumas that can cause PTSD (we call these *big-T traumas*, the life-threatening ones that are central to a PTSD diagnosis), but almost all of us have experienced small traumas (we call these *small-t traumas*). Small-t traumas can include everything from non-life-threatening injuries to emotional abuse, racism, bullying, loss of a significant person, harassment, a messy breakup, unexplained losses, unplanned expenses, or a job change. They might seem less significant, even part of everyday life, but when they happen frequently enough, they can affect our emotional and nervous systems even more significantly than big-T traumas.

The Staircase of Stress Response

Although our bodies prefer to be in a rest state rather than a stress state, when something threatens our survival—whether the threat is real, remembered, or perceived—a branch of our nervous system is designed to help us get through the danger and back to a rest state, where we feel calm, playful, and present. Because these survival systems developed a long time ago when threat of attack by wild animals was much more likely, the following wild-animal analogy will illustrate what these processes look like in action.

On a sunny afternoon, I go for a hike in the mountains near my home. Suddenly, I see a cougar on the trail. My survival systems kick into gear: my body releases a cascade of stress hormones to help me move fast, spot additional threats, and pause things not currently a priority, such as digestion, rest, and preparing for a lecture. All this energy helps me back away slowly until the cougar is out of sight and then run down the trail back to safety. When I get back to my car and close the door, I breathe heavily as I feel my body begin to return to normal. I might then call my husband or a friend to tell the story, processing it verbally and establishing a connection that further helps me feel safe and not alone.

That's a best-case scenario. But life, and our brain-body response, is often more complex than a stress-response system that turns on or off like a light switch. Because we are social creatures who need connection and relationship to survive, the threats we experience most often happen between us and other people (not cougars). Instead of an on-off switch, think of the stress response as a staircase with three steps on it. Each step represents one of three responses our body might have to stress: social engagement, mobilization, and shutting down (see fig. 1).[3]

When a stressor threatens our safety, our bodies are wired first to seek help through social engagement, then to mobilize

Figure 1

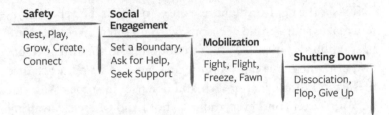

Safety	Social Engagement		
Rest, Play, Grow, Create, Connect	Set a Boundary, Ask for Help, Seek Support	Mobilization	
		Fight, Flight, Freeze, Fawn	Shutting Down
			Dissociation, Flop, Give Up

ourselves to action, and finally, if the first two responses fail, to shut down.

Step 1: Social engagement. Imagine I'm back on the trail, and I see the cougar. My social engagement instinct might be to yell for help, look around for someone else, or grab my phone to make a call.

When we sense danger but still have enough distance from the threat, a branch of our vagus nerve[4] is activated that cues up our throat and inner ears. This helps us speak up and hear specific vocal tones. When this stress response is activated, we do what is called *social referencing*: we pay close attention to what's happening socially, and the messages we get back can help us feel reassured or more at risk.

One of my best friends, Kelsey (who is also a trauma therapist), has told me about times she has noticed this reaction in her eldest daughter. When they are watching a movie and a scary scene (for a kiddo) comes on, her daughter instinctively looks to her mom to make sure everything is okay. When Kelsey cues her that it is safe—through her voice, words, and reassuring smile—her daughter happily turns back to the movie to keep watching.

Step 2: Mobilization. Let's go back to the hike. If no one is around, if social connection won't help me, or if it could put me at greater risk, another branch of my vagus nerve is activated, along with my hypothalamus, pituitary gland, and adrenal gland. These activations trigger the release of stress hormones so I can have all the energy I need to get to safety.

This is the fight-or-flight response, in which the nervous system makes split-second decisions, without our conscious awareness, about whether we are far enough from the threat to get away, or whether escape is futile and we stand a better chance of survival through approach and defense. In some cases, our nervous system puts everything on hold and we freeze, waiting for something to change or hoping to be invisible.

When we are in danger and need to spring into action, we are more likely to choose fight or flight based on what has helped us survive in the past and what has been rewarded or modeled by others. Because we are wired for survival, our nervous systems learn and adapt; the more something has worked in the past, the easier it is for us to form a neurological groove and default to that pattern in the present. That means, for example, that people are more likely to fight back in the present if they grew up in situations where fighting back (with words or action) was the most effective adaptation—even when it's not the most ideal or effective response to a boss's passive-aggressive comments or a partner's query about the dishes in the sink.

Step 3: Shutting down. If neither social engagement nor mobilization systems keep us safe, the final step is shutting down. In the hike scenario, this might look like losing consciousness, feeling a total drain of energy and becoming immobile, or going somewhere else in our minds. This response has many names: flop, defeat, feign death, dissociation, collapse, or the dorsal-vagal complex. It happens when our nervous system decides that we have no other options. You might have seen or heard stories about this happening with animals in the wild. When a predator is too close or actually catches the prey, the prey's only chance of survival is to feign death, hoping the predator will give up and move on.

Because human beings in the West tend to think of ourselves primarily as thinking beings, we overestimate the degree to which conscious thought is responsible for what we do—that every action we take is a choice. But when it comes to the shutdown response, there is no choice at all. It is completely automatic. Shutting down does not mean that you are weak or that the trauma was not real—it means your nervous system is the one calling the shots.

At the moment we are overwhelmed to the point of shutting down, we are experiencing something categorically traumatic. Whether we experience shutting down as floating above our bodies or mentally disappearing into a happier time, this is what our body has determined is our best chance to get through this. And so our bodies get floppy and limp, we curl up, we faint, we dissociate (present in the body, but elsewhere in the mind), or more commonly, we feel like all the life has drained out of us and it is easier just to stay in bed all day.

It is widely understood by researchers and clinicians in the trauma world that depression is often the result of an ongoing shutdown response. Depression is not a feeling but a nervous-system state we move into after having been overwhelmed (by what is around us, memories, or big feelings inside) or mobilized for too long. A brain-body system that learned it couldn't survive by staying engaged, running away, or fighting back decides that its best strategy is to shut down and disengage. Burnout is not so different.

Going Up and Down the Staircase of Stress Response

If every stress response were a textbook case, we would move up and down the staircase one step at a time and in order: We would first use social support. If that fails, we'd move into mobilization. If that fails, we'd shut down. Then we would move back up the staircase in the same progression: from being shut down to mobilization to social engagement and back to feeling safe again. But sometimes when we are in acute danger, or when we have lots of practice hanging out on certain steps, we can skip a step.[5]

While the staircase model can help us make sense of being human more broadly, the stress response itself remains unique to each of us depending on our life experiences. Whatever patterns we have used most in the past are the ones that form neurological grooves in our brain-body system. Just as water running over rocks changes the shape of the rocks, our thinking/behaving/responding changes our neurobiology, making it easier for our nervous system to instinctively take that pathway in the future. For example, if asking for help in the past has worked, it's going to be easier for us to take that social engagement step now than it would be if we had tried it in the past and were shamed or mocked, or we experienced even more violence or hurt as a result.

Climbing Up the Staircase to Safety

Each step of the staircase has a purpose. Based on what step we are on, our bodies do what they need to do, inhibiting or activating certain actions or sensations. When we are on the social engagement step, our bodies communicate to others that we need support or want a boundary to be respected. When we are on the mobilization step, we have huge amounts of energy running through our body. When we are on the shutdown step, our nervous system keeps us disengaged to protect us from risk or threat.

The body-based messages that accompany each step on the staircase communicate what is necessary. For example, the energy of the mobilization stage signals the need for movement and the release of all the energy. Then, when we use up that energy, the body sends a message to our stress-hormone release centers and the higher-brain thinking structures: "Since we used up all this energy, we must have fought or fled our way to safety, so you can stop making all those stress hormones now."

This might make all the difference for us when we are in a stressful situation. For example, it could prevent us from moving from stress into trauma, or it could help us stave off depression, dissociation, or burnout. Our body is giving us everything we need to get to safety; we need to listen to what is happening within us and honor it.

We move up the staircase in the same way we climb down, by passing through each of the steps on the way up. So, if we find ourselves on the shutdown step, it can be surprising to learn that we won't necessarily jump from shutdown to safety. Instead, we're likely to find ourselves on the mobilization step before we move back up to connection with others and ultimately to a state of rest.

Animals who survive a predator attack typically get up, shake themselves vigorously, and then go back to their usual routine.[6] This is one of the theories about why wild animals don't hold on to trauma the way humans do: by shaking and making running motions, they are able to release the trauma response mechanisms that get stuck when they are overwhelmed and shut down. We complete the stress cycle when we release our trauma response mechanisms by moving the stress-related energy out through the body. This often happens involuntarily, through shaking, but we can help ourselves by doing it on purpose—by running, dancing, wiggling, jumping, or squeezing our muscles for a few moments with all our might. Using up this energy sends a signal from one internal monitoring mechanism to another to let the brain-body system know that we are now safe.

After the second car accident, when I was unable to move and my clothing was burning, all of my stress response impulses were activated, but I couldn't do anything. I was trapped at the scene, which was part of what made it a trauma for me. In the ambulance after the crash, I was shaking a lot. As I was coming out of the shutdown state, my body wanted to use up all the energy it had generated to help me fight or take flight but that couldn't be used up while I was trapped in the car. So I shook, just as animals shake when they escape the jaws of a predator.

Trapped in Trauma

Not everyone gets a chance to work their way back up the staircase to safety. Sometimes we don't receive safe and gentle touch, hear loving words, or have the opportunity to discharge the stress energy. When that happens, we can become trapped in our trauma. In fact, I believe one of the reasons trauma and depression are so prevalent is that our social context actually prevents us from listening to our body's need to release the trauma we are carrying. Sometimes what keeps us from shaking out our distress is not the tight seat belt and discharged airbag but the constrictions and inhibitions around emotional expression, race or gender scripts that make our innate capacity to heal seem dangerous or untrustworthy. I have worked with people who shook while processing trauma or who were confused about why their whole body went limp when we started talking about their childhood abuse.

In a societal context that celebrates bodily dissociation and mastery of physicality as a sign of maturity or status, the body's natural desire to heal can be perceived as a threat. We take pride in pushing ourselves beyond our physical limits, reward workaholic employees for their commitment, praise people who eat restrictive diets for having enviable self-discipline, and celebrate "mind over matter" as a sign of moral fortitude. Meanwhile, we are suffering.

This is how trauma gets stuck. This is what makes it hard for our nervous systems to know that we are safe—that what happened was indeed scary and overwhelming but is now over. When we cannot move through the processes that allow our nervous systems to climb the staircase to safety, or when we try to socially engage and all we get is more judgment and criticism, our systems never get the message that the pain is over. As a result, instead of moving from pain to safety, our systems move from pain to pain.

Anything that happens after or in response to the trauma is called a post traumatic factor. These factors influence whether or not we get stuck and how long it takes for our system to recover. For example, whom did we tell and how did that person respond? What happened right after? Did we get the care we needed? Did we have access to medical attention? Were our injuries and symptoms taken seriously? Were we told, "At least you didn't . . ." or other statements that minimized our experience? Or, in the case of rape myths or other horrific sociocultural biases that reinforce victim-blaming, were we told that our trauma was deserved?[7]

What happens before and during a trauma also affects whether or how it gets stuck in our body after a traumatic event. We call these pretraumatic and peritraumatic factors. Physician and trauma specialist Robert Scaer, author of *The Body Bears the Burden*, believes that "the most common complaint in current medical practice, that of persistent and unexplained chronic pain, has its roots in the actual changes in brain circuitry associated with unresolved trauma."[8] (If you are hungry for more information about this, we'll get to that in chapter 6.)

The phrase "return to safety" implies there is safety to return to. But what happens if we never got to return to safety? When hurts occur repeatedly at the hands of those who are supposed to protect us, or when there is no safe place to return to, we call this complex trauma. In complex trauma, unrest might actually feel like the easiest, most comfortable place to us. What should feel safe can feel dangerous, and what should feel dangerous can feel safe. It often means that we never learned it was safe to trust, which leaves us feeling desperately alone inside without knowing how to be connected. And often, if this happened at a young enough age, that overwhelm was managed by a shutdown state of shame, the fundamental sense of being "broken."

Memory Cookies

Imagine you are making cookies. You gather and mix all the ingredients and then bake the cookies in the oven. At this point, it is impossible for you to remove the sugar, flour, or vanilla from the dough but keep the salt. The ingredients are combined in such a way that separate things have become something else in combination. This is my favorite way to think about memories formed during intense experiences.

When we go through trauma, every ingredient of the experience combines in a way that makes it impossible to separate one from the other. So the brain combines the separate elements of a trauma into one memory package, engaging in some extremely helpful processes to keep us safe later. The elements might include things such as a smell, the time of day, the body's posture, close and faraway sounds (including music), lighting, who we're with, where we are, and what happened just before things got scary.[9] Whatever is in the memory bundle associated with the trauma gets neurologically coded as deeply threatening to our safety.

This packaging process is both helpful and unhelpful. It's helpful because if we encounter any of the trauma ingredients again, our brain can quickly activate a stress response mechanism to keep us safe. It's unhelpful because the mere presence of a trauma ingredient doesn't mean the trauma is happening again. In other words, even though you are in a similar situation, smell the same smell, or hear the same song, you are not necessarily repeating the trauma. Instead, you're experiencing a *trigger*—your nervous system is remembering something in the past based on something in the present.

My favorite name for a trigger is the "false positive" response. That is what happened to me while on the massage table. When the therapist put her hand onto a certain muscle in my shoulder, my body remembered the moment of the accident when that muscle first constricted.

Dr. Lorimer Moseley, neuroscientist and pain expert, tells a story in his TED talk about a near-death experience.[10] He was walking in the bush when he felt a nick on his calf. Then, he says, a message went from skin to spinal cord and up to the brain, and it was contextualized by the brain's ability to recall all past similar experiences. The conclusion of his brain activity: "You probably just got scratched by a twig." So he kept walking. Not long after, however, he fell unconscious. It turns out he had been bitten by the deadly Eastern Brown Snake.

Moseley survived, but the next time he was out for a walk in a similar area and felt a nick to the same part of his leg, he fell to the ground writhing in pain. As it turned out, this time it was just a twig. But as before, the messages went from skin to spinal cord to brain, and the brain interpreted the sensory information in light of what had happened in the past. Based on the ingredients from the traumatic memory, his brain sent out messages that said, "We must have been bitten again by an Eastern Brown Snake."

The memory of trauma affects us on a genetic level. We call this epigenetic change. The scientific community has explored epigenetics, or stress-related genetic changes, since the 1940s, when children conceived during the wartime famine in the Netherlands were found to be at increased risk for certain biomedical conditions, such as diabetes.[11] More-recent research has also identified a connection between epigenetic changes and the fear and stress response. For example, what was dangerous to one generation can activate or deactivate certain genes in a way that is passed down to the next few generations, predisposing them to instinctively fear what was dangerous to their parents and grandparents. This can range from specific traumatic events to more widespread cultural trauma.[12]

It is painful to know we could pass on our trauma responses to the next generation. And it helps us explain why some things activate our stress response even if we don't have a trauma of our own around those things. This makes a compelling case for why we would all be better off if we did our own trauma work: while our stress has the ability to turn certain genes on and off, our efforts to heal can do the same.

These findings about epigenetic change not only help us better understand intergenerational trauma but also highlight that embodiment and trauma work are political as well as personal. For example, those in marginalized communities are more likely to experience bodily based trauma—both *to* their body (such as violence or sexual assault) and *about* their body (such as commentary and policies designed to devalue them and subjugate them to the dominant culture). All this is stored in the body just as personal traumatic content is. Epigenetic research helps us better understand how those in marginalized communities bear the heavier burden of intergenerational trauma, and it enables us to marvel at the intergenerational resilience that has helped people survive.

Knowing how our brain-body systems work helps us respond more compassionately to ourselves and others. When we notice ourselves reacting to a trigger, we can respond with "of course" instead of shame, building safety within ourselves regardless of what happens around us. And when we see someone else who is activated, we can offer them the same tenderness we have learned to hold within ourselves.

How to Heal and Be Here

Our whole-person system is adaptive. That means we can learn on our own to adapt to stressful, painful, or traumatic situations. But we can also learn how to get back to a state of rest and safety through relationship cues, safety cues, and the mindful use of skills. It can take time and intention, but it is never too late to start. Here are nine ways you might take a next step.

Work with a trauma therapist. In research and theory about trauma treatment, the first step is always to create safety in the present moment. Only then do we begin to process the trauma actively. Working with a therapist specifically trained to treat trauma is one of the best ways to establish safety.

If the body is where the trauma happened, going back into the body itself can feel threatening, especially when doing so brings up memories and emotions that caused the shutdown. It can be hard to go back to the scene of the trauma alone. This is why it is helpful to do so with a safe and attuned other.[13] The other person's loving and gentle presence communicates to your nervous system (through a process called neuroception) that it is safe for you to stay engaged. When your nervous system has settled, your thinking about the world, yourself, and others can begin to change.

Thanks to research done on trauma since the Vietnam War, we now know that trauma does not happen to our thoughts but to our bodies—and it remains in our bodies until we know we are safe.[14] Therefore, we cannot process trauma only by thinking; we have to use our whole selves, including our physicality. Fortunately, several body-based (or somatic) therapies are designed to help us get beneath thinking to the parts of the system that store the trauma. These include Eye Movement Desensitization and Reprocessing, Brainspotting, Observed and Experiential Integration, sensorimotor psychotherapies, neurofeedback, Accelerated and Experiential Dynamic Psychotherapy, Somatic Experiencing, Trauma Center Trauma-Sensitive Yoga and other trauma-informed movement and expressive therapies, Focusing-Oriented Therapy, Internal Family Systems, and Emotion-Focused Therapy.

Talk to your body. While it's best to have an attuned other present to cue our nervous systems into safety, we can learn to be that supportive and caring person for ourselves. Regardless of where you are on the stress-trauma continuum, if you notice yourself getting stressed or activated, try this: place your hand on your chest or somewhere else on your body (perhaps somewhere that helps you settle, or where you sense distress rising). Then say: "I know you're feeling scared right now. This makes sense in the big picture, even if it's hard to make sense of right now. What is happening is just your survival response in action. You are working so hard to stay alive and safe, and I'm so proud of you for that. You're doing such a good job of getting me ready just in case something awful is going to happen again. Thank you, you are so good." And then, if you really are safe, try adding this: "But you are safe now, and as soon as you're ready, it's okay to let go and come back into rest. I will stay with you the entire time. We will do it together, one breath, one day at a time, as long as it takes."

You could also do this by imagining that the afraid or activated part of you is another person. Sometimes when this part of you is sitting across from you, you know what to say because you have said kind, reassuring things to other people you love.

The example I gave earlier about memory cookies, where all the sensory components get mixed together, applies to positive experiences as well as trauma triggers. Sensory elements can be combined to form memory cookies that help us know we are safe, cared for, and loved. So if you are alone and it is hard to access your truest self, imagine that a loving friend, your therapist, or anyone else who makes you feel safe is talking to you or sitting next to you. The memories and emotions you associate with loving people, or even by thinking of them, can help you access that feeling of love, which you can then use to help yourself feel safe.

Learn about grounding and orienting. Grounding and orienting are skills that help our brain and body remember that we are "here," even when we are remembering something traumatic or anticipating something traumatic or overwhelming. Grounding can also be useful when our stress level has peaked and we are not coping in the present moment. Orienting helps us focus on our environment and the cues that our surroundings are safe. Below is a list of some simple grounding and orienting techniques to try. You may want to keep a copy of this list on hand to access regularly.

1. Use a technique called 5, 4, 3, 2, 1. Notice and list out loud five things you see, four things you can feel, three things you can hear, two things you can smell, and one thing you can taste (or a taste already in your mouth). You could even try picking out five things for each of the senses.

2. Reach out and touch an item near you. Perhaps it is a wall, the floor, the chair on which you are sitting, a rock, or the grass. Feel the sensation of that item in your hand.

3. Put your hands in water or splash cold water on your face.

4. Count backward from a large number by 7 or 13 (such as 12,567 by 13s).

5. Describe aloud the physical sensations you are experiencing in your body.

6. Go for a walk, or take your shoes off and stand on the earth. Feel your feet meet the ground.

7. Describe what you see around you. Pick an object or shape and trace it slowly with your eyes, taking in all the little details.

Practice having choice and power over your own body. During a trauma, you have no choice. But learning that it is safe to be back in your body does require a choice. In a yoga-based trauma

73

therapy called Trauma Center Trauma-Sensitive Yoga (TCTSY), you might hear an instructor say, "I invite you to bend forward at the hips. You can choose to stay here, or you can choose to add movement by swaying from side to side at whatever pace or intensity feels right for you. As you're swaying to the left, you might notice some of the following sensations down your spine. . . ." This invitation to choose what you want to do with your body is about bodily agency. This kind of movement is one way to begin practicing *interoception*. Interoception is the ability to sense what is happening inside your body and to know yourself from the inside out. Some examples of interoception include noticing hunger cues, physical changes that come with emotion, heart rate, or even if you feel hot or cold.

Use your imagination or memory to help you shift your emotional and physical state. Because everything that happens inside of you is connected, you can use what you are thinking about or your memories to help cue your body into a different emotional state. Just as remembering a trauma can make your body feel unsafe, you can remember a time you felt safe and calm to help your body feel at ease again.

Try remembering a time you felt completely safe or at peace. If it is hard to remember, you might try thinking of a split-second memory. Remember what was going on around you, what it felt like in your body, what you were thinking. Pay special attention to as many of the sensory elements as you can. You could also try visualizing yourself doing a task you find calming, picture the face and voice of someone you love, or think about something you are looking forward to and visualize yourself experiencing it.

Update your interpretation of your stress response. Interestingly, some new evidence shows that *how* we think about stress affects the measurable effect it has on our health (research done in this area has been called Stress Mindset Theory, mentioned earlier in this chapter). In studies, those who perceived stress

74

as helpful—as a way that their bodies were equipping them to navigate difficult situations—had fewer long-term negative health effects of stress, and many performed better at whatever task they were attempting to accomplish. In contrast, those who perceived stress as negative had worse health effects from stress.[15] If we can shift our thinking about our bodily response when stressed, it can be protective and even corrective.

Here is how this could look: First, notice a stress response, such as a racing heart, buzzing energy in arms or legs, hyper-vigilance, perhaps even wide eyes and racing thoughts. Then place a hand somewhere on your body and say to yourself, "Thank you for responding to help us get through whatever is going on. I know you are doing everything you can to keep us safe." If you don't need a stress response in that moment, you could try adding, while still keeping your hand pressed against your skin, "I'm so glad that you are there, helping me get ready for danger. Right now, I am safe, and I am going to take care of you. So, you're welcome to step aside for now, and I am so relieved to know you will be right there as soon as I need you to protect me."

Learn about your own stress response staircase. Find a journal or set up a secure digital document and create your own version of a stress response staircase (based on the model from earlier in the chapter). For each of the steps (safety, social engagement, mobilization, shutting down), make a list of the behaviors, thoughts, or internal sensations that let you know when you are on that step. Try thinking about some of these questions:

- What does it feel like to be on this step?
- What sensations are in your body?
- What goes through your mind?
- What feelings do you have?

Then focus on safety:

- What people, situations, or environments signal that you can move up the staircase to safety?
- What people, situations, or environments signal that you should move down the staircase?

By beginning to be conscious of stressors and the sensations that accompany them, we can learn to put specific strategies in place to manage feelings when we do find ourselves experiencing a stress response.

Use your breathing to regulate and shift your state. I've noted how the vagus nerve responds based on the level of danger or safety you are in. The nerve itself runs bidirectionally, meaning it sends information from the brain to the lungs and from the lungs to the brain. That makes intentional breathing a very powerful skill you can learn and practice to tell your body that it's safe. It is particularly powerful when you take breaths that

- come in through your nose (breathing through your nose helps you take in more oxygen and more nitrous oxide);
- go deep into your belly (pushing bottom ribs to the side and belly to the front);
- have nice, long exhales (exhales are more calming, inhales are more activating); and
- are slow, with gentle pauses between the inhale and exhale (ideally, when at rest, we take about four or five breaths per minute).

Try researching nasal breathing techniques, box breathing, or guided-imagery exercises for breathing. Partner breathing can also be a helpful way to experience safety cues. If your partner is feeling calm and engaged with you, try matching your pace of breathing to theirs, or simply watch them breathe. A word on breathing: sometimes it can trigger a paradoxical effect by making a person who has been through trauma feel even more overwhelmed and unsafe, triggering a panic attack or other state of overwhelm. If that happens to you, you are not broken, but breathing may not be the best practice for you at this moment, or it may be something to work on in the presence of a trained professional.

Practice going slow. The speed at which we engage healing practices is just as important as the practices themselves. This is where titration comes in. *Titration* is the clinical word for exposing ourselves to traumatic content in small portions so that we do not become overwhelmed or retraumatized. "Touching" on difficult and stressful content in small doses helps us build our tolerance over time, and it helps us practice getting into and out of the traumatic content safely.

Learning to Be Safe Again

Our stress and trauma responses are constantly sending us messages. Our distress signals sound the alarm to indicate that something is wrong or that what is happening presently reminds us of something scary from the past. These signals alert us to change a pattern or to develop a skill. Instead of ignoring these signals, we can learn to listen to them as they help us move into compassionate relationship with ourselves, learn to care for others in meaningful ways, and prompt us to take steps toward healing. In this way, learning to listen to and honor our trauma and stress responses, even in how awful they feel, can serve our ability to grow and heal.

It is our ability to heal and reclaim our bodies—rather than what happened to us—that punctuates our stories. As with the stress response, healing is also written into our DNA. Like a million little resurrections waiting for us, there is healing and victory each time we notice our breathing, speak kindly to our body, or work to change a harmful pattern that was woven into our DNA long before we knew it was happening.

I had proof of my own healing after a therapy session not long ago.[16] I have been seeing a psychologist who specializes in trauma to help my body remember that I am not still in that car about to get hit by the truck. When I think about the accident, I typically go back to one of three moments, sometimes in succession: the moment before my car was hit head-on, the moment my car was spinning before it hit the parked cars and came to a stop, or the moment I was sitting in my car and heard people screaming that I was dead. After a recent therapy appointment in which we were using a therapy process called EMDR,[17] I wobbled down to my car feeling completely exhausted but also more settled than I'd felt before the session.

As I got into my car, a new memory of the accident came back to me. I was in my smoke-filled car and people were outside the vehicle screaming when a young woman opened the passenger door. She softly but firmly asked, "Are you okay?" I didn't answer because I couldn't move my neck to turn to see her. I heard her run off and talk to someone else. They were on the phone with the ambulance, and then I heard her footsteps running back to me over crisp snow and broken glass. She paused, only for a moment, and then climbed into the passenger side of the car and said, "My name is Paige, and the ambulance is on its way. It's going to be a little bit until they get here. There are lots of accidents because of the snowstorm, but they are on their way."

As soon as she crawled into the wreck, I let out a sound I don't know if I've ever heard myself, or anyone else, make before. Part scream, part cry. She got closer to me. Like she was lacing a shoe, she wove her left hand around the back side of me and her right arm around the front side of me. I cried harder. And she said, "You must have been so scared. It was so

78

scary. You are alive, you will be okay, and the ambulance is on its way, and I'm going to stay with you until they get here." She rested her head on my shoulder and said the same thing over to me about a hundred times.

After therapy that day, I remembered that Paige had been there when the ambulance drove up and I thought I was getting hit again. She calmly told me that I was going to be okay, and that it was scary, but the ambulance was there. When the EMTs got to the car, she climbed out so they could get in. As they were trying to get me out of the crushed vehicle, she thought one of them was being rough with me and said with striking firmness, "Stop it! Be gentle with her."

That was the last I heard or saw of her. An angel disguised as a university student, I am certain.

Another thing clicked into place after that therapy session. One of the first times I had a flashback while driving, I was on a highway just outside of Los Angeles driving to an event, and I thought I was about to be hit again when an oncoming car temporarily swerved into my lane. It was enough for my body to react. I pulled over and told myself some of the same things Paige had told me. *It was scary, but you are alive, and you will be okay.* At the time, I wondered where those words had come from. It seemed that they too had become part of the trauma memory, buried under the more horrific parts and waiting to surface when I needed them.

Eager to reach the venue, I got back on the road, still shaking but not far from my destination and wanting it just to be over. As I pulled up to the venue where I was meeting some friends, Mike McHargue saw my car pull up, and he noticed how I uncharacteristically remained sitting in the car. Mike is one of my closest friends, and when I see him, I almost always drop all my possessions and run over to give him a hug. This time, I was stuck in the car. He came over and opened the door, and again I burst into shakes and tears. He helped me get out of the car, brought me inside, and held me as I cried and shook until it felt like I had crested the top of a wave of fear and was coming down the other side. Solid, but with so much gentleness, he held my shaking body in an embrace. In an experience of complete attunement and safety, I knew he would not let go until I was ready, and that however long it took would not be too long for him. Without knowing it, he said some of the same words Paige had said to me in the car. His words and embrace merged into the old memory of the accident, adding new ingredients of safety and care.

What is striking to me now is that I didn't remember Paige coming into the car until I had processed some of the trauma. It was as if, in the processing, my body could change how it remembered the event, and something deeply sacred, beautiful, and miraculous came to the surface: the memory of an unknown young woman holding me in the scariest moment of my life. Her body against my body. Her arms and head against my side. Her body reminding my body that even though I was scared, I was not alone.

I am so incredibly grateful for both of them, a stranger and a best friend, who helped me in moments when I needed it most. If strangers and friends can offer so much compassion to me, then I can certainly offer the same level of compassion to myself. And if I can learn to do that, so can you.

Being a trauma therapist, and healing from my own trauma, has convinced me that we can heal. When we do the work to change our patterns, to get out of stress and into safety, to be kind to our pain and distress instead of judgmental, to let someone into our trauma to help us experience it differently, we can experience transformation in the same way that our body experiences stress and trauma. We can integrate memories. We can learn to be safe again. We can leave behind a story categorized by a choppy, fragmented, silent scream, certain parts under a magnifying glass, others seemingly invisible. Healing is written into our bodies. Just as they can go down the staircase, our bodies can come up the staircase. It takes time, support, and openness to receiving the safety and care of others, but our wise bodies know how to heal.

For the first time since the accident, just now as I wrote out this story, I didn't feel afraid when remembering. Surprisingly, what I do feel is a deep, wide, open warmth in my chest, gratitude in skin and muscles, comfort in the voices of Paige and Mike, and sheer safety on the other side of overwhelming fear. People nurtured me in moments that proved to me that the danger, and the aloneness within the terror, was over. Slowly, I can feel my body climbing the staircase to rest.

SOME THINGS TO THINK ABOUT

Try thinking about some of your reactions to things that catch you off guard or things you know are related to a trauma trigger. What might you do or say to create safety in yourself when those things happen? How can you respond compassionately to yourself afterward? If you don't know how, imagine being with someone who is compassionate, and think of what they might say.

SOME THINGS TO TRY

- If you haven't been to therapy before but have a history of trauma, unexplained or chronic pain, or big gaps in memory or choppy memory, try doing therapy with someone who has advanced training in one of the therapies listed in this chapter, or take the small steps to prepare for when you're ready, like researching therapists who do this kind of work or getting recommendations from friends.

- Make your own grounding toolkit. Put together a collection or list of grounding items, practices, or resources for when you feel yourself starting to head down the stress staircase.
- Make a voice recording of yourself saying what you need to hear when you are overwhelmed or triggered. Play it back to yourself as a reminder that you will not always feel that way and that you can comfort yourself.
- Notice if you need to discharge any energy that is in your body after something stressful happens. Identify one or more of the strategies suggested in this chapter that you can use to help your body move up the staircase toward safety.

4

Appearance and Image

How We See Our Body from the Outside

As usual, Jazmyn was early for her appointment. I found her in the waiting room with a book, a mug of coffee, and a bag of miscellaneous things, as if she were ready to be there for hours. I had been seeing her in therapy for almost two years now, and she trusted me. She had always been fun to work with, her jokes cleverly disguising her mistrust of others and the fear knit into her muscle fibers. But as we peeled back layer upon layer and had enough Monday evenings together that she began to relax into my care, her defenses dropped and the stories she told me became less curated.

She came from a family fraught with stressors. She learned to keep the peace by acting in ways that put everyone at ease. Around puberty, her body became the playground for an extended family member for several years. When she tried to tell her parents about the abuse, she was ignored. She described the interactions with her parents as being just as disorienting as the violence done to her body. They never spoke of it again.

And yet her parents' silence about the abuse posed a stark contrast to the surprising amount of detailed commentary and attention they paid to her body in other ways. Without hesitation, Jazmyn could rattle off the comments and circumstances under which they occurred—all the times she'd been told her body was bad. Usually, comments were paired with a smack of the back of the hand to the skin folding over her waistband. She was constantly reminded that someone else was monitoring her size, her shape, her very self—and reminding her to monitor it too.

It was no wonder that decades later she talked about living her life as if watching it from the outside. That Monday night she told me about a recent experience at a restaurant. As she was ordering, she could not stop thinking about two things: what the waiter thought about what she was ordering and what everyone else in the restaurant was thinking about her body, from whatever angle they saw her. She was doing what she had been trained to do: to think of herself as being monitored, to think of herself from the outside, and to anticipate judgment. Long after the back of her mother's hand had stopped smacking her, she continued to smack herself mentally, punishing herself for the "sins" of her body. As she described it, at least then she could control her unruly body before someone else tried to or made her a target for more violence of any kind.

Learning about the Body as an Image

Just as Jazmyn did, most of us have learned to forget being a body and to think of our bodies in terms of how they appear from the outside. This is so pervasive that when I speak and write about the body, most people think I'm talking about appearance. We have learned that we are objects, two-dimensional versions of ourselves, images that can be liked, not liked, criti-cized, or praised. Often, seeing the body as an outside object becomes our starting point long before we understand what it even means to be a *self*.

The term *body image* first showed up in the mid-twentieth century when Austrian psychiatrist Paul Schilder defined it as "the picture of our own body which we form in our mind, that is to say the way in which the body appears to ourselves."[1] In short, body image is what we think about our appearance. More research and other theories have resulted in expanded defini-tions of Schilder's term. But most of the time when we read or talk about body image, we're referring to how we perceive and evaluate our appearance, how accurate those perceptions are, how we feel about all of that, and how we behave as a result.

Body image is about evaluating our appearance, but what criteria do we base our evaluations on? What are the metrics for a desirable body? Our experiences influence our percep-tions, which means that the criteria we use are handed to us through comments people make about our bodies, images we view, and how other people talk about their bodies. The explicit messages, the subtext, and what is not seen or said all contribute to shaping our criteria. In body image research, we call this the Tripartite Influence Model. Culture has ideals about bodies—what is considered a body to prize and what is a body to change—and the ideals are communicated through three primary sources of influence: parents, media, and peers. Messages are passed through these three sources via indirect and direct communication.

The work of my first book focused on how messages about body image are passed like heirlooms between women from one generation to the next. What I found in my research is that kids notice all the subtleties of their parents' beliefs about bodies, even when the parents did not know the kids were watching or listening. This was true even when parents didn't know they were "saying" anything. For example, adult children remember that the men in the family got two servings at dinner, while the women got only one. As children, they remember piecing together that "fat is bad" because they overheard their mothers making disparaging comments about their own bodies in the mirror or in a changing room. These are examples of indirect communication from parents.

Shame-based indirect communication is just as damaging as direct communication. After observing and hearing enough of it, a child can start to build a belief system about desirable and undesirable bodies without even noticing it. This is not meant to be mother- or parent-blaming, but it does remind us that we influence others. Each of us is shaping or reinforcing the culture that is also hurting us. If you are a parent, an educator, or someone with the privilege of shaping lives, it is important to become aware of your self-perception, self-talk, and body ideals—and model what you hope to see in those you are raising or influencing.

Parents also use direct communication, as Jazmyn's parents did. Parents might say things such as, "A good body looks like . . ." or, "Make sure you never wear . . . or never look like . . ." Those messages are hard to miss. Sometimes children are fortunate enough to have direct communication that supports a healthy appearance story.

Media and peers also offer direct and indirect communication about bodies. In the media, we are sometimes told directly "fat is bad" or "get smoother skin" or "whiten your teeth" and on and on. Direct messages like these are meant to make us feel so bad about ourselves that we buy whatever is being sold—weight-loss programs, skin cream, whitening toothpaste—to resolve the dissatisfaction or disgust we feel about our appearance.

Indirect media communication about body image happens, for example, when we see only certain kinds of bodies in ads.

Why were no fat bodies in that ad? Why are so many white movie stars in mainstream-media award shows? Why do we only see television characters that look *that* way (whatever *that* way is)? What people look like when they are selling certain products, and the people we don't see in those same advertisements, also shapes our internalization of the ideal appearance.

When it comes to our peer group, direct and indirect messages about appearance often take the form of a greeting. We say things such as, "You look good" and use appearance comments when we first see each other. Especially if appearance has been important to us, our brains notice inconsistencies in our friends' responses: we ask ourselves, sometimes without knowing it, what is happening on the days when no one makes a comment about our appearance at all.

A frequent pattern identified by eating disorder research, and by those with lived experience, is that celebratory comments from others increase after losing weight through experimenting with food restriction and disordered eating.[2] Instead of seeing a person's distress or need for support, we praise the behavior supporting an illness. Celebrating another person's weight loss and believing it to be complimentary supports cultural messages about weight bias that end up hurting us all. This praise reinforces the idea that our appearance is connected to our social belonging. It can hook us into a cycle of trying to change our body to earn value in the eyes of others. This system fuels conditional self-worth, which in turn keeps us endlessly chasing affirmation.

A conditional self-worth and appearance-based value system is damaging wherever you are in life, but it becomes particularly problematic as we age. This is more true for women than for men, as there is a double standard in aging: aging men are seen as having increased prestige, whereas aging women have less importance as they are no longer seen as sex objects. Although not as obvious, the "problem" of the aging body is challenging for some men as well, particularly when it comes to hair loss, protruding bellies, difficulty getting or sustaining an erection, or anything else that creates the feeling that one is moving away from the ideal.

One of the fascinating findings that showed up in my doctoral research was that as women age and move further away from beauty standards associated with youth, thinness, fertility, and sexual objectification, they have a choice to make: they can put more work into maintaining a socially valued image, or they can quit the game altogether and find freedom in letting go of the body expectations they have carried since puberty.[3] When it comes to appearance, aging can feel like a loss at first. Sometimes moving away from the ideal is a reminder that the ideal was an unrealistic construct all along, offering none of the self-worth and freedom it promised. For some, this creates the possibility of opting out of body shame—fueled efforts to change the body. When what we had oriented our life around slips from our grasp, we have the choice to either hold on tighter or open our hands and let go.

Moving onto the Front Lawn

We are told many things about the ideal body, but we are never told that the promises of what will happen to us when we arrive at the ideal are false. Complete lies. We are told, for example, that when we have the ideal appearance, we will be carefree, sexually irresistible, and self-satisfied. What research about body image and dieting shows is that for those who find self-worth in appearance, working hard to arrive at the body ideal does not render us more relieved and secure; rather, it can make us more afraid of our appearance changing in ways we do not want, rendering us more preoccupied with the strategies that got us there.[4] And those who cannot get as close to the ideal as they wish often end up feeling some sense of moral failure, as if there were something fundamentally wrong with them because they could not fit their perfectly normal body into the box of an impossibly unrealistic ideal.

We have been objectified and we have played along, learning to objectify ourselves as if it were our moral duty to do so. But in the process, we have lost sight of what it costs us. Imagine you are fortunate enough to own a house. You have all sorts of resources within your home that help you live your life: a pantry stocked with food for nutrition, plush pillows for resting in the sanctuary of the bedroom, a walk-in shower in which to get clean. But after living in your house for a few years, you happen to peer out the front window and notice all your neighbors on their lawns. Everyone in the neighborhood is outside, and they're all talking about their houses. One of them waves to you from across the street and calls out, "I love the new trim above your door. Looking good!" It feels good to be seen. Then your next-door neighbor says, "You should be really happy about your roof. Mine is so much worse than yours." Down the street, two neighbors are comparing house size. All of this is news to you. You were content living life inside your house until the compelling dialogue about colors, shapes, and house sizes drew you outside.

Pretty soon, you start spending more time outside on the lawn comparing your house to the other houses. Your house doesn't look quite like it used to, so you start doing what you can to fix it up. When people notice the changes and comment, it feels good. Pretty soon, you find yourself spending more time on your front lawn than you do inside the house. And because your house tells the story of rainy winters and hot summers, including wear on the garage door and some faded paint, you're working hard to maintain the outside. But over time, you lose sight of the fact that your house was made to inhabit, not just evaluate; you were meant to live inside your home, not on the front lawn. You also forget that your home is *yours*—which means it doesn't have to look like the neighbors'. Your home is a place that allows you to express your own style, to entertain, and to store the resources you need to get through the demands of life.

When it comes to our bodies, most of us are living on the front lawn. We are looking at our bodies from the outside only, and we have not yet learned how to move back in. In other words, we are so fixated on our appearance that we lose the ability to sense what is happening inside. Even if all our attention is on the outside, the house still exists—for us. We are all born living on the "inside"—it really is the only option. But as we start to realize we have a *public body*—that other people comment on, celebrate, use, grab, or critique—it gets harder to resist leaving the home that has always been ours.

Self-objectification is the clinical term for living on the front lawn. Objectification Theory was first made public in 1997 by psychology professors Barbara Fredrickson and Tomi-Ann Roberts, who explained objectification as the experience of being female in a patriarchal culture that sexually objectifies the female body.[5] Girls and women are highly likely to be objectified, but increasingly boys and men are objectified as well. When this happens, a person can begin to self-objectify—to internalize the observer's perspective as a primary way to view themselves. Objectification and subsequent self-objectification are central to disembodiment and are linked with a variety of health concerns, including depression, eating disorders, substance abuse, self-harm, and sexual dysfunction.[6]

Psychologist Carol Gilligan's topical work has been important for helping us understand the process by which we "move out of our house," especially when it comes to girls and women. Gilligan and her research colleagues demonstrated that when girls' bodies change during puberty, they start to see themselves differently because of how others begin to treat them.[7] One year, the walk to school is characterized by hopscotch and talk about friendship bracelets. The next year the same walk comes with unwanted attention from the man driving by or the boys catcalling while riding by on their bikes. The changing body means a changing experience of the world and the newfound awareness that one can exist in the minds of others as a sexualized object. Gilligan's research showed how girls' changing experience of the body was connected to how they experienced themselves in relationship with others and consequently how girls used language. This included how confident they were in sharing their ideas or speaking up in conflict and the actual words they used when interacting with someone.[8]

Girls move onto the front lawn when, during puberty if not before, the world tells them it's time to do so. Sadly, boys learn to do it even earlier. This often happens around age five when they are socialized at school in groups of other boys who have already learned to tuck away anything associated with femininity. For boys, the ideals are reinforced by mockery and physical force. There are social consequences for boys who feel their tender feelings in a hypermasculine world, which paradoxically rewards both rationality and irrational violence. While girls learn to live on the lawn when they become preoccupied with appearance for desirability, worth, or belonging, moving onto the lawn can also be motivated by a desire to flee what is in the house.

Body Shame, Neutrality, and Positivity

Walking outside the house, hanging out on the front porch, admiring how it looks with someone we love, or planting our favorite flowers in the garden are all part of enjoying the house and making it our own. Having a body image isn't wrong. Our appearance allows us to interact with the world in a mostly coherent way. The reason my friends recognize me when I show up at their back door and let myself in is because of my appearance and its relative continuity over time. My appearance is mine, it belongs to me, and it expresses who I am.

The primary way many of us talk about bodies is through shame-based dialogue about appearance, even in covert forms, such as praising body changes like weight loss. This is one of the many expressions of negative body image. Shame and disgust about our appearance has become normalized. We even use shame to connect with other people, commiserate, protect ourselves from what we think others might be thinking, or maybe even make others feel better about their body shame. Social psychology research calls this "fat talk."[9] Fat talk is what happens when individuals bond over hatred or frustration with their appearance. It shows up for individuals across the weight spectrum, with those in larger bodies feeling even more pressure to speak this way. Sometimes, people do this accidentally, because the way they think about their bodies in private spills out into the conversation. It can also be a tool to create connection and reassure someone we care about: "You have nothing to complain about. My [weight, shape, skin, pant size, cellulite, etc.] is way worse than yours." We put ourselves down to make other people feel better. But all this does is reinforce the comparison game and suggest that your body is only "okay" because it's not as "bad" as mine.

All this shame-based dialogue can be exhausting. And talk about bodies, especially talk about how bodies should look, can be so painful for us that we just need spaces where no one comments on bodies at all. We need a way to detox. We need breaks from the constant reminders of our public bodies. We need spaces where we can interact with others in a way that helps us remember other parts of our lives. For people whose bodies have been the focus of public commentary, trauma, or self-objectification, having spaces that are free from dialogue about the body can be revolutionary. It can also be a form of resistance, especially when people are relegated to their body in ways that disconnect them from other important parts of their social identity, and when their skills are devalued or neglected because of a focus on obvious "different" or oppressed aspects of their bodily identity. And as the body-positivity movement[10] gains popularity, a person might even feel frustrated or ashamed for how their relatively unchanging body image persists in the face of other people's newfound body positivity. I have a friend who says, "I don't want to hear about how someone else is totally in love with their cellulite when I'm still trying tirelessly just to not hate myself. I have been obsessed with my appearance in an unhealthy way for so long that I am working hard to remember the other parts of my life that make up who I am."

The term *body neutrality* has been coined by those in the body-image movement who are seeking an alternative to the term *body positivity*. When a person has felt disgust for their body, the thrust of body positivity (think "radical body love") can feel grandiose or like too much of the same thing—a singular focus on appearance. Body neutrality offers an intermediary step on the way to body positivity, or it can be a completely satisfying result in itself. Body neutrality suggests that instead of love, wild affection, or enthusiasm, acceptance is an option. Acceptance might sound like, "This is my body. As is." An optional addition would be, "Can we talk about something else, please?" Body neutrality is a viable option especially for someone working to move away from self-judgment fueled by an appearance-focused social context. What body neutrality offers us is an invitation to consider that our value, strengths, and personhood are separate from our appearance and from how others or we ourselves have evaluated our appearance.

My one concern about body neutrality has to do with the language; it seems to be a misnomer to reference the body, in its entirety, when the movement is mostly focused on appearance. The body is not simply about appearance. Perhaps a more accurate term than *body neutrality* would be *appearance acceptance* or *appearance neutrality*—the idea that appearance just is. Part of body neutrality is remembering that the body is more than appearance. Additionally, given that our bodies are also the place of oppression, and inherently political, I'm not sure we can be neutral about our bodies. When I use the term *body positivity*, I am referring only in part to appearance and also to all the other aspects of the body. For example, I believe it's possible to be body positive by placing your hand against your beating heart and saying "thank you" to this organ that is keeping you alive, without once thinking about how you look in the mirror.

If body positivity means that we must have unwavering affection for our appearance without any complexity or negotiation, I don't think such a thing exists. Such all-or-nothing thinking fails to dignify the multitudes and nuances at work within us all. After all, body positivity itself backfires when it becomes another metric to chart our failure.

If we are moving from body negativity to body positivity, the *way* we do it has to change too. There must be room for flexibility and compassion. As with any healthy relationship, when there are misunderstandings and hurt happens, the repair of that rupture is what matters most and ultimately determines whether the relationship is healthy. The same is true of the relationship we have with our bodily selves. Just as in a healthy romantic relationship, in the relationship we have with our body we want the arc of time to point toward safety and connection, even if there are repairable disruptions along the way. Regardless of the language we use or whether we better identify with body positivity or body neutrality, we all want it to feel good and safe to be us, and we want to know that harmful scripts about bodies don't define our worth.

A non-appearance-related, healthy, and realistic body positivity invites us to consider the following affirmations, some of which we touched on in chapter 2:

- My body is good, without conditions. The word *body* includes more than just appearance; it encompasses the fullness of what it means to be human.
- I do not need to change my body in any way to be more valuable, even if my culture says otherwise.
- I do not need to punish myself for a changing appearance or for looking different at two points in time.
- If it is hard to understand why my body is doing something, I can assume there must be a reason, even if I don't know it now.
- My appearance is a part of me, but it is not the only or most important part of me.
- Being a body invites me into deeper connection with myself and those around me.
- I can respond to negative body-image thoughts with curiosity and kindness, and doing so can deepen self-trust and create safety within myself.
- My body is not bad, but cultural scripts have gotten lots of things wrong when it comes to bodies, and sometimes I get the two confused. This is true of my abilities and my limitations—instead of seeing my body as the problem (the medical/pathology model), I can see society's narrow definition of the ideal body as the problem (the social model).
- My body is made up of all sorts of experiences, some of which I don't even remember because I was young or because they were handed down to me by past generations. These experiences shape what it's like to be me in the world. My body is a living map, a nonverbal intergenerational biography, tracing me back to my ancestors and, ultimately, to all humans.

Try reading through this list and listening to your bodily cues. Notice what feels connecting or relieving, and what is uncomfortable or disorienting. This list is just a place to start; consider it something to come back to, write out on your own, or add on to.

There are spaces where body neutrality is essential. For example, it's inappropriate for an employer to comment on a person's weight during a work lunch or for us to evaluate a political leader's policies based on how they look. There may even be points in a person's life where body neutrality feels like the most victorious place to land after swimming in the sea of negative body image. However, we needn't settle for body neutrality—there is so much more for us than neutrality. I understand that appearance is confusing and that it's challenging to think about our body as more than just our appearance—particularly an appearance we learned to see through the eyes of others. Yet goodness, or we could call it love, is all around us, always happening. And part of why we became so fixated on appearance and negative body image is that we were never taught that the same goodness that is out there is also right here—in this body, in this beating heart, flowing through me into the world. Treasuring our bodies in a way that extends beyond appearance is an invitation to recognize that right here, in this breath and in this space I take up on the earth, I have autonomy, agency, creativity—and it is good. In *The Body Is Not an Apology*, Sonya Renee Taylor implores us to consider how this kind of radical self-love is essential for building a world where every body can belong. She says that creating a world that works for every body "is an inside-out job. How we value and honor our own bodies impacts how we value and honor the bodies of others."[11] Learning to love ourselves well inspires us to interrupt the systems of body shame and oppression. While we can be appearance neutral (what I see as a main thrust of the body-neutrality movement), disrupting body hierarchies invites us to be decidedly non-neutral about bodies in general. Regardless of how we feel in the moment about our appearance, believing in the goodness of our own body is one place we can start.

Building Body Positivity and Embodiment

You might have heard someone say something like, "My head is saying one thing, but my gut is saying another." In other words, "What I know in the higher-order part of my brain has not trickled down into the lower, felt-sense part of my brain. There's a disconnect." When it comes to changing our sense of self and moving away from an over-fixation on appearance, the best way to get what we know about body positivity into our felt sense of ourselves is to have new experiences and to savor them.

Earlier I described changing our thinking using the metaphor of planting a new bulb, not ripping off a flower head and gluing on a new one. Think of experiential learning as "bottom up" learning, like watering the roots of that daffodil plant so the flower can grow, instead of watering the blossom itself and hoping it trickles down to the soil. This is true of body positivity too. If the list of affirmations above feels terrifying or impossible, forget about the list for now. Instead, allow me to offer you some ideas—all based on evidence from current research, including my own—about healing body image and coming into wholeness. Think of these as practices (dealing with the roots) you can use to change your body image (the blossom).

When we are hyperaware of our outward appearance, our inner awareness often suffers. Learning to tune in to the inside of ourselves interoceptively (for example, noticing sensation in bladder, heart, stomach, and lungs), and practicing that regularly, has been shown to improve body image.[12] Interoception is possible because of all the messages that run from our body to our spinal cord (through something called afferent nerves), up

97

to our brain stem, and then into a region very deep within our brain called the insula. Interoception is essential for creating the experience of balance and homeostasis, regulating emotion, having a sense of body ownership, and experiencing continuity as a person over time. When we have these experiences, we are training our attention to remember ourselves as more than an appearance, and we are less likely to try to manage our appearance as a means of creating agency in our lives.

Just as it is with any other sense, we can fine-tune interoception through practice. One exercise involves sensing our heart rate without taking our pulse, a technique pioneered by psychology professor Rainer Schandry.[13] It provides a way for researchers to measure, with relative objectivity, how aware a person is of their interoceptive cues, and then how accurate that awareness is.

To practice this skill, trying to become aware of your pulse, without using your fingers on your wrist. It can take patience and practice. My friend Dr. Jerome Lubbe has suggested that if we have a hard time sensing our pulse, we can try puckering our T-shirt in front of our belly in such a way that we can see the belly's pulse through how the T-shirt moves. Seeing our pulse creates a sensory foothold we can use to begin locating the interoceptive sensation of the pulse, like leapfrogging from one sense to another.

Another way to practice interoception is by paying attention to when you are hungry, full, tired, or need to use the toilet. If sensing your own heart rate seems too difficult, try paying attention to hunger and fullness cues. Because most of us feel hungry and full at least a few times each day, there are multiple opportunities to practice. Try asking yourself next time you are hungry, "How do I know I'm hungry? How would I explain this to someone who had never felt hunger before? How do I know that I'm full? What is it like? What senses are telling me that I can stop eating?"

Even if body image is not your concern, practicing interoception is worthwhile. People who are able to notice their interoceptive cues and do so with a high degree of accuracy are better at completing complex cognitive tasks and using intuition for decision making. In contrast, people who have a low degree of awareness and accuracy around interoceptive cues are more likely to see their body as an object, and they are more likely to struggle with depression and eating disorders.[14]

Seeing ourselves as a human being with an appearance, recognizing ourselves in the mirror, and using appearance to express ourselves are normal, developmentally appropriate tasks. But our excessive focus on appearance and the associated tie to worth and value is not healthy; neither is it a skill any of us needs to focus on more. Our image-saturated culture ingrains this harmful idea enough. While the ultimate goal is for our embodiment to be the predominant moment-to-moment way we relate to our bodies, there are a few things we can do to help heal our body image specifically.

The first is media literacy. Media literacy is the ability to view and analyze media critically so we can see through the behind-the-scenes communication strategies and portrayals of bodies. Developing media literacy makes us an active participant rather than a passive consumer. It requires educating ourselves about how images are altered to portray bodies in very specific ways, and what those alterations communicate about which bodies are valuable. It also requires noticing bodies that are underrepresented, which means looking for what is missing in media. We start to pay attention to why only thin people appear on a magazine cover, or only white people, or only people who don't appear to have disabilities. Research shows that people with strong media literacy are inoculated against unhealthy body messages and have a healthier, more positive, and more resilient body image.[15]

Although our use of social media has us exposed to more images than ever before, we are also more freely able to choose what we view. Our social media platforms allow us to add, mute, or delete accounts that are harmful. We can also give power to or share power with groups of people who have been underrepresented in traditional media by using our "follows" and "likes" as a kind of voting system to change cultural norms around what is ideal.

Take some time to look through the social media accounts you view regularly and try to think critically about them. Ask yourself the following questions:

- How do I feel when I look at this content?
- What are some of the values about bodies that are communicated in this content?
- What is added to my life because I engage with this content?
- Do I feel better or worse about myself as a body after viewing it?

Our sense of the goodness of being a body comes through experiences in which we get to encounter ourselves outside of the restrictions placed on us. We can do this through movement, play, and dance and through creativity with our appearance. We can ask, "What would I do about my visual self-expression if I weren't concerned about what other people might think? What would that look like?"

Our bodies might be telling us we like something—a color, a pattern, a haircut—but our thinking brain, trained to judge us before anyone else can do that, shuts down the quiet sense we have about what we like. This is where interoception comes in. We can practice getting back to that quiet sense by paying attention to the creative nudges that linger within us related to our appearance and by stepping into them in spaces that support us to do so. Sometimes there are external restrictions placed on us, such as work uniforms, finances, or hairstyles that work with our particular hair texture, but we also have the right to play within the spaces that allow us freedom. Consider this your permission slip for creativity, authentic expression, and the practice of creating safety and play within yourself.

Imagine yourself as an artist sitting in a studio with all the tools in the world to use to create whatever you want. You look down and realize that you are holding a black marker in your hand, and every paper in your studio is scribbled with black marker. But maybe you don't want to draw only with black marker. Maybe there are times you want to use oil paints, pastels, acrylic, or graphite pencils. You are the artist, and you are responsible for choosing the medium that helps you create what you most want to create.

The medium represents your thinking. As the artist, you are not the medium, but you get to choose the medium. You understand that you are different from the black marker, that your thoughts are different from your person. Sometimes a black marker has worked, or it was just what was handed to you by those in your life, or by the larger social context. But sometimes you wake up to your life and realize that what you want to create inside yourself is an impressionist-style painting with gentle pastel colors. Sometimes the way you think about yourself and the world has just been your go-to way of thinking. But you can step back and remind yourself that you are not the black marker but rather an artist in a room full of choices. You can choose a medium that works best for you.

Begin by noticing how you are thinking about your body. Then decide if you want to set down the black marker—any shame-based, critical self-talk—and maybe pick up a different color or maybe even some paint and a brush.

Here's what this sounds like when I've done it in connection with my appearance: "I don't like how I look in this dress. I used to . . ." At this point in my train of thought, I catch myself (black marker in hand) and make a change by choosing a marker of a brighter color: the thought picks back up and goes a new direction. "Nope, I'm not going to do that anymore. I used to do that, but it didn't work for me. I wouldn't say that about anyone else, so I won't say it about myself."

While experiences, or the bottom-up way, are the most meaningful way to create lasting internal change, our brains tend to do more of what they have had lots of practice doing already. So giving our brains new things to practice can help, as can repairing the wounds that we acquired along the way by apologizing to ourselves. Sometimes I put my hand on my chest and say to myself, "I am so sorry I used to believe those harmful things. There is so much more for me than to be stuck there again."

Those of us who have struggled with body image have spent so much time focusing on what we don't like or what we would change about our bodies that we have trained our brain to effortlessly notice those things. But to support our resistance and healing, we can also look for ways to connect with our bodies that incite gratitude and wonder.

For example, the big toe. We almost never think about our big toes unless we stub them, but our big toes are miraculous appendages. Think of your big toes and thank your big toes for all the unnoticed work they do.

What about teeth? They are bones on the outside of your skin. It is the weirdest thing to think about. Teeth do so much and we rarely think about them except for when they ache.

For me, a wonderful way to connect with myself recently has been to get up close to the mirror and stare into my eyes. Sometimes it seems like I could get lost in what feels like a whole universe in there. And I've been amazed at how practicing wonder and gratitude related to my body has spilled over into how I feel, experience, and encounter other people. Everyone is a walking miracle! And I often linger a bit longer with people's eyes just to get a glimpse of the universe inside of them.

Seeing Something Else

Two years and a month to the day after Melissa started coming to me for therapy, she wanted to revisit our first session. In that session, she described herself as someone who loves helping others but who keeps everything inside, including her distress. She told me that she'd had an eating disorder from a young age, eating whenever she was able in order to manage all the stress she carried inside. This led to notable weight gain, and her family eventually enrolled her in a weight-management program. Later, she joined a support group that came with meetings and an eating paradigm that encouraged controlled food intake through measuring and weighing foods. But it did not deliver only the outcome she had hoped for; the system also increased her phobias around certain foods and created overwhelming shame and disproportionate emotional reaction when she ate foods that were not part of the "plan."

After decades of being at war with food, she sat across from me on the couch and with tears in her eyes said, "I hate the cycle I'm in with food. I hate the size I'm at. I feel so frumpy. I just . . . I hate my body." She had brought two photos to show me: one photo from when she was at her lowest weight, and one photo from when she was at her highest weight. She displayed them in front of me in the lamp-lit therapy office, and I took both photos in my hands. I could see her waiting for a reaction, first looking at my face, then down at the photos, then back at my face again. It seemed important for her that I see these images, representing the journey she had been on as a body.

When I am working hard to say the "right thing," or it feels like a moment in which the words need to be chosen just so, I usually remember it. But I don't remember what I said when I saw the photos. I said something, and we moved on.

Two years and a month later, she wanted to talk about my comment. She told me that the first day we met, when she handed the photos to me, I pointed at one of the photos and said, "Oh, I love that dress." I had pointed at the photo that carried the most shame for her, where she was at her biggest size. She told me that a few things happened in that moment. She thought to herself, "Oh, she's not playing the game," and she felt a major disturbance in her existing worldview. And she knew she could trust me. Up to that moment she had believed that her bigger body was somehow a "worse" body. When looking back at the photos, she couldn't even see the dress. It was through my unexpected reaction—without commenting on her body at all, without validating how awful it was to have been a larger size—that she learned she could begin to see herself differently. Maybe everything she had learned about her body from a young age could be unlearned; and maybe a new perspective of her body that was much more whole could begin to take root.

What I want for you, and for all of us, is to have our appearance-focused worldviews disrupted. I want us to re-member the experiences of ourselves as bodies that pull us out of what we think is going on in the minds of others and place us into our very selves. I want us to torch the ideals that are restrictive, damaging, and often unattainable, and learn instead to be present to and compassionate toward what is. Not at some later time—after we think we have changed our body until our appearance is acceptable—but now. And even if the stories about our appearances have been not so good, our bodies are good. All bodies are good.

SOME THINGS TO THINK ABOUT

- Reflect on the media you consume. What do they say about bodies (un)like yours? How does that impact how you feel about yourself and how you think about your body?

- What is missing in the media you consume?
- When did you first learn to see your body from the outside? What was lost when that happened?
- If your body did not change, but you could wake up one morning and feel differently about your body, what would you want to be different? How would you live, and what would that be like?

SOME THINGS TO TRY

- See if you can notice your heart rate without checking for your pulse. You could also check your pulse with your fingers and notice the different rates of pulse in different areas of your body. Or you could interoceptively match the pulse you feel through your fingers with the blood pumping in other areas of your body.
- Investigate the media you consume with the goal of purging accounts, shows, and other content that get in the way of your self-acceptance or are problematic in their portrayal (or lack thereof) of other bodies.
- Look at your eyes in the mirror. Perhaps set a timer for a minute or two, and spend the time really connecting with yourself. You might even try looking at your body in a full-length mirror, talking to the image of your reflection with kindness and compassion, or perhaps neutrality. This is particularly effective when naked.

5

Feeling Feelings

Getting to Know the Emotional Body

It is 8:15 a.m. Eastern Time, but my body clock is still on West Coast time. I am awake, but I put my pants on backward twice, burned myself while wrapping my hair around a curling wand, and I'm about an hour away from talking to an audience of almost four thousand. I am both half-asleep and terrified. I have been practicing my words for days, and I even recorded my talk so I could play it back to myself while going about my day. But the mix of fatigue and terror has me missing words I have practiced incessantly for weeks.

The morning event run-through ends, and the other speakers and I are ushered to a green room where I make tea and wait. As the start time approaches, I notice my legs are bouncing, my heart is thumping in my chest, and I am both clammy and sweaty, a mix of hot and cold all at once. Fear is here; it has announced itself. I am sitting next to another speaker, perhaps the steadiest person I have met and one of my intellectual heroines,

107

and I reach for my cup of tea with shaking hands only to knock it over onto my stack of papers. This was certainly one way to show the entire room that I was also feeling oh-so-steady.

I could sense my thoughts starting to spin, and so I excused myself and found a quiet place to sit on my own. I did everything I could to settle myself: I took deep breaths; I tried to "discharge" the energy from my body by tensing and releasing my muscles; I examined my thinking patterns. I asked the fear to go away and told it that it wasn't useful in this situation. I even used EMDR, an anxiety/trauma therapy I do with my clients. I was trying everything I could—and my training as a therapist meant I had a lot of things I could try.

At some point, a knowing bubbled up in me that seemed to say, "You're trying to get rid of the fear, aren't you?" Under this, it seemed, was the belief that if the fear were present, I could not deliver my speech effectively: I believed the fear had to go away for me to do what I needed to do. While that may seem obvious, it was a piece of knowing that rerouted me into something else. If I could sum up all my years of clinical training and research in one statement, it would be this: *We heal when we can be with what we feel*. In other words, trying to make feelings go away, and in a very authoritarian, cognitive, and seemingly disconnected manner, wouldn't do it. It is ironic that turning toward our emotions instead of exiling them is what helps us move through them. So I tried a different approach.

I grabbed a scrap piece of paper, wrote the word *fear* on it, and tucked it into the breast pocket of my shirt. Then I put my hand on my chest, where I could feel the corners of the paper tucked under my fingertips, and I began a conversation with my fear. I imagined there were two parts of me. One was young and scared looking. We can call her Scared Hillary. The other part was the "me" I know well now, an adult who is calm, present, caring, attentive, curious, creative, and patient. We can call her Calm Hillary.

I imagined seeing Calm Hillary approach Scared Hillary, my child-self, and wrap her up in her arms. Then I imagined Calm Hillary saying something like this: "It is so okay for you to be here. You don't have to go away for this to be good. It is not when you are gone that I get to do the things I feel excited about doing; it is when we are together. I want you to remember that you don't have to be in charge right now—I can do that."

I felt my exhale deepen, a steady stream of air coming out through my lips. I continued the conversation. In my imagination Calm Hillary, still holding scared, child Hillary, said, "I know you don't want to be embarrassed. It is so hard to be seen, because when we are seen, we can be judged and rejected. I know you are just trying to protect me from shame. You are rattling me from the inside out to get my attention, thinking that if you get loud enough, I'll listen, and we can stop this before we get hurt. This won't be like other times we got hurt. No matter what happens, we can handle it together. Will you come with me onto that stage? I can't wait to tell everyone what we've learned." Another deep sigh, and a loosening of what felt like a belt around my throat. My heart rate, though still faster than normal, had slowed, and I let my hand linger on my chest for a few more moments. I didn't need to rush away from that moment of intimacy within myself that I had spent years working to create.

The What and Why of Feeling

Feelings can be hard for us to get close to because our culture is widely feeling-phobic, or at least feeling-illiterate. The fear and confusion that arise around feelings—when we don't know how to feel them, worry we will get lost in them, or wonder how it is going to look to others if we express them—is enough to cause most people to move in the other direction. But stay with me, and stay with this, if you're able—it is going to be worth it.

Let's start at the beginning. We are born with emotion hard-wired into our brain-body systems. Neuroscientist and psychobiologist Dr. Jaak Panksepp spent his entire career studying the science of emotions, why they matter, and how they develop among humans and animals. He defined emotions as "inherited ancestral tools for living."[1] They are powerful signals to self and others written into our biology to help us survive. Emotions move us toward what feels good and what we need, and away from what feels not so good and what might be threatening to us in some way.

Emotions are central to our survival and also to our ability to adapt. This is why, when we are feeling something, especially intensely, we are more likely to create, store, and retrieve memory about that thing than we would be if there were no emotion at all.

Although we use many words to describe how we feel, there are seven categories of primary emotions that have their own circuitry and function within us: anger, excitement, sadness, disgust, joy, fear, and sexual excitement. Each emotion emerges depending on what is happening within and around us.

Anger helps strengthen us to fight, assert or defend ourselves, and make a change or get what we need. *Excitement* gives us the energy to move toward something, to investigate, or to explore. It's part of how we expand and lean into life. *Sadness*, which can lead us to feel heavy and pulled down, signals to us and to those around us that we might need some support. It helps us to grieve and to learn what is painful to or meaningful for us. *Disgust* was originally an emotion that activated our gastrointestinal tract and certain facial muscles to keep us from ingesting something dangerous, but it has evolved to include all manner of things we find harmful (including policies and behavior). It can signal to others "This is harmful," whatever "this" is at the moment. *Joy* helps us expand, heal, and continue to thrive. It drives us into an open-

110

hearted state in which we can connect and share. *Fear* puts us on alert, helping us to anticipate and perceive threat and to move toward protection and out of or away from situations that might be damaging to us. *Sexual excitement* or *desire* originally developed to keep our species alive through procreation. It motivates us to meet unmet needs, fulfill ourselves, and experience pleasure. Each emotion has a purpose and comes with its own physiological signature and action tendency—or the pattern of what we want to do when we feel that specific feeling.

Emotions influence our sense of self more than our thinking does. That's because the mental structures that process emotions are located deeper in the brain than thinking structures. Because emotions are so central to our survival, they are meant to take over or "hijack" our thinking brain when we are in a situation that threatens our survival or that is deeply meaningful for us. In a society that devalues the body and overvalues rational thought, this can be a disruptive discovery. Some of us might be tempted to imagine a world without emotion—nothing to complicate the workplace, the to-do list, dating, or parenting. But from people who have disturbances or deactivation in the emotion centers of their brain, we learn that they are actually *unable* to make decisions or connect with others. Emotions have a purpose, each of them, even in a culture that hushes this innate wisdom that is available to us all.

Emotions happen inside the body and are expressed through the body. This means that emotions can signal to others through the body what is going on within us. You might have heard it said that emotion is e-motion, or energy in motion, and the landscape for that movement is our bodies. But some of us have confused our ability to feel our feelings as they move as energy through our body with our ability to talk about what we feel. We can sit in therapy, tell sad stories, and talk about feeling sad without ever having the bodily experience of sadness.

111

Psychology has historically focused too much on cognition and behavior while neglecting the process that underlies them both: emotion. But current neuroscientific research reveals emotion (also called *affect* in the scientific literature) as the central driver behind why we are the way we are, and how we develop and heal.[2] We now know that most psychopathology, or mental illness, is the result of the inability to effectively regulate emotion.

Feeling in Context

All of these emotions happen in the body, and each body exists in a social context. We are wired for survival, but we cannot survive alone. This means that the human organism needs belonging and connection, both to stay safe and to fully develop. So our nervous system picks up cues from our context about its conditions for belonging, and this shapes how we express, or do not express, our feelings.

In our earliest days, these cues most often come from our primary caregivers, particularly through tone of voice and eye contact. For example, even before we have a command of language, we can learn to feel shame about emotions if our caregivers scoff at, mock, or roll their eyes at our expressions of feeling. Or, with the reassuring gaze and soothing tone of voice of a parent, we can learn to feel feelings, tolerate uncomfortable emotions, and make meaning of it all. As we age, our sense of belonging extends to wider and wider circles, and we pay attention to cues about emotions while at daycare, in school, in social clubs, with peer groups, and in faith communities. All of them give us feedback about emotions, and our ways of being in the world adapt in response. Through repeated social experiences, we learn to internalize the responses others' give us to our own emotions, often replicating in our internal world the spoken and unspoken messages we receive, whether internalizing loving care we receive from someone else to lovingly care for our own feelings or internalizing shame from a critical person to shame our own feelings.

Unfortunately, not all of these contextual learnings are healthy, even when people love us and mean well. And sometimes we learn conflicting messages, with different groups saying contradictory things about how to belong "when you are with us."

Think about each of the primary emotions described above: anger, excitement, sadness, disgust, joy, fear, and sexual excitement. Whether you were aware of it or not, you learned something about each of these emotions growing up. You learned how and with whom to express yourself when feeling each emotion, whether you could anticipate shame or praise for feeling them, and what each of them revealed about you.

Consider sadness, for example. Some of us grew up in families in which sadness was interpreted as weakness, so feeling sad would result in criticism and isolation. If we were sad, we were told to "quit being a baby" or to "grow up." The underlying messages were that this emotion, this self-expression, must be controlled as a condition of belonging and that we must prevent further sadness. Because belonging is essential, we learned how to "shut off" the feeling in order to stay safe and close to the people who met our needs. Some of us may never have picked this up at home but learned out in the world, based on our body, that sadness was not available to us—such as when boys are told "Real men don't cry" or when girls are told "You're being manipulative."

Although many of us grew up with damaging stories that some emotions are negative, some of us grew up learning that even the so-called positive emotions were bad. We were told that pride—a mix of excitement and joy and self-directed value—was selfish and immoral. We were punished socially— through shame—for feeling this incredible biological impulse.

The words "don't get too big for your britches" or "don't get too full of yourself" have been used to quiet people's impulses toward ambition, mastery, and self-satisfaction.

We also learn stories about how to express emotions. Although the impulse and the sensation for each emotion are hardwired into our body, how we express each emotion can be shaped. For example, we can be shown that violence is a sanctioned expression of anger. We can learn that it is okay to feel fear with someone close to us but never with strangers. Even the idea that some emotions are negative and some are positive shows our emotional socialization.

Not long ago, I was leading men in a psychotherapeutic group context in which we were talking about how men in a patriarchal context express emotions. When sharing about emotions, they had the strongest reactions of suspicion and rejection toward the notion that even sadness and anger were good. Upon further exploration, it became clear that they had never been allowed to feel sadness, or supported to feel it, with any measure of confidence. In fact, they had been shamed for expressing sadness, which resulted in avoidance and fear of sadness in both themselves and others.

On the other hand, anger was something that was modeled for them—by their fathers and other men—as violent words and actions. This left them feeling confused because it communicated that anger was acceptable, likely inevitable, but also dangerous. Never was it communicated to them that what they had witnessed as violence was an ineffective strategy to manage sadness or fear (the hurtful behavior being a way to demonstrate and accrue control when feeling powerless), or an unhealthy and inappropriate response to the inability to feel and be angry internally. Without condoning either of these responses to anger, I suggest that the truth about emotions might be different from the stories we have been told about them.

Why It's Hard to Feel

Even now, we usually have trouble feeling emotions for a number of reasons:

> We were discouraged from feeling through shame, punishment, rejection, isolation, or the sense that our feelings would overwhelm the person we were hoping would help us.
>
> When we did feel, it was unbearable. We didn't know how to feel, how to soothe ourselves, or how to get through to the other side. Or we had to do it alone, but it was overwhelming and terrifying.
>
> We learned that feeling wasn't allowed for our particular identity or context.

Regardless of the why, when we weren't supported to stay with our emotion, we failed to learn that emotions rise and then eventually fall, and that we will be on the other side of the feeling at some point. As a result, we need to learn, through supportive connection, that it is safe to feel and how to do so.

Never being shown—consistently and frequently enough, if at all—how to ride the wave of an emotion can make it terrifying to start feeling because all we know is that the sensation in our body is rising, rising, rising with no end in sight. So, when we are faced with emotion moving in us, it can be overwhelming and shame inducing. This can keep us stuck in a loop that reinforces a shutdown, fear, or avoidance response.

Without the ability to move all the way through an emotion, we cannot get to what is on the other side: rest, presence, calm, connection, playfulness, and curiosity. This is what we call a "core state"—or our openhearted, authentic, self-at-best state. Just like emotions, it is available to us all, written into our biology, where we can access our confident, engaged, creative, and kind self. When we can be with emotions in our bodies (watching, tracking with sensation as it moves through us), emotions can release and move through us, allowing us to get back to our authentic self.

Getting Away from Feeling

If we have never been shown what is on the other side of feeling and all we know is that intensity is rising in our bodies, we will do whatever we can to get away from that sensation. This is where defenses come in. A defense is a catchall category for anything we do to avoid our feelings. Sometimes we do this consciously, sometimes unconsciously. Often it began consciously but now operates unconsciously. Some examples of defenses are sarcasm, laughing, overeating or undereating, overworking, substance use and/or addiction, changing the subject, numbing out or spacing out, procrastination, perfectionism, projection, racism, intellectualizing, violence, avoidance, blaming and passing judgment on ourselves or others, self-harm, eye-rolling, denial, and the list goes on.

A defense is different from an otherwise acceptable activity because a defense is used to get away from what it feels like to be us or to avoid the emotion that is trying to get our attention. A defense isn't necessarily a bad thing; sometimes it's too much of a good thing, or sometimes we're using an otherwise good thing to get away from feeling something. Having a glass of wine to get away from our feelings is different from having a glass of wine because it complements the meal. The same is true of learning, laughter, and eating.

Although defenses keep us away from our emotions, they do serve a purpose: they protect us from emotional experiences that we feel unable to tolerate alone or experiences we feel scared to move toward; they also protect us from emotions that we have been shamed or punished for feeling in the past, either by those close to us or by cultural scripts. These defenses were and sometimes still are helpful. This is especially true if we have never been shown how to feel our emotions all the way to their end. Consider this analogy: A thick wool coat is helpful for keeping us warm while we are outside in the winter, but at some point the seasons change, and if we're still wearing the coat in the middle of summer, we could get heatstroke. Defenses are like winter coats. At one point they helped keep us safe, but now that we are somewhere new, or the seasons have changed, they no longer serve us and can actually hurt us.

To get to the emotions that need to be felt, and the open-hearted state underneath, we need to work with our defenses. This requires identifying that they are present at all and getting curious about what they might be defending us against. In her book *It's Not Always Depression*, psychotherapist Hilary Jacobs Hendel invites us to ask the following question of a defense when it comes up: "How is it trying to help me right now?"[3] Asking this question moves us toward what might be lying beneath the defense without ignoring the defense or creating more shame, and it affirms that the defense is there to help us.

Defenses are one way we get away from feelings that we don't know how to stay with, and another way to get away from feelings is through inhibitory affects. Inhibitory affects are particular emotional responses that allow us to push down feelings so we can go along to get along. The three forms of inhibitory affects are anxiety, guilt, and shame. When we learn from our family, culture, or community that particular emotions are not okay, we find a way to block those emotions from coming up. If sexual arousal is forbidden, especially when it happens in *this* context for *that* person, we lock it down. If we feel sad and are told it is embarrassing, we find a way to reject sadness within ourselves to stop it from coming up again. Like defenses, inhibitory affects let us know that our bodies are trying to communicate something. Inhibitory affects rise up

117

to push things down, thereby signaling that we are entering territory into which we have been told we should not go.

Both inhibitory affects and defenses are ways that we do our best to get away from emotions we can never actually be rid of. A large percentage of people who come to therapy do so because they have realized that their defenses are not working or are hurting them or others, they are stuck experiencing inhibitory affects (the shame, guilt, or anxiety), and it feels awful, or they are oscillating between their defenses and inhibitory affects.

To make this more concrete, let me tell you about Yuchi. Yuchi is kind, tall, and extremely bright—always the top of his class and always one point ahead in the argument. We started working together because his partner was concerned about how much Yuchi was drinking (spot the defense). Yes, he was into craft beer culture, but he was also drinking too many beers almost every night of the week.

When Yuchi and I started working together, he would often look down or away, or sometimes keep talking as if looking straight through me. He was in the room, but it felt like he was somewhere else entirely. I regularly paused him to invite him back into the present, to connect with himself and with me, and asked him what he noticed was happening for him as he was talking. I often got a blank stare in response. The more I persisted in stopping Yuchi and inviting his awareness back to his body, the more it became clear that his body was not a place where he spent a lot of time.

As part of therapy, Yuchi and I did an experiment. Between appointments, Yuchi would pause before opening the first beer at night to ask himself how drinking that night might be helping him in some way. We were helping him explore the function of the defense, or what it was defending him from. Over the course of that week, as he gained awareness about his drinking as a defense, he seemed to lose interest in drinking. It seemed as though the inability to drink mindlessly made him aware of himself and of the underlying process at play.

When Yuchi came the following week, he told me that whenever he went to drink, he felt anxious (inhibitory emotion); he was keyed up and tense. As he was telling me that, I noticed that his face pulled downward, and his eyes started to glisten more than usual. I again interrupted and asked him to pay attention to what was happening. He paused, and then tears began to form in the corners of his eyes. "I didn't realize how much sadness I was carrying around and how elaborate my strategies were to get away from it." It was as if he opened cabinet doors inside his chest to let me see inside. He had experienced many losses and much grief but also a corresponding need to make the grief go away, to "move on," and to protect himself and his family from what it might be like to be with all the sadness.

As he began to practice staying with his sadness and moving it through him—instead of running away from it—he noticed that anxiety emerged only occasionally, and he could actually enjoy a beer after work, really savor it, without mindlessly consuming bottle after bottle. What was most interesting about Yuchi's experience was how much more deeply he was able to feel love for his partner. With the ability to feel came the pleasure of rich connection.

This way of thinking about emotions comes from the work of Dr. Diana Fosha, through her development of a theoretical framework and approach to therapy called Accelerated Experiential Dynamic Therapy (AEDP).[4] In this model, the interaction of core emotions, defenses, and inhibitory emotions is called the "triangle of experience," which Hendel refers to as the "change triangle" (see fig. 2).

Within this framework, the goal is to nonjudgmentally observe where we are on the triangle; and if we are in defenses or inhibitory emotions, we invite ourselves back to feel and be with core emotions so that our bodies can return to our core state.

Figure 2

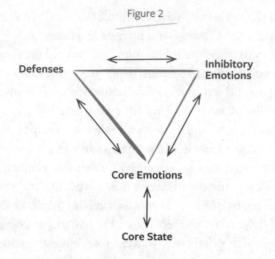

The Man Box

Perhaps one of the greatest contributors to emotional repression is something called "the man box." I first learned about the man box a few years ago through the work of Brian Heilman, Gary Barker, and Alexander Harrison.[5] The researchers surveyed over 3,600 men, asking them questions about what Western culture says about being a man and about how much men identify with these beliefs. Men feel pressure to perform a supposed ideal version of masculinity as described by the seven pillars of the man box: self-sufficiency, acting tough, attractiveness, rigid masculine gender roles, heterosexuality and homophobia, hypersexuality and sexual prowess, and aggression and control.[6]

In this study, the men who had broken out of the box had rejected these masculine ideals and had decided to think more freely about what it means to be a man. But the men who were most "inside" the man box were those who had most internalized the seven pillars. Just as getting closer to the ideal body image increases rigidity and fixation on the ideal without delivering on the self-worth promised, the more "inside" men were, the more concerning factors began to emerge. Specifically, those who were more inside the man box had lower levels of life satisfaction and self-confidence. They had poorer mental health, displayed less vulnerability and emotional connection in their friend and romantic relationships, demonstrated riskier behavior, had poorer body image, and were more likely to both perpetuate and experience bullying and harassment.[7]

The results are compelling: Compared to men outside the man box, those inside it were far more likely to have symptoms of depression and suicidal thinking. They also felt unable to talk about their concerns with others, or they had no close friendships within which to talk vulnerably at all. Those inside the man box were also far more likely to have perpetrated sexual harassment or sexualized violence against a woman or a girl within a month of being interviewed for the survey.[8]

As I read the research report, I was both shocked and not surprised to see the role emotion played in the pillars of the man box. The messages that men had been told growing up about how to "be a man" had left them hurting, lonely, and disconnected from themselves. They were more likely to hurt themselves, hurt others, and feel insecure. Being told to "man up" and shove down their feelings, while putting themselves and others in harm's way to show just how manly they were, was not working. And when their pain, loneliness, and insecurity caught up with them—in the form of depression, anxiety, and suicidal thinking—the man box kept them trapped, preventing them from reaching out for or receiving help because of their deep implicit belief that vulnerability was off-limits to them.[9]

The study also holds hope. The men who had climbed out of the man box were sometimes socially punished for their rebellion against this toxic form of masculinity, but they were also healthier psychologically and more connected to themselves and to those around them. When they struggled, they were much more likely to tell others and to seek help. They also engaged in the following rewarding emotional behaviors: crying in front of another male peer, providing emotional support for a friend, and letting a friend into something difficult that they were going through. They had places to take their painful emotions and know that they were not alone. Not suprisingly, this translated to a decrease in suicidal thinking.[10]

If we are going to change our relationship with emotions and give boys and men a better chance at health and meaningful lives, then it is important for all of us to deconstruct the man box. This means identifying when we are propping it up and observably standing in opposition to the systems that maintain it. But most importantly, it means treasuring when men step outside the man box, reminding them that their value is found not in this harmful performance of masculinity but in who they are as people.

Emotions as Doorways, Invitations, and Teachers

Emotional intelligence and embodiment go hand in hand because emotions are experienced and released through the body. As it turns out, this may be what we need in order to survive in our emotion-illiterate, body-phobic culture. And even if our culture has not given us permission to feel, the wisdom of our bodies is always calling us into awareness of what does not work and what needs to heal. You might remember from chapter 3 that unprocessed emotions do not just disappear but linger, speaking through our bodies in the form of trauma reponses and pain.

To become healthier mentally and physically, we have to get to know our inner landscapes with more curiosity, kindness, and compassion. We do that by understanding emotions as our guides to self-understanding, identity, and fullness in life. In this way, emotions are like colors in a crayon box. Knowing them means we can use them more skillfully. It is hard to have a life of wholeness if we have only one color or if the crayons seem to chaotically spew out of the box. This process of learning to use a full box of crayons, deciding how to best use colors and when it's the right time to do so, is called emotional regulation: it is our ability to notice, manage, and respond to emotions effectively and appropriately given our context. Emotional regulation enables us to prevent and treat mental health issues, facilitates better academic performance, helps us parent with more ease, and equips us to have more peaceful, intimate, and satisfying relationships.

The following practices can help you change your relationship with emotions. The better you get at identifying what emotions feel like on a sensory level, as they emerge and then pass, the less scary they become and the less you'll need your defenses.

When an emotion emerges, direct your attention toward your bodily sensations. What do you notice? If we were in therapy together, I might ask, "What *tells* you that you are feeling that way?" You could start at the top of your head, slowly sweeping your awareness down through your body, looking for anything that stands out, such as temperature, tightness, openness, or movement of energy (swirling, rising, pressing, weighing, undulating, sinking, etc.). The purpose of noticing sensations is not to take us away from the emotion but to help us attend to it in a way that moves the emotion through us without blocking it. When emotions signal something in our body, turning kind attention toward that helps us regulate our emotions and also connect with ourselves—a connection that cannot be taken from us regardless of what stirred the feeling.

Think of an emotion as a wave. Emotion usually rises and falls like a wave. When we turn our attention toward it, we can observe it ascending, peaking, and then resolving. It can feel scary when we notice the wave of emotion building, as if it

123

might last forever or boil up outside our control. So we move into our defenses, or our inhibitory affect rises to inform us that we are going into what was once a danger zone. But when we feel an emotion rise and fall by observing the sensation in our body, it helps us get to the other side. Riding the wave of each emotion enough times gives us confidence when the next wave is building that it too will recede.

There are some good things on the other side: usually we get a mix of relief, internal space, and some insight about what matters to us or what we need to do next. Even in situations of danger, when we need to react immediately for safety of ourselves or others, planning what to do next is more effective when we have started to come down the other side of an emotion. Diana Fosha has said that feelings are the experiential arc between the problem and the solution.[11] When we stay with that arc, our bodies lead us to what needs to happen next. Sadness helps us ask for comfort, helps us grieve, or gives us the release of letting go. Anger helps us set a boundary and protect ourselves or someone else. And joy takes us into full expression, sharing our experiences to help them expand. Remember the last time you were really angry and started furiously typing an email or text and learned the hard way that it's better to wait and send a message after cooling down and doing some heavy editorial revisions? That's an example of coming down the other side of an emotion; it is often the best time to harness the wisdom of the emotion and then decide how to act. When we are more emotionally regulated, but haven't forgotten the message the emotion gave us, we can integrate our thinking into our feelings to figure out our best next move.

We tend to want to rush the wave, which usually means we are experiencing a mix of the emotion that was originally there as well as a new defense related to our impatience. The goal is to become aquainted with emotion, noticing our unique wave patterns (and the waves unique to each emotion), without judgment or a timeline.

Watch what your thoughts are doing. Sometimes when we are learning to stay with emotions, we confuse that body-based process with the thoughts that made us feel that way in the first place. That is the equivalent to pouring gasoline on a fire (great if we want a bigger fire, not so great if we are struggling to manage the fire as it is). For example, you might think of something sad, but as you try to stay with sadness, you continue to think about what someone said to you and what you think it means about you. Instead, try to step back and notice only the emotion, setting the story aside in order to be fully with the bodily sensation. This can take practice, especially when we aren't used to focusing on our inner experience this way.

Respond to yourself compassionately. The best way to midwife ourselves through emotion is to do so tenderly. Think of an emotion that surfaces often or one that you have a hard time with. Perhaps it is fear. Then think about how you would respond to someone you love if they told you they felt fear. Without even knowing the story, what might you do? You might give them a hug, help them take some breaths, remind them that you are present, or reassure them that they are safe, if they are in fact safe. We can borrow from the loving responses we would offer to others to help us tend to our own feelings. If you have a hard time thinking about who you might care for, you can borrow a compassionate "inner script" from someone you know at a distance, such as an author, a friend's parent, a therapist you have had or know about, or even something in this book.

Get curious about your values and your past. Emotions are wired into us because we are human, but the specific emotional response we have to a scenario is unique to each of us. These responses tell us what is important to us and what we have been through. Even if two people are experiencing the same event in the same moment, because of what they have been through in

125

the past, one person might feel afraid while the other person might feel excitement or not notice much of anything. Feelings offer us insight about ourselves, if we let them. When we are frustrated, it is easy to blame another person, but doing so means we miss a chance to see where we need to heal, seek comfort, get out of a situation, or understand ourselves more deeply. Believing that a feeling is about someone else might make us think that the other person, or the situation, has to change. That can trap us in a cycle of codependency, making us think that we can never be okay until the other person changes. When a feeling happens in your body, you are responsible for exploring, understanding, and regulating that emotion.

Although feelings are personal (in that they are about us), there is a direct link between emotional regulation and conversations about social justice. Because of how our brains are wired,[12] we are meant to feel emotions in our bodies in response to the emotions of others. That is empathy. But when we cannot feel our feelings, or haven't been allowed to, we can be confused about how to respond to the emotional expression of others. We may even try to make someone else's feelings go away or dismiss them to avoid having to feel the emotions that get stirred in us when they invite us to see the hurt they have experienced. Improving our ability to tolerate discomfort, take responsibility, and soothe ourselves when we experience big feelings helps us stay in uncomfortable, meaningful conversations without making them about us or making the other person's emotional expression go away.

Feeling, but Not Alone

Not long ago, some friends and I were in the California desert leading a men's retreat devoted to deconstructing the man box. For men socialized into the man box, one of the core and problematic values is resistance to emotional vulnerability, especially with other men. I began by inviting men to experience emotion in their body. I asked them to remember a time early in life when they learned that they had to shut down their emotions. I invited the men to imagine bringing their younger self into the present moment, to join other men who were also on a journey to envision a new way of being men. They told their younger self, in many cases no older than five or six, that he had not been forgotten and that he was not stuck in the past but that he was loved and free to be fully himself.

In this quiet circle, sobs began to emerge. These men were grieving for themselves and for everything they had lost in an effort to stay connected to those around them. But they were also experiencing relief. The need to shut down parts of themselves was coming to a close; tenderness for themselves—when they imagined themselves as children—invited warmth and compassion into the places that had felt cold and dry.

At the next break, I overheard one of the men approach another man and say, "Will you walk with me while I cry?" The second man simply nodded, unphased, and the two of them walked together out toward a crop of walnut trees. When we came back together after the break, the first man shared that the walk was the only time in his life he had cried with another man present. He described feeling that for the first time, almost unbelievably, he knew he did not have to be alone in his sadness. Because he was not crying alone, his sadness was bearable and began to dissipate.

I was in awe. His courage and authenticity were so moving that most of us sat with mouths agape. It was a stunning, real-time demonstration that change is possible and that when we are not alone, we can take risks to feel the pain that was otherwise unbearable. Each of us was reminded that emotion itself is never the problem; the problem is the stories that keep us apart from each other, create conditional belonging, or require us to shove things down in order to stay connected.

I think of this memory often because I never want it to leave me. It gives me hope. In fact, I can't imagine a better picture of hope than those two men walking close to each other on a path into a grove of trees. One man cried, and the other man helped him write a new story—a story in which being a body, with all its feelings, did not have to exclude him from connection but could draw him more deeply into it.

SOME THINGS TO THINK ABOUT

- What stories did you learn about emotion growing up?
- What emotions were you allowed to feel or not allowed to feel? How did you learn that?
- What do you wish you could tell your younger self about emotion?
- What is your relationship with emotion now? What about in the spaces you move in?
- With whom do you feel free to experience your emotions?
- How would you like to be accompanied when you are feeling specific emotions (such as anger, excitement, sadness, disgust, joy, fear, or sexual excitement)? What would it be like to do that for yourself?

SOME THINGS TO TRY

- Draw or print out the outline of a human body seven times, one for each primary emotion listed in this chapter—anger, excitement, sadness, disgust, joy, fear, and sexual excitement. Using markers, colored pencils, or crayons, draw each emotion as it appears in your body, using different colors to represent movement, temperature, and intensity.

- Make a list of your defenses. Next time a defense comes up, try exploring the emotion underneath it.
- Read *It's Not Always Depression* by Hilary Jacobs Hendel or *Living Like You Mean It* by Ronald J. Frederick.

6

You Are Not Broken

A New Perspective on Pain

It is twenty-five minutes before my next appointment, and I have snuck an ice pack out of the freezer in the staff kitchen and returned to my office without anyone noticing. It is very important for me that no one notices. Right now, I want to be with the pain in secret.

I'm lying on my back on the floor of my office, and the door is shut. When I'm settled, and only then, I allow the tears to come out of hiding, pouring out of each eye, down the sides of my face, and tracing a path into my ears.

I feel conquered. This is what most days are like since the car accident three months before. I wake up often in the night. When it's morning, it seems wrong to be waking up to enter the world—as if the throbbing in my body is sure proof I have not been resting.

Changing positions helps—moving from the bed to the shower, sitting in my car, then slowly rising out of it. But because of an injury to my leg, it hurts to walk. It is too painful to be still, too painful to move. The pain feels like fire, flames licking up and down either side of my spine, spreading out from top to bottom, then out to the sides, slowly burning embers singeing everywhere.

Sitting helps until it doesn't. Standing helps until it doesn't.

Then ice or heat, then the massage ball, lying down, tapping, breath work, progressive muscle relaxation, the list goes on. And it helps to know there *is* a list: try this next—something to remind me that I am not out of options. Until I am, and I am at work, and I have hours to go until I get home, and I am trying not to let my supervisor see that I'm crying behind closed doors.

My research and writing about embodiment was birthed out of understanding the goodness of my body as both the medicine for and the fruit of eating-disorder recovery. But since the accidents, I have been in pain while sleeping, walking, standing, and sitting. And I have been kept from the experiences that had helped me feel the goodness of my body—the running, the yoga, the dancing. It now seems my remedy has turned on me, and the things that used to remind me that my body has always been good are just out of reach, create more pain, and are for now forbidden by my treatment team. I find myself wondering, *Do I really believe my body is good—even now?*

With years of practice, it has become natural to think that my body is good, that all bodies are good. But it requires something different to say that now—it carries a different weight for a person to say it when there is pain. Or illness. Or injury. Or disability. I was becoming aware of how much others might have to negotiate to know and believe that their bodies are good, especially when prevailing cultural values are against them.

Still on the floor, condensation from the ice pack leaking into my blouse, I realized I felt embarrassed. In my campaign to join the existing voices helping us tell a new story about our bodies, I had neglected to see the privilege in my obvious physical ability. I suddenly understood a bit more of the challenge some may face when hearing this message, especially those who do not have the same access to movement, sensation, bathrooms, or stairs, or those who cannot know with certainty if a venue they are invited to socially will be physically accessible to them.

While I understood what it's like to move through the world as a woman in a misogynistic and patriarchal culture, my vision was widening. I am European Canadian and light-skinned in a culture that has valued light-skinned people of European heritage. I was young, was in good physical health, and had a body that others might suggest resembles the ideal female form. I was educated within an academic tradition that has favored the wealthy, white male way of understanding the person, which meant I could move through many spaces and be respected and protected while using my voice. Even within this slice of society where my body was devalued in one sense, in other ways my form was also prized above others.

This led me back to one unifying truth: my body is good in a kind of moral sense and not because of appearance, function, or labels I use or others give me. My body is good simply because it is my home. What is true of me, underneath the stories we tell about our body, is true of you too. Your body is good simply because it is your home. Your body is good, no questions asked—though it may be the fight of our lives to remember and reclaim this essential truth for ourselves and each other.

My next appointment was about to begin, and I had to return the dripping ice pack to the freezer down the hall. With my hand on the doorknob, I paused to stay with this for one more moment. In my decision to be alone, I found myself very much not alone. And although I would never have chosen to endure the trauma of the car accidents, and feel the pain of it still, I was understanding what it means to be a body in the world in a more empathetic, wide, and complex way.

Good Body—Even Now

It is systemically oppressive, and simply untrue, to say that a body is good only when it is physically able, in full health, or developing in a typical way. It is problematic when ability and health are defined only by those whose bodies hold the most social power. To say that bodies are good, without promoting any kind of "ism"—racism, sexism, ageism—requires making that statement of all bodies.[1] For those of us who have lived with pain, illness, or injury, this necessitates working through some challenging questions:

- How can my body be good when it seems to be breaking down?
- How can my body be good, when the pain is not caused by an injury that will heal but exists because of a chronic illness or autoimmune disease?
- How can my body be good when the limitations, pain, or messages from my body interfere with the plans I have or what others expect from me?
- Why this pain? Why this suffering? Why my body?

A few weeks after my second accident, I asked my physiotherapist why I was still experiencing so much pain. Evidently, I had asked this before. Without pausing her work to arrange the treatment bed, and with matter-of-fact gentleness, she reminded me that her previous response to that question was still true: my body was doing its best to protect me from further wounding.

When a trauma happens, the muscles around the injured area tighten to create stability. This tightening holds things in place, but it feels almost like another injury. When I'm lying in a treatment room, what feels like an injury is my body's response to the actual injury: the trauma, the accident, the thing that happened to me. But woven through the physiotherapist's explanation, I hear the message: *My body isn't bad.* What happened to me was scary and painful. My body did what has kept so many bodies safe for millennia—it tightened.

Realizing that the pain, the tightening, was a natural response to something scary and unpredictable gave me instant compassion for myself, for my physicality, and even for the tightening. I could notice myself in pain and say to my body, as if speaking directly to the wise force entwined with my DNA, "Thank you for how you tried to keep me safe. You are doing the only thing you know how to do when something very scary happens. And although we are safe now, you do not know that yet. Instead of being angry with you, I promise I will show you that we are safe by treating you in such a way that reminds you that we really are safe."

My body softened. I took a deep breath.

That breath went so deep that I wondered if what I had been telling myself about the pain—that it was a problem—was compounding it. What if blaming myself for the pain and feeling frustrated with my body was actually making it harder for me to heal? I started to see what wove together the experience and story of the ongoing pain, even now after the accidents had happened.

The map of my experience appeared:

- I saw the truck coming and braced for impact. I thought I was going to die, and my body tightened. Then the truck hit my car head-on, resulting in injury.
- I was sent home from my time in the hospital and told I needed to rest. Be careful; everything was about being careful.
- When I wasn't lying down, it felt like a risk to do something. I did so suspiciously, and it often hurt. I would tell myself it was too soon, not to push myself. I would avoid the pain.

- I would get frustrated that I could not do the things I wanted to do, so I would lie back down, disappointed.
- Doing nothing was relieving, but I became more afraid of it hurting again when I tried something else.
- More avoidance. I thought, *Don't do anything and it won't hurt.* I reached a point where I could not do nothing, and then it hurt more. Then the confirmation-bias thinking kicked in: *I knew I shouldn't have done anything.*

Our thoughts and bodies are not as separate as we have been led to believe. In fact, they influence each other constantly. What we *think* about what is happening in our body shapes both our thinking and what is happening in our body. At the same time, what we are thinking is more informed by our body than we give our body credit for. All this is central to changing our understanding of pain.

A word of caution: In sharing some of the ways I have made sense of these things, I hope to offer another thing to try. Perhaps this gives you hope and insight. I cannot know all experiences of pain, illness, or injury. I will miss something. I may see this all from an angle that cannot get at what you are living through. I have no intention of offering you a remedy you are not interested in or that grates against your pain. Please know that what is most important in this chapter is the sense of shared experiences. There are others who have felt what you have felt, who are asking the same questions you are asking. And you are more like them than unlike them.

Making Sense of Pain

First, speaking generally, pain makes sense. Pain means something is happening in or to our body and the appropriate systems have been activated to respond, keep us well, and help us heal; our nervous system is also communicating some of that to our conscious awareness. Thank goodness.

Our bodies' messages about pain, fatigue, or soreness help us know what is needed in the moment. It might be rest, medicine, intervention, touch, or guarding of the injured area. For example, pain and swelling in a broken ankle tell someone, and their physician, that *this* needs attention.

How we respond to pain, and some kinds of physical illness, often exposes the "mind over body" mantra. We are so used to living life at an uninterrupted pace that we often experience the time and rest necessary to heal from a time-limited illness or injury as extremely inconvenient. In our frustration, we use language that assumes it is our body—not our plans or pace of life—that is the problem. *Why won't my body just hurry up and heal?*

We also push ourselves to keep going—to work, to produce, to play sports—perhaps even wishing away the sensory information our body is providing that tells us what we need to know in order to heal.

And yet, if anything demonstrates the reality of the mind-body connection, it is pain. Did you know that pain itself does not occur at the site of the injury in the tissues? What you experience as pain is the end result of a set of messages sent via nerve endings throughout your body to your spinal cord and up your brainstem to a series of structures in the middle of your brain. The messages say that there is an injury, or at least that you should pay attention because something is amiss. This messaging system also involves the frontal lobe of your brain, which helps process the sensations received by other areas of your brain, such as the thalamus. None of this means that pain is not real or that it is "all in your head" (a phrase we use to minimize or devalue people's experiences of suffering), but it does mean that the networks in our brain interpret sensation and that impacts the experience we have of pain.

Research conducted by clinical neuroscientist and pain guru G. Lorimer Moseley and his colleague Arnoud Arntz led to fascinating discoveries about how the brain interprets pain.[2] They asked people to rate their levels of pain when a piece of cold metal was placed on their skin. The catch was that participants were simultaneously shown a light—some a red light, others a blue light—without any explanation for the light or its color. The temperature of the metal never changed, but those who saw the red light felt much more pain and described the metal as hotter than did those who saw the blue light. Because for most of us red means "hot," the metal felt hotter when the red light was shown. Moseley and Arntz proved what clinical neuroscientists and philosophers had long assumed to be true: the meaning we give to sensation makes it more or less painful.

What about When the Pain Is Chronic?

While pain is a healthy response to an injury, appearing and fading away as the injury heals, there is also a kind of pain that seems to have come out of nowhere, an unwelcome guest staying for far too long: the pain that is chronic and that often comes with long-term illness, disease, or disability, with no sign of letting up.

When we've lived with physiological distress or discomfort for an extended period of time, it can be especially confusing to figure out where we end and the illness or disease begins. Too often a person's pain has not been believed or taken seriously by their medical providers or loved ones. This can drive them further into an awareness of pain necessitated by the distress of being disbelieved and the desire to prove that what they are experiencing is real. For others, what has been just as problematic is having their pain so medicalized and pathologized that it reinforces that the pain really is horrific, and the only way they will ever live ordinary and fulfilling lives again is for the pain to disappear completely. On both ends of the spectrum of response, a person's identity becomes enmeshed with the pain, making it more difficult to envision living in the presence of it, the body again becoming the scapegoat for creating the sensations that interrupt a full life. The more this enmeshment takes place, the easier the route to shame, criticism, and fear that overwhelm us, making it harder for us to heal and pay attention to other information and sensation.

Following the accidents described in the previous chapters, the pain I was experiencing in my body intensified dramatically to unbearable levels, but before those two accidents I had already been living with chronic pain for eleven years. It had gotten so embedded in my narrative of personhood, and I was so familiar with all of the richness of life that the pain had stolen from me, that if only slightly provoked I could easily access a well of resentment and loathing at my body that seemed to scream out for no reason at all. On top of this was isolation, avoidance, and dread of when the sensations would come up next.

It was, ironically, tsunamis of pain that allowed me to begin to renegotiate my relationship with pain more deeply, experiencing embodiment in a way that allowed me to remember that I am so much more than the pain I live with. In the end, the pain invited me into healing that was deeper than just the sensory level and helped me reorganize my entire relationship with myself. But first I had to see that there was no way around the pain without entering more fully into how I understood and experienced it.

But, as you are well aware by this point in the book, our self exists within this body. As much as we might try to disconnect our sense of self from our physicality, our tissues experience everything that our minds think about them. How we think about our pain matters for two reasons: it affects the processes within our body (increasing or decreasing actual pain, and the ability to heal) and our quality of life (creating relief and comfort, or increasing our suffering). We can think of pain as coming *from* the body and attacking the self—something that not surprisingly activates the mobilization response discussed in chapter 3. After all, we are wired physiologically to respond to threats, even if we believe the threat is our very own physicality. However, we can also think of pain as something happening *to* the body, or something the body is responding to. In therapy, we call this externalizing. Externalizing allows us to center the hard and good work the body is doing to keep us alive and healthy, building compassion for our bodily selves.

We might recognize externalization in how we talk to other people about the illness they experience. When my mother was diagnosed with cancer, my first instinct was to say, "I am so sorry this is happening to you." I never thought, "What is wrong with you that a clump of your cells multiplied in a strange and dangerous pattern?" In other words, I never confused her cancer with her identity. A friend told me recently that while hospitalized for a sudden, life-threatening infection, the most helpful thing anyone said to her in the hospital came from a nurse: "It's so obvious how much your body wants to be alive; it's doing its very best to fight this right now." The language we use helps us remember that a part of us is *not* the pain—and that the not-the-pain part is doing the very best it can to heal. This kind of language is called "person-first language," and I have learned it from the disability community. For example, we say "David, my friend with the developmental disorder" instead of saying "the disabled guy." This helps us center the person and their feelings, rights, and dignity instead of what society has labeled as the problem or the barrier.

For some the pain journey is connected to illness, or more lifelong conditions, and they see their bodily response as the alert to what needs to change or to a story their body is telling about childhood trauma. I also write this knowing that for others, given how they have been discriminated against or marginalized, centering their pain and illness and its connection to identity is a form of activism; what is lived through the body cannot be separated from who they are and how they live in a social context. I name this to address the complexity and individuality spread across the spectrum of pain journeys, and to honor that what is medicine for one person might be compounding trauma to another.

The Weight of Our Thoughts

Let's back up for a moment. What happens in our thinking is intimately connected to what happens to our physiology, and the influence is bidirectional. As I described in chapter 3, when we remember or think about something scary, our body activates to protect us as if the scary thing from the past were happening again in the present. A similar dynamic can happen with pain. For example, if we have a history of missing out on fun things because of gut issues, any stomach sensation we experience in the present might create a sense of tightening in the belly and cause us to feel afraid, wondering if it is a signal that we're about to miss out on another opportunity.

You've likely heard it said, "Sticks and stones will break my bones, but words will never hurt me." Many of us understand the problems of violence, but we often overlook how words and thoughts can also damage our body. When people say hurtful things, use a threatening or shaming tone of voice, or create a damaging social experience, a massive amount of stress-related hormones is released into our bodies. That is part of why our faces crumple and we turn our heads down when we feel shame, and why our blood pumps faster and our eyes widen when we are afraid. The words other people say affect our physiology.

But what if the hurtful person isn't out there but inside our heads, and we are the ones who are saying the shaming things? When that happens, our brain releases the exact same stress hormones. Our body goes into the same states of hypervigilance, activation, or shutdown and defeat, creating the same neurological activation that can make us sick and cause our bodily system to break down. The only thing that may be worse about doing this kind of thing to ourselves, versus it being done to us by others, is that we can't get away from ourselves. No matter where we go, we take the bully with us.

We call this the inner critic. Often it emerges because we borrowed a script from someone else. Before we had an inner critic, we had an outer critic—someone who beat us up verbally or criticized us to make us change or disappear, or someone we heard shame themselves verbally. The inner critic emerges internally from what we learned externally. Even so, the inner critic can have a role in providing temporary protection. We think, "If I beat myself up badly enough, I'll perform well enough and change my behavior so that no one else will pick on me—I'll beat them to it." While this is not a healthy kind of protection long-term, a part of us learned to do this to keep ourselves from getting hurt even more.

As with the stress-response system, this might be an opportunity to imagine thanking your inner critic for all the ways it has helped you—and, if you feel able, to then imagine saying to the critic, "I'd like for you to step aside to give me some more room in my life."

The Two Arrows

Psychologist and researcher Ron Siegel specializes in the psychophysiology of pain, illness, injury, insomnia, and gastrointestinal issues. He has a helpful tool he calls "separating the two arrows," drawing from the "two arrows."[3] From a teaching found in Buddhism, this framework suggests that life shoots the first arrow: something difficult happens. We get an injury, we get sick, we face a loss, we struggle with a disease, and that is the first arrow.

But we are the ones who shoot the second arrow. The second arrow is shot when we add to our own pain and suffering by how we talk to ourselves and others about what is happening with us.

The Second Arrow: Our Inner Critic

To better understand how the second arrow works, imagine that you go over to your friend's house for a barbeque. The winter was cold, the days were short, and you have not had a chance to be outside without a down jacket or umbrella in months, but you're at the barbeque, and someone suggests a genteel game of badminton. And you think, "Sure, why not?" You feel out of practice, but after a little bit of play, things heat up. At one point, you land funny on your ankle while reaching wide for a pass, but you don't think much of it.

The next morning as you're waking up, you can barely move your back. It is next-level stiff. You lean over to turn off your alarm, and your wrist is screaming with sensation. As you step out of bed, you put weight on your ankle and feel a sharp and sudden pain. You look down and see that it is purple in places it should not be purple. That is the first arrow.

Here comes the second arrow.

As you reach behind your neck to try to massage your stiff shoulders, you mumble to yourself, "I should never have played that stupid game." Maybe it stops there, or maybe it keeps going: "I can't believe how much that hurts. I'm so out of shape." Or "What is wrong with me? I can't even play a little game without . . ." Or maybe even, "My body is a piece of trash." And before you know it, you've shot the second arrow.

Once you start noticing the second arrow, you realize there are a few kinds of arrows. The self-blame arrow, the blame-someone-else arrow, and the scary-prediction-of-the-future arrow are popular favorites. The second arrow we shoot is often modeled after the ways people responded to our pain when we were growing up.

Blaming others has its own purpose. It makes us feel in control or puts up a defense against owning our responsibility in this. The arrow that forecasts the scary future also has a role. It sounds like this: "The awful thing will happen again, and I won't be able to handle it." And it helps us feel in control, for a moment, thinking we can predict the danger ahead and then plan for it. Most of us acquainted with pain, illness, and injury know too well the arrow of self-blame.

We might choose self-blame for any number of reasons:

- It can help us feel in control. If something bad has happened and we have someone to point the finger at (us), someone we have control over (us), then it gives us a feeling of power over unpredictable or scary situations.
- It is something we learned to do because we have blamed or been blamed by others.
- It can seem helpful for motivating us to make changes in the moment, even if it ends up causing more damage in the long run.

Research on the psychophysiology of pain helps us understand how what we think about our bodies in general, and how we respond to what's happening to our physiology, can either help us heal (or improve our quality of life) or make it harder for us to heal (or decrease our quality of life), no matter how the first arrow was shot.[4] This is true even in cases where the original arrow is having a long-term illness, disability, or

144

degenerative condition. The main idea is that no matter what caused the pain, it is usually awful and so we have a natural frustration-based or fear-based response to it. But guess what happens when we are frustrated or afraid?

Our bodies tighten.

The organ systems and biochemistry that make our muscles tense are activated, even if we don't know it is happening. That is our nervous system trying to protect us. If the triggering event is indeed something from which we need to be protected, great. Otherwise, the activation is not so helpful.

When our body tightens, the muscles compress around our nerves and cause a lot of pain. It is real pain, not imagined pain. Think of a charley horse or a leg cramp. While it is happening, we know that no major injury has occurred, but it can hurt like hell. No matter how the pain happened, how we choose to respond to it can ramp up, or lessen, the pain.

This pattern is a cycle we can get stuck in when we have chronic pain; we will call it the pain cycle. The research on chronic pain[5] and stress-related disorders[6] (irritable bowel syndrome, insomnia, TMJ, and even some forms of headaches or autoimmune diseases) and the psychophysiology and behavioral aspects of how we respond to our own pain show us a pattern: we get stuck in a cycle of tightness → pain → second arrow (repeat). Figure 3 illustrates this.

Something happens (the first arrow), it hurts because our nervous system gets amped up (tightens), and we are in psychological distress. What we do in response contributes to the cycle. we might stop doing things we enjoy, which increases our stress, and then our capacity to move with ease decreases. And the cycle repeats.

What makes this more complicated is that all of this is happening in a social and cultural context that makes us afraid of our bodies and afraid of pain. Maybe we know someone with the pain or illness we are experiencing. Or we might watch

Figure 3

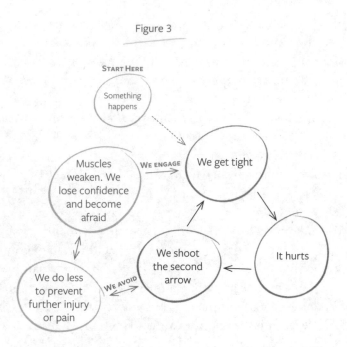

a news program about the epidemic of back pain in North America. Having all this information about how bad pain is makes us more likely to fear it when it happens, like we are preloaded to shoot the second arrow.

Figure 3 offers us a way to look at ourselves head-on. We have no idea what we are working with if we only ever give our struggles the side-eye. I have been in this cycle too. And if you find yourself there, it in no way means you are weak or broken, just human.

Once we understand the pain cycle, we can identify the parts we can work with and do something about. This often starts with naming the second arrow using a skill called mindfulness, which helps us become aware of how we are thinking about our pain, illness, or injury.[7] Here's what mindfulness might look like:

- Start by recognizing what your inner critic is saying about your body (or the pain, illness, or injury, if you are using externalizing language). Ask yourself, "What are my go-to thoughts when I shoot the second arrow? How do I know when I am doing that?" It can be discouraging to notice how often it happens. You are learning, and there will never be a time when we are perfectly mindful.
- Imagine what you might say the next time you notice the second arrow. You could start with, "Oh, there's that second arrow," or "Wow, this is hard to catch. I'm doing that thing again where I criticize myself."
- Learn to shift your attention by replacing your inner critic with something compassionate. Take a breath or shift your body into a more relaxed posture.

It takes time to feel comfortable with something we're just learning. And if we're counting on what we're learning to help us heal, that can add pressure, which can make us afraid and tight. But we can always begin again with a breath, a noticing, a shift in posture or attention, a decision to not do the same old thing. Hope becomes available when we become more aware of our inner process and learn to see off-ramps from the old cycle available in any moment.

The Inner Nurturer Instead of the Second Arrow

We also need to attend to the first arrow and find a salve for the initial injury. The first arrow invites us to develop a fierce inner nurturer who stands opposite the inner critic. The role of the nurturer is to witness and tend to the pain (or whatever the first arrow is) and to comfort ourselves in it. After all, our body hears everything we think. While we may never have chosen to be in such a tangled relationship to pain, learning to develop

the inner nurturer is a way that we can begin to heal our relationship with ourselves, transcending the boundaries of when
the pain began or when it will end.

One way to practice is to begin responding to ourselves with
kindness when we become aware that we are hurting. Here are
some ideas of what that might sound like: "I'm so sorry you
are hurting right now"; "This is hard, and I'm glad I get to be
with you in the midst of it"; "I haven't left you, and we will do
it together"; "You did not deserve this, and this didn't happen
because you're bad." When the pain we feel is the result of the
way our bodies were speaking up for so long, without being listened to, we can also say, "I'm sorry I didn't hear when you were
whispering. I'm listening now." Compelling research shows that
safe, loving touch, even from ourselves, can decrease pain and
speed healing, while increasing our comfort and shutting down
the systems that cause us to get tight and feel afraid.[8] Here's an
experiment to try: Place your hand on your chest or wherever
feels right and say each of the above phrases to yourself. Pause
between each phrase and notice what it feels like. If you find one
that works, try saying it a few more times and see what happens
as you do. If none of the phrases feel quite right, rephrase it to
make it your own.

If speaking to yourself with kindness feels hard, perhaps
expressing curiosity will be easier. Here are some questions
you can use to ignite wonder:

- What other sensations can I feel right now besides the
  pain?
- If I saw a piece of art that captured what this is like,
  what would the image be?
- If my pain had a voice or words, what would it say?
- Speaking to the pain: What do you want me to know
  about what this is like?

148

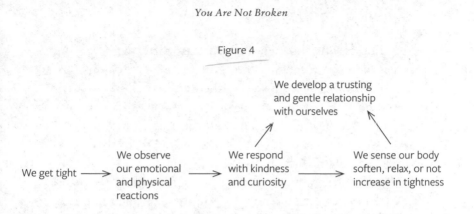

Figure 4

When we are able to choose kindness or curiosity to at least interrupt the second arrow, it looks like the progression in figure 4.

This new way of responding builds confidence in our ability to respond to our pain, helps us begin to heal our relationship with ourselves in a more global sense, and starts to reverse the pain cycle by undoing the tightness, fear, and avoidance we experience in the presence of pain. And when pain comes up again, we know we have agency in the process: we can choose how we respond to it. That makes pain less scary and hopeless, and it makes it easier for us to refrain from picking up the second arrow. You might remember from chapter 3 that having agency over our bodies is one way to heal from trauma. By not adding more distress to our bodies, we can make space to heal what is already there without heaping more pain on top of it. Although pain may still be there, we can learn to respond in ways that don't cause more pain.

Where It Started

I have had allergies for as long as I can remember. When I was young, my mom says she often washed my sheets and clothing three times—once with soap and twice without—otherwise, I would get rashes. Allergies have shown up over and over again in my life, cycling through different categories with varying degrees of severity, ranging from mild rashes to anaphylaxis. Having a lifelong relationship with allergies helped me learn early to be aware of my sensory cues, but it was also another reason to hate my body—after all, this seemingly disorganized nervous-system response was what kept me from sharing so many experiences with others I loved.

When I started graduate school and learned how to use research databases, I made a hobby of combing through empirical evidence and clinical trials to learn about psychobiological development. That's when I came across two interesting findings.

First, some allergies can be caused by significant maternal stress during pregnancy.[9] In short, the mother's stress bathes the baby's nervous system in stress hormones, and the baby's nervous system becomes activated, confused about what is and is not a threat. This produces reactivity to things that are not otherwise dangerous. I sat at my computer and felt my body relax, as if something clicked into place. My mom's older sister had died, suddenly and tragically, when my mom was pregnant with me. I thought, "Oh, of course." A reminder, again, that my body is not bad. I just got a lot of stressful chemical information before I was ready for it, and some of my settings have been on high alert ever since.

Second, there is a meaningful relationship between having allergies in childhood and having disordered eating later in life. Kids can learn to be hypersensitive to the sensations they have when eating and digesting. They can become afraid of food, be confused about whether their bodies and food are good or bad, or form a complicated relationship with food.[10]

For me, this was another important insight. Through having so many allergies as a kid, food became more of a focus for me than it was for my friends. My body was communicating powerful messages that some things in my environment were not a good fit for me. My nervous system made the association between those things and the reactions I had. That is where the fear came from. It was my body saying, "Stay away."

The information helped me feel more compassion for myself and for my mom. In different ways, we were both going through a lot when she was pregnant with me. This is another way I can see my body telling the wordless story of what I went through before I could form conscious memory.

Some people will never know their parents or their ancestral history. Some people do not have access to academic journals where emerging research findings are shared before they are accessible to the public. There is privilege in knowing how to access, understand, and apply information. Not everyone can get the information I was able to get. But the research into epigenetics as a whole reminds us that while we may never know the exact cause of our bodily suffering, we may be living out the end result of genetic changes that occurred generations before to keep our ancestors safe (we call this epigenetic change). And just as our genes, and the genes of our ancestors, can change to adapt to stressors and circumstances, so can they adapt to learning that we are now safe, held in the arms of our inner nurturer.

The Invitations

I'm going to put an idea forward here about pain that may be uncomfortable to consider, so I want to be clear that how you interpret it is wholly up to you. Ideas of this magnitude are best considered for oneself, not offered to others as platitudes, spiritual bypasses, or cop-outs when we do not know how to sit with our own discomfort or other people's pain.

Here is the idea: pain can be a doorway into the present. Even more, pain can be the invitation into loving and caring for oneself, sometimes learning how to do that for the very first time. The intensity of the sensations of pain are cause for us to try to escape into our mind, but they are also an invitation into the present. When we feel nerve activation in our bodies, it is a reminder that we are here, in the right now, alive and feeling.

Sometimes the body is saying, "You went through something" or "Stop ignoring me." Sometimes the body is saying, "This is new" or "This is hard." My favorite is imagining the sensations as my intricate and beautifully evolved tissues speak with nerve and electrical firings: "I am in desperate need of some care right now." We can only learn what the message is if we stop to pay attention. Whatever is going on for our body can make us afraid, but it can also reconnect us to ourselves.

It was through the pain and injuries following my accidents that I learned to more deeply commit to the practices I so readily offered others. My accidents exposed my integrity breach and invited me into all the things that I know work but had not practiced with any degree of commitment myself. The pain flung open the front door of my bodily self, my home, through which self-compassion and attunement could enter. While I do employ moment-to-moment strategies to ease my suffering, the overarching narrative had to change from avoiding or dismissing my pain to learning to be in dialogue with it, realizing that I could decide to respond to it in a way that took me closer to myself.

Changing-Room Dialogue

Several months after the second accident, my leg had not yet healed, so I advocated for myself until the doctor I was seeing agreed to order an MRI. Because I live in Canada, my tests and treatment come at no added expense. Instead of being afraid of extra medical bills, I could focus on coordinating my treatment, finding my voice when communicating with medical professionals, and learning how to better understand my physiological distress.

My mind was constantly going back and forth between the two stories I was telling myself about my body. A dialogue of sorts, like shooting the second arrow, pulling it out, shooting it again—maybe in the same place, maybe somewhere new—and pulling it out again.

The bow was loaded: "They said things would feel better by now. I'm doing everything I've been told to, so why won't my body heal?" Then: "Okay, lots of criticism and frustration today. Let's slow down. You got hit head-on by a truck. That's something people usually use as a metaphor for a disaster, and it actually happened to you, and you're still alive."

I became accustomed to the back and forth. Where there had once been only a critical monologue, I learned to talk back to the inner critic with something more supportive and compassionate. Over time, as far as my recovery was concerned, the unhelpful way of thinking about my injuries became less prominent.

Then, half a year later, the morning of the MRI came. Everything was right on schedule, and I was ushered into a small changing room, next to three others, with a sliding curtain for privacy and a mirror on the back wall. I slipped on the seafoam hospital gown. It was silent in the changing room, but I could hear others adjusting their attire.

I started moving at half-speed and gently placed my warm hands on every part of my body, pausing and lingering at the places with pain or injury that I was there to investigate. Feet first, then ankles, shins, knees, hips, belly, and chest, then my neck, scalp, and finally my hands came to rest on my cheeks as I met my own gaze in the mirror. I was standing there, hands tenderly on my face, like a mother would place her hands on the face of her beloved child. To the parts that were hurting, that had worked hard, had endured, survived, were afraid, I said aloud to all of me, "Well done. You have worked so hard. You have been in so much pain, so vocal about where it hurts.

Thank you for speaking up. I am listening. And the doctors are listening too. Thank you for working so hard to protect me after such an awful and scary thing happened to you. You are safe now." It just tumbled out of me; perhaps it was all the practice I'd had doing this in the mirror before and after physiotherapy, late at night in bed, on the floor of my office, or every time I got in a car after the accidents.

There was an older man in the stall next to me struggling to put on his seafoam suit, and he chuckled at my profession of compassion. I had forgotten for a moment that anyone else was there. But I smiled, wondering what it was like for him to hear all that. Perhaps this was a kind of dialogue he knew well. Perhaps I was simply the mysterious lady with a soft voice one stall over having a very strange conversation with herself.

I pulled back the curtain, and there stood a nurse, motionless, with tears streaming down her face, hand over her mouth. She said, almost with disbelief, that in thirty years of working in the imaging department of the hospital, never had she heard anyone speak out loud about themselves with such kindness. I took a breath, lingering in that moment with her. We wondered together how much more difficult it is to heal when we are also contributing to our own pain by how we respond to ourselves about it. Her expression lives preciously tucked into my memory, a souvenir of the magic of that moment.

I survived two successive car accidents, one of which more likely than not should have ended my life. Somehow, I lived. And I have scars, visible and invisible, to remind me of something terrifying that happened outside my control. But I have chosen powerfully to refuse to let my inner dialogue contribute to the injuries that happened to me.

I refuse to shame, punish, ignore, or discipline my body for telling the truth about what happened to me in those very scary moments, moments that somehow linger on in the present through pain and injury. My body is allowed to tell the truth for as long as she needs to, and I will not stop her. We have been together this whole time, and with my words I will remind her that even though she thought she would die then, we are safe now.

SOME THINGS TO THINK ABOUT

- How do I normally speak to myself when I'm sick or in pain? Where did I learn that?
- If I could choose some other way to respond when this happens, what might that sound like? What might a loving person say to me?

SOME THINGS TO TRY

- Notice the moment before you shoot the second arrow and pause there.
- If you have never practiced mindfulness before, try it for one minute. Set a timer and pick something to focus on (a sound, the feeling of your breath, a sensation in your body, something you can see). When you get distracted and notice that your mind has wandered, bring your attention back to the thing you are focusing on. You will get distracted at some point, so don't beat yourself up. Try this practice daily, and when one minute feels comfortable, try increasing the duration by a minute or two.
- Write a list of kind things to say to yourself next time you are in pain or hurting. Use your list when you need it most and see how it feels.

7

The Body and Oppression

When Bodies Are Political

My friends and I had just arrived in a tiny town about a two-hour drive north of Los Angeles where we were the main speakers at an event. When we speak together, we find that most of the attendees are typically people who listen to *The Liturgists* podcast, and we know them well. On this occasion, however, it took only moments to realize that this group was different. It was a smaller group, about forty people, and most of them were over the age of seventy, had never heard of our work, and had never listened to a podcast. But the most obvious difference from our usual audience was the notable absence of people of color.

The event had a few parts: we were doing a live recording of the podcast that morning, and we were each invited to talk about something we were passionate about. The podcast seemed to be relatively well received, with minimal overt pushback, despite the podcast being about questioning "evangelism" and the fact that I characterized many kinds of mission work as forms of colonization and cultural genocide. Later that afternoon, William, a Black man who was the only visible person of color in the room, presented a documentary he had made based on his visit to the Arctic National Wildlife Refuge. As an advocate for climate change understanding, he had been invited to go with some friends to meet with and learn from the Gwich'in people who live there. This was spurred by threat of oil drilling on the land, which would disrupt the ecosystem within which the Gwich'in people live, hunt, and carry on their traditions.

After William showed the documentary, the first question he got was overtly racist and included obvious misunderstanding about colonization. I remember being so moved by his ability to educate while being both boundaried and assertive in answering the question.

As the conversation evolved, it seemed to become more constructive as people from the audience joined in and shared their concerns about the changing state of the earth and our responsibility to adapt our ways of living. There was palpable concern in the room, and the longing for a better way of being in relationship with the earth was echoed.

In response to the emerging dialogue, William described to almost exclusively white Europeans that as a Black man he has hope that springs simply from knowing that he was there, in that room, because his enslaved great-grandparents had hope and refused to give up. The room was rapt; it was so moving to hear him speak about how a legacy of horrific oppression and violence against Black people had not been and will never be as powerful as their resilience.

When William and I returned to the hotel after the event, we sat for a while in the bar to debrief. We ended up talking about what it was like for him to be in a room where he had to educate so many people about things that are inescapable for him. The threat and weight of systemic oppression of bodies like his move with him from space to space and are in his DNA, while everyone else in the room buys a ticket to learn about injustice done to others and can easily leave it behind after the event is done.

Even in that moment, as William shared this with me, he was giving me the gift of education. He was inviting me to know something about his experience that I—as a person whose skin color has never made me more likely to experience covert and overt violence—did not know. He paused for a moment and looked away, almost as if collecting a part of himself, and then looked me squarely in the eyes, "There is nothing quite like being in a room full of people who are the descendants of slaves. Not only is it energizing, but it feels like it connects me to who I am and where I come from. In spaces like that, I don't have to explain what it's like to be me."

Politics of Bodies

The body is the site of oppression. So whenever we are talking about oppression, we are also talking about people's bodies.

Oppression happens to the body in at least one of two ways, if not both—through artificial divisions that exist systemically and through the interpersonal lived experiences of those divisions that have an observable psychophysiological cost. First, the hierarchies created by societies, in which some people are conferred more power than other people, exist because of the artificial labeling of certain bodies as more or less acceptable, right, or "normal" than other bodies. To do this, clearly delineated categories must be created, such as white/Black, ability/disability, man/woman, straight/gay, cis/trans or cis/nonbinary, young/old. The less we are forced to see these divisions or feel their effects, the more likely it is that we are somewhere near the top of this constructed hierarchy. In other words, privilege is blinding.

159

These divisions are reinforced by macroaggressions and microaggressions. Macroaggressions are large scale, ongoing, and overt, such as violence, hate crimes, and political decisions that are made at the national or local level. Microaggressions are small, brief, and often subtle, such as making some bodies (in)visible in advertising, asking questions about hair texture, or telling someone they are a hero for leaving the house in a wheelchair. It can also include who makes eye contact with whom, what looks a person gets from others when entering a room, who is followed around a store, and who is never called on or whose opinion is disregarded in the boardroom. In many cases, oppression of one body is perpetuated not only by abstract systems but by how two actual bodies interact within a space.[1]

Second, all forms of oppression affect the body. From research about the brain, especially through the use of neuroimaging, we know that it is factually *incorrect* to say that physical violence is the most hurtful, and thus most valid, form of injury. Our brains and nervous systems process verbal, social, political, and physical injury in the exact same way.

A pivotal moment in my understanding of humanity, pain, and our need to take responsibility for our interactions with others came when I learned of research that showed that the exact same structures and systems in the brain were active whether people were hurt emotionally (through damaging words and social rejection) or physically (through injuries to their tissues).[2] Even if oppression is happening "out there," is seemingly invisible, or seems so subtle that it is only felt but hard to describe, it affects a person's body.

Oppression is a form of trauma, a collective trauma,[3] but it often goes unrecognized because there is rarely one single event a person can point at to say, "That is why I feel this way in my body." One study concluded that people in oppressed or marginalized groups can meet all the criteria necessary for a

160

diagnosis of PTSD without having experienced the single life-threatening event usually associated with PTSD.[4]

Whenever talking about power and oppression, it is important to also talk about how systems that give some people power and keep it from others are both *constructed* and *concrete*. To say they are constructed means that the categories of value are created by our minds or made up. To say they are concrete means that the impacts of these made-up categories are decidedly not made up but very real and tangible in how they affect the people who experience the oppression and in how they benefit people with power. No one person is *actually* more valuable or better than another person. However, when we have been told for long enough that these divisions of power are real and necessary, it becomes part of our inherent belief system and shapes how we act in the world. As a result, we start to reify the thing that was made up in the first place. That's social constructivism: the cycle of how our created ideas and frameworks shape our lived realities, which feed back into our ideas and frameworks.

Take gender, for example. The gender binary is a story we are told about ourselves that feels so reinforced and concrete that it is hard to imagine it being just a story: *If you are born with a penis, you need to act a certain way. If you are born with a vulva, you need to act a different way. Don't stray from the story, otherwise you will get hurt or be ostracized, and you will be excluded from the social resources you need to survive.* If we hear the story often enough and have little to no access to another story, everything keeps flowing along as planned (by those who hold power).

It can be hard to see with clarity the systems within which we live, especially when these systems seem abstract and ideological, or when we benefit from them directly. But they shape the social landscapes within which we live, and they have observable and experiential consequences on our bodies, individually and collectively. In the words of somatic psychology expert Christine Caldwell, "The marginalization of the body has such a long and cross-cultural history that we barely notice or care that the oppression of our bodily selves is constant, insidious, and potentially devastating."[5] To begin to undo the nature of these damaging stories, we have to name them as what they are—oppressive, which means that while they are hurtful for some, they are highly beneficial for others.

Telling a New Story

It is humbling to admit that my interest in bodies was initially about my own body and my own freedom. As others have said, research is often me-search. I found that narratives about my body as a woman were constraining, damaging, and even life-threatening. But as I began to explore the politics of the body, I started to see how my body was not only hurting because of oppressive systems; it was also benefiting from them. It was again humbling to realize that I had much to learn from those whose bodies are oppressed in ways I have not experienced.

Through listening to their voices, I learned that not one positionality or identity sees everything. In taking responsibility for my learning, and unlearning, it is important for me to keep listening to the voices of people who have lived as bodies different from mine—especially bodies that have been marginalized—to better understand what they can see that I cannot about the systems of which we are all a part.

As I listened and learned, I became increasingly interested in disrupting the systems that label certain bodies as problematic or dangerous. As an outflowing of that, I wanted to find out how I had internalized those systems and body-stories and how I continued enacting them against myself and others.

Feeling restricted to only two options was a trope of myths about power and oppression that I was implicated in. I believed

I had to choose between perfection or inaction, with no space in between. For all my trying, I am failing at this constantly. Often in public. And as messy as these public failings may be, they invite me to continue to learn, and they make me responsible to pull at the threads that are hard for me to see at first but that are creating real hurt for others. To do that, I want to invite you to get to know four people in my life who have taught me some of the most valuable things I have learned about oppression and the body—Melaney, Malcolm, Kathy, and Heather.[6] It is worth stating that although each of these people represents a different intersection of identity, and each experiences injustice toward their body in a particular way, they are not speaking on behalf of all other people with similar identities and experiences.

Melaney: "My Body Is Political"

Melaney is one of my greatest teachers. Whenever I introduce her, I'm never quite sure if I should introduce her as my mentor, a friend, a sister, an aunt, a mother, a teacher, a healer, or my hype woman. She feels so deep and vast, as if her presence is limitless, and she is equal parts fierce and tender. She has a particular way of slicing you open with a question, reminding you she is really paying attention, almost always in ways you had forgotten to pay attention to yourself.

As an Indigenous woman born in Canada in the sixties, Melaney was taken from her mother in the hospital by the government, and she was given to a white family (she is part of what's known as "the Sixties Scoop"). From the moment she was born, she was separated from her culture, her family, her land, and her language. The family to whom she was given became her family too and loved her well. But it wasn't until she was in her thirties that she "came home," moving back in with her biological father, on to her people's land, and learned about the traditions and language that she had been ripped away from. The horrors of what was done to the Indigenous people of Canada and across Turtle Island (the pan-Aboriginal term for North America) are easy to ignore when we simply read about them in social studies textbooks, believing that the trauma of colonization is contained in the past. But Melaney's story proves otherwise.

As we sat down together to talk, she pulled fresh focaccia bread from the oven and ladled hot lentil soup into a bowl. I started by asking, "What does it mean for you to be a body?"

She paused for a moment, stirring her soup with a spoon. "As an Indigenous woman, holding a status card highlights that my very existence is political. We are still defending our lands, rights, and titles when the government didn't think we'd still be in existence. When our land was taken in the 1800s, they most likely thought we would be dead, disenfranchised, or assimilated into the Eurocentric culture, and not have any connection to our Indigenous identity. That was actually the plan. All of their directives and policy-making were done to assimilate the 'red children of the queen.'"

Her voice was soaked with sarcasm and defiance, and she had a twinkle in her eye. I offered back, "You're saying to the system that tried to make you disappear, 'Oh, you thought I wasn't going to be here? Well, guess what? I'm still here!'"[7]

"Yes, we are still here, suckers," she said with a sly smile.

"So, yes, you're here, but that racism is not just in the past. Even from the moment you were born, you were taken from your family," I added.

"Yes, being born Indian, you get a status number like a birth certificate. I am a ward of the Federal Government of Canada. I mean, it's not something I had to think about as a kid or a teenager. But now, as an adult, an adoptee from the Sixties Scoop, there are different things that I have to figure out. I understand more of the government assimilation tactics as I listen to our stories and reconnect and continue to reclaim my Indigenous identity."

She paused for a few beats, dipping her bread in her soup, then turned her body to face me. "It feels like my body is more political than ever. As we are protesting the abuses of Indigenous rights by the government, I have put my body on the front lines to protect the lands. At one of our original village sites, I put my body in front of trucks and construction workers. It's pretty intense when you're standing up against some big men who are trying to get their job done.

"A number of my relatives and I go to public events to use our bodies to protect and defend Indigenous lands, rights, and titles. We need to be seen and to put our bodies on the front lines. Nothing else is working. I believe Indigenous peoples are always ready at the table to negotiate and make positive changes. It's not that we are trying to get our own way. We're trying to honor the treaties or agreements that have been put in writing over the 150 years of the existence of this place called Canada."

"So when you go to the sites to protest, you're saying with your body, 'I am here. You can't ignore my voice'?"

"Yes," Melaney answered. "Or, 'You can't ignore the voices of the people we are supporting.' Because we are not only defending our own rights but defending other Nations' rights. . . . Showing up as a body is a way to create solidarity. We are fighting for all people, as stewards of the land, Nation to Nation, protecting the earth."

"Your body, your existence, is political, yes!" I said, wide-eyed with excitement. "What is that like? What is the experience of being this body, this way?"

She settled into her chair, resting her elbows on the table. "I always say that I am a spiritual being embodied as an Indigenous woman. And I can't separate those things. My spirituality, my physical body, my mental state—they all coexist in my body."

The tone of her voice changed from declarative to pensive as she began talking about the effects of finding her Indigenous family later in life.

"Knowing my heritage, my genealogy, my DNA, it's another way of being in my body," she said. "Most non-Indigenous people do not know our story, they haven't even listened to our story. That's why we are frontline activists and truthtellers, rising and standing our ground to get our stories and our voices heard. We are trying to get to the ears of the people who make policies and decisions, and not just educate the general public."

"It's so unjust," I said, "having to put your body in the line of sight, in front of construction vehicles and government buildings, just because no one is listening to your voice. The irony, it's just absurd, of having to put your bodies in unsafe places just to advocate for the safety of your bodies, and the body of the earth."

She sighed and nodded. "Brown bodies are policed. We walk into the store and we're followed by security. We walk down the street and someone thinks we are in the wrong place. We get questioned and stopped. We are stopped at checkpoints on the road, and officers immediately assume we've been drinking. It's all the stereotypes. Even total strangers yell at me on the street."

As we talked about what she and others have endured, she began talking about their resilience. And she made it clear that even stronger than the violence endured is her connection to her culture. "My spirituality is probably the most important thing to me," she continued. "What I say and what I do with my body hold the teachings of my ancestors. I want to continue all the things my ancestors brought that I carry with me in my body. . . . As I age, I know that I'm part of the next generation of elders who need to be able to hold on to our stories, our heritage, our genealogy, and our cultural roots to pass on to the next generations. . . . My existence means keeping our cultural roots and our family and community stories alive—it's our living culture."

Melaney began to tell me more about coming back to her culture after being raised in a family with white European heritage. She described it as living between two worlds.

"I am a bridge," she said. "I walk between two cultures, between a colonized society and my Indigenous heritage. I get angry that I was taken and put into the foster-care system, that I lost all ties with my Native family as I was growing up. Even though I was raised in a great family and never lacked anything in one sense, I was without ties to my Indigenous community, my language, our traditional ways of being, hunting, fishing, gathering, our laws and teachings. I've gained some of it back, but not what I would have had if I had been raised within my biological family. But that was the intention. That was part of the Canadian government's assimilation tactics—to disconnect us from our Indigenous identity. There is so much brokenness in our communities because of that."

We paused for a moment to boil more water for tea. When we sat down again, she said, "I met my birth father when I was in my mid-thirties. Because I was raised by a white family, I didn't look like anyone [I grew up with]. When I looked in the mirror, I didn't know who I was identity-wise. But a month after I met my father, I went to put on my makeup, and I saw my father in my reflection. And I was like, 'Oh my God, I look like him.' For the first time in my life, I looked like someone. It was huge. All my life, I was the brown kid in the pictures with all these white siblings, going to church with all these white people, and then it was like, all of a sudden, I'm connected. It's in my DNA."

Melaney paused here, tears in her eyes and in mine. We sat in silence for a few moments.

"I carry the DNA and resemblance of my ancestors," she said. "It just blows me away. Yes, colonization goes back a few hundred years attempting to disconnect me, but in every single cell of my body I hold thousands of years of DNA of the people who walked before me. My body holds resilience and resemblance."

She ended our conversation with her head up, eyes gleaming, and both a strength and a softness in her voice. "I see resilience, resistance, and reclaiming. I am reclaiming Indigeneity. I desire that settlers decolonize and reclaim their stories. I learn something every time I sit with people, and I try to find the common ground between the European Canadians and the Indigenous people and try to walk in this movement called reconciliation. I want that for the world and hope that someday there will be an end to war, oppression, and racism."

Malcolm: "Being a Body Is Lonely"

Malcolm and I met a few years ago through mutual friends. I was drawn to his mile-a-minute intellect, mischievous smile, and thoughtful analysis of everything he encounters. He is the kind of human I trust deeply to inform my thinking about matters of the world, and I often find myself asking and thinking about his opinion on a particular matter—everything from a popular TV show to a political leader. I was eager to ask Malcolm to share with me some of his experiences of being a body as a gay Black man in his thirties.

The vulnerability and honesty with which he shared was a gift for me. I didn't realize how much pain there would be in listening to him talk about embodiment. It was another reminder of how being the body that I am—and the social construction of that body—means I will never have to live through certain experiences. Instead, I have the luxury of learning about these experiences from the outside.

We had this conversation in the car while taking a winding mountain road up to a viewpoint of the valley below. He started our conversation off with a gut punch. "My experience of being a body is lonely," he said. He paused before continuing. "I don't often feel like a self, a person sometimes. I have to take a shower to remind myself that I'm a body. Maybe because I don't take time to fully be my body. I'm always on the go and doing things."

When I asked if he thought that the experience of being Black in a white America and being gay in a straight America makes it harder to be a body, he immediately said, "Yes."

"I have always had to see myself from outside myself," he said. "It's like I'm always having to see myself through another person's gaze just to be okay, just to navigate the world. I think that part of that is being Black, but I think another part of that was growing up religious, constantly having to wonder if I was pleasing God just to be okay. I feel like my whole life is a constant experiment in pleasing someone else."

When talking about the meaning of being a gay Black man, he said, "I always feel wrong. I always feel like who I am and what I desire is wrong. Always. It's like a constant hum or a buzz in my ear or inside of me that says, 'You're disgusting, you shouldn't have that, don't touch that, don't be that, don't be here.'"

I wondered if that was connected to the feeling of needing to please. "Yeah, because I learned I can never trust myself," he said. "I always have to trust someone else's gaze of me rather than my own. I like to think that maybe there are people out there who grew up differently from me who don't feel as wrong. But it took me a long time to begin to accept myself." We sat in silence for a moment, taking in the view as the car rounded the corner and there was a clearing in the trees.

"Living my life so that my body would meet other people's expectations actually opened me up to the idea that maybe, in and of myself, I was okay. And that was more of a mental exercise rather than a feeling exercise because, like I said, there's always a buzz that tells me I'm not okay."

"What are some of the spaces or social contexts where that buzz is quieter, where you can be more at rest?" I asked.

Malcolm responded, "Where I'm living now. The city is open to so many people who are same-gender loving. It creates less judgment. There's still judgment in the city, but it's far less.

There is so much representation in seeing people who are you out in the world. Whether it's coming out of the downtown area or just a corner coffee shop or restaurant, I can walk into any place and a quarter or half or more of the people in the room are gay, and you can feel it. It's just a different energy."

"One of the things I've learned about oppression and the body is code-switching," I said, "that how you move, walk, talk, act, sit is based on what space you're in. I am curious if you notice what it's like to be a body in other spaces that are not as free or supportive or that don't have as much representation."

"That was my whole life from childhood onward," he said. "I was in spaces that were oppressive, in spaces that really touted heterosexism. Those spaces have enforced it. They established order on how to live, how to talk, and how to be a man—and if you don't play by that social order and those social cues, then you're off and weird. I think there's something inherently violent about those oppressive spaces. . . . It's like they create a reality where only one answer or one version of you can come forward. Everything—the logic, the talk, the social norms—demands a certain response out of you. And to live like that is suffocating.

"Leaving an oppressive space doesn't mean that the oppression isn't still inside of you, because it has been trained in you—it's in your body, it's in your nervous system, it's in your way of being. So, yes, it's liberating and freeing to be in a freer place, but that doesn't necessarily mean that you are free, because that buzz and that hum is still there."

Malcom and I ended up going for a walk at this point. We talked more about what it was like for him to be in spaces with people who are like him, whether that is with queer people or Black people, and he shared about how that felt effortless, as if there were one less layer of weight in his body and he could set down the hypervigilance. Those spaces, he said, allowed him to rest in a country where there was always the threat of violence.

Kathy: *"I Do Not Want to Shift Myself Anymore"*

In a hypothetical dream scenario in which a genie in a bottle gives me a few wishes, I would use one of them to see the world as Kathy does. She is brilliant, full stop. And she always seems to have some hidden talent or profound insight that a person would only find out about if they took just the right combination of conversational turns. She is wise, and I have never had an encounter with her in which I didn't walk away wondering about something I'd never considered.

When we met to talk about bodies and embodiment, we sat down at a busy downtown diner for brunch. There was constant chatter at the tables around us and there were plates clanking in the kitchen, but we talked for hours, and my attention was rapt the entire time.

"I have been working through different social categories around who I am for a while. I'm a woman. I'm Asian. I'm queer. And I'm a Christian." She went on to describe growing up Korean American in a predominantly white neighborhood in the San Francisco Bay Area. She recalls realizing when she was "different," largely prompted by her appearance. "For kids, social currency is a dance between what makes you the same and what makes you stand out. Often differences are not good, and kids aren't shy about letting you know. The evolution of internalizing certain negative narratives about my race and ethnicity began very early.

"It wasn't until college that I started to engage in conversations around race and ethnicity in a positive way. I went to UC Berkeley in the early 2000s, which is now a majority Asian school. That afforded me this exposure to so much diversity among Asians—I mean, we're just as diverse as anybody else. That much diversity makes it harder to make assumptions. Suddenly I wasn't viewed as a representative of a homogenous conglomerate. I don't think I was able to articulate this at the time, but looking back I realize that was the first time I was proud of my race and ethnicity, in contrast with the negative associations I had held."

Her tone changed slightly, and she gestured with her hands like she was turning a corner. "Then I moved to Vancouver to attend a largely white seminary. I had left an extremely diverse environment, known for its historical relationship with certain justice movements, but I didn't have something to hold on to when I moved to Vancouver. At seminary, I forgot about my body." She went on to describe how she focused on other elements of her identity, such as her belief system.

"I wasn't asking what it means to be a woman," she said, "or an Asian person of Korean descent. And I definitely was not asking what it means to be queer. There was no space for that."

"Coming out actually helped me move back into my body by forcing me to make room for my sexuality," she said. "Sexuality is not just about someone else interacting with your body. It's also how you experience yourself. It's not just an externalization. But without thinking about it, I internalized certain negative associations with my body as a function of my sexuality.

"As a Christian, I learned: sex is gross, you are not a sexual being, but save it for somebody you love. Like, what? So many Christians experience this negative narrative around sexuality in general. But it's difficult when there is this added piece that your particular expression of sexuality as a queer person is not just for later, it's for never. I internalized those narratives without them ever being articulated."

There it was, the theme I had also heard from Melaney and Malcolm, about receiving messages that their bodies were bad. Because that was the water in which they were swimming, those messages somehow got inside of them, even when another part of them knew they were not true. Their environments were telling them they were bad, or needed to be changed, and this shaped how they experienced life inside their bodies.

"Without knowing it, I had adopted so much mythology in both arenas for me," she said, "around my Asian identity as well as my queer identity. There was so much I had to undo, unwrite, to rejig—so many cultural narratives I had to break down about myself before I could start building something new. That work is not straightforward by any means in the face of all these insidious competing messages.

"That was something so important about my experience at college around my Asian American identity. We were all helping each other be proud. It didn't necessarily involve naming internalized racism, but we could come together and talk about various forms of discrimination and laugh together to alleviate some of that experience.

"But as East Asians, we are also light skinned. Our history in America is such that our defense mechanism was to adopt white supremacist thinking and then play the game within that framework to accept a kind of second-class citizenship. The manifestation of that is complex yet profound privilege, even though we are people of color. Because we were light skinned, we had the privilege of just playing along. There is this internal work that still needs to happen among Asians so we aren't continuing to perpetuate problematic narratives about ourselves or others."

She looked away, then back at me. "My sister has been really pivotal in helping me rethink a lot of this," she said, "my rights, my ethnicity, my sexuality, and my role in view of my privileges. She was the one who taught me about internalized racism, where I had adopted the dominant negative view about my own identity. I was learning a lot, and I started using this phrase, 'White Kathy,' to describe the defense mechanism I had adopted."

"It sounds like making the invisible visible helped you see what was going on inside of you," I said, "to have your sister articulate your experiences in a way that you could see yourself, and then maybe do something different." Once again, I was noticing a common thread between what Kathy was saying and what Malcolm had said about internalizing hurtful narratives and code-switching to minimize social discomfort.

"Yes," she said, "I try not to do that anymore. I've practiced that way of being for so long in order to be accepted, to belong and feel safer. Sometimes I would mimic or parody or outright make fun of myself as an Asian. I was saying to white people, 'I'm not like those people who are sensitive about race. You don't have to worry about me; I won't cause trouble here.' I was basically putting myself and my community down to make someone else feel comfortable and not have to change something. But I'm in my mid-thirties now, and I'm asking myself the question, 'What does it look like for me to be proud of who I am, with my race and ethnicity and sexuality?' I don't want to shift myself anymore just to make it comfortable for other people. That is for their sake, for my sake, and for the sake of people groups who experience far more oppression than I do."

I paused to absorb her potent words. The waiter came to refill our waters, and I asked Kathy about the spaces where she feels most safe.

"I think representation is one of the most powerful ways to cultivate justice at every level," she said. "For example, if I see a woman in leadership, I know that part of my experience is being represented and vocalized behind closed doors in meetings. The more representation, the stronger those voices are. But when there is a group of people who are really different, like this church I was at, when nobody belongs, we all belong to each other, and it just works. You can feel more ease about being yourself, because there isn't this caricature of who you're supposed to be."

We finished our meal, and the server came to clear our plates. I asked Kathy why embodiment matters, and why it matters to her that we are not just brains being carried around by these fleshy bodies.

"I want to say that it matters and that I don't have a choice in how it matters," she said. "Embodiment matters because it should, but also because everyone is making it matter to me. I have been handed certain narratives about my body, my identities, that have shifted me into a space where I'm seen as a body, and I see what people think about that body. Because of that, I've had to shift into a more curious relationship with my body, where I've had to do the work of reconnecting with myself as a body in newly positive ways. I wish that bodies mattered for purely positive reasons. But for so many of us, our bodies are perceived negatively. Because our bodies are not the 'thing' that someone said they are supposed to be—because they deviate from the mythology of normativity—suddenly our bodies are perceived as inadequate. I hope we can use embodiment to shine a light on structural mythologies about which bodies have power and which ones do not."

Kathy said it so poignantly. One of the reasons that bodies matter is because of the vilification of the body, especially bodies that are different from the socially constructed bodily ideal. We have focused on bodies because we have learned to become afraid of them. However, to right the narrative, we need to center the experiences of those who have lived as bodies that have been rejected, demonized, and shoved to the margins. This is part of the "righting" of our relationship with bodies in general—to point out what has been missing in order to disrupt the narratives of bodily exclusion that do harm to members of our human family.

Heather: "Disability Is Not the Opposite of Ability"

My friend Maggie first introduced me to Heather. Maggie sent a group email to those of us who would be speaking at an event about body politics, asking for our topics. A few moments

175

later I saw Heather had responded: "I will be speaking to the experience of living in a fat, trans, disabled body and living with other people's judgments, stereotypes, and misperceptions placed on me." I immediately thought, *Heather is a person I really want to talk with about the politics of bodies.*

Heather is the executive director of Creating Accessible Neighbourhoods (CAN), a non-profit they[8] founded in 2005. They speak regularly on disability, inaccessibility, and ableism as an advocate, activist, and educator, and they have paid close attention to the way that the disability community is composed of people with intersecting identities.

I met Heather at their home, where we found our way to a living room near the back of the home and sunk into overstuffed couches. When I asked Heather about how they got into activism, education, and advocacy, this is what they shared.

"I have had disabilities throughout my entire life," they said, "but for a large portion of it I didn't recognize them as such. I had mental health issues in high school but didn't realize what disability was or how to label it. Then at age seventeen, my body just broke down, and for a good five years I didn't leave my house except for medical appointments. Then I started using a power wheelchair.

"I was trying to use public transportation, but the buses only came once an hour, and half the time the drivers would lie and say the ramps weren't operating because they didn't want to take the time to get the ramp down and to load me on. It was particularly frustrating because I had spent so many years being isolated. I felt that this power chair was my freedom, and then to have the gatekeepers stop me from accessing the world was quite difficult. I couldn't find an organization that could help me, so I started my own. Previously, all my letters to transit authority had gone unanswered, but as soon as I was the executive director of an organization, I got a response a week later."

"It sounds like the barriers weren't what we might typically think of with a disability, but that other people and the systems they created were significant barriers."

"Absolutely," they said. "One of the most frustrating things is the consistent use of the phrase 'wheelchair-bound' because people who don't have wheelchairs see it as something you're trapped in, and it's a bad thing. But with my wheelchair, I had freedom, I had mobility, I had access to my community, and I went all across Canada. I've traveled all over with my wheelchair and mobility aids. It's a completely different mindset because for those who really need wheelchairs, it is a freedom and a relief. Because of my internalized ableism, it took me a long time to make the decision to go into a wheelchair because I thought it was quitting, giving up. While getting in the wheelchair was freeing in one sense, it came with the constricted and limited perspective of others and their comments. People said things like, 'Good for you for getting out of the house today.' Getting congratulated for leaving the house? I've even been asked, 'Oh, is this a special occasion that you're out of the house?'"

I was starting to see how social stigma is part of what makes disability particularly disabling. Heather told me that they know a lot of people who don't use mobility aids when leaving their homes because they don't want other people to comment on their bodies. Even when we think we are protecting people and respecting the rights of people with disabilities, sometimes our goodwill can be harmful. Heather said, "I blame the international symbol of accessibility for this because the sign for the washrooms, the sign for parking—it's a figure in a wheelchair. That is what people think of when they think about disability. But in reality, 93 percent of disabilities are invisible. There is a lot of variability to disability, and I don't think that's talked about enough."

Heather told me that some disabilities are seen as more legitimate or real, while others aren't. They also identified how different systems work together to create more barriers for people to access care. For example, weight stigma and anti-fat rhetoric compound access to care for someone with a disability. So a person who has PTSD and who is in a large body might find it difficult to access medical care because of a traumatic experience with a health care provider. Then, when they finally arrive at the doctor's office to talk about the PTSD symptoms, they are told to lose weight. "It's really difficult," Heather said, "to find a health care provider you don't have to educate about your identity."

Heather highlighted two ways of thinking about disability: the social model and the medical model. The medical model views people with disabilities as needing to be fixed by the medical system. In this case, disability is the problem. But the social model views harmful perspectives on disability, or ableism, as the problem. Ableism creates an inaccessible world, and we all have a role in either creating it or dismantling it. The social model shifts the problem from the person and bodies to systems and ways of thinking about people and bodies.

When I asked about how people with disabilities were forgotten, Heather politely corrected my assumption.

"We've not been forgotten," they said, "because we had to be thought about or considered in the first place to be forgotten."

"You're right," I said. "And without people at the table, or who have authority in government or leadership positions in organizations, there is less of a chance that the perspectives of people with disabilities will be heard or considered, especially at key moments when decisions are being made."

"It's also hard for people with limited energy to gather and advocate for themselves," Heather said. "First of all, can they get there by transportation? Can they gather? Is it too cold or hot to stay outside for very long? What about people's pain levels? In fact, this even impacts something as basic as voting rights. The last two times I've gone to vote, I've ended up in tears because there were so many barriers—and I'm a full-time advocate! It's so easy to think, 'Why do I try?' It invalidates you as a person. It makes you feel like you're unseen, unwanted, and a nuisance. That's so disheartening—and it's also a reason why so many people with disabilities don't vote.

"So often, people are trying to do the right thing," they said, "or help out a person with a disability, but they end up making decisions for the person instead of letting the person with the disability ask for what they need, or decide if they need anything at all. When our efforts to help and good intentions are misinformed, they can create barriers to community and experience that increase the barriers for people with disabilities. One of these barriers is the assumption that ability and disability are dichotomous, like a person who has a disability in one area is defined by that disability and the rest of them isn't seen. But everyone is inherently valuable, even if their productivity looks different from others'. That does not mean they have less to offer."

As our conversation came to a close, we talked about comparative suffering, and how we sometimes use other people's perceived limitations or challenges to make ourselves feel better. How we tend to talk about disability reinforces the trope that the lives of people with disabilities are bad or that they need to be rescued. Heather also talked about the distinction between person-first language ("a person with a disability") and identity-first language ("a disabled person"). We talked about how each phrase has its place, especially given what the dominant and hurtful social narrative about disability has been. But ultimately, different communities have different perspectives (for example, the Deaf or Autistic communities versus the community of those with eating disorders), and each person within those communities has their own relationship with disability. In the end, Heather highlighted that while each person feels differently, language matters as a tool either for devaluing a person or for helping a person gain social power.

The Global Human Body

Our bodies are the sum of smaller components working together to create a functioning whole: the nervous system, the endocrine system, the digestive system, and more. All the parts within each system, and how those systems function together, help us move toward growth, health, and life. Humanity functions as a body as well—we are all connected to each other. That means we have a responsibility to be aware of the systems that are hurting one part or different parts of the larger human body. It requires paying attention to how we devalue bodies—our own and others'—and working to eradicate these systems because of the deadly infections they are to the body of humanity.

Because the body is where our identity develops and resides, we cannot be fully ourselves in the world, fully free, or fully safe until our bodies and all bodies can be free and safe. It is essential that those who continue to be oppressed have spaces to meet with people who are similar in identity or experience to work through and name how oppression is impacting them.

For people who have been oppressed and marginalized, freedom and safety can come from belonging to a group that validates oppression as real, especially when others have denied or failed to see that oppression. Belonging to a group that names oppression as an outside force and expresses a commitment to protect one's community is a protective factor against myriad health concerns attendant to existing within an oppressive framework.[9]

The work of undoing the systems that create marginalization of bodies is ongoing. I am committed to better understanding how I perpetuate these narratives and how they are

180

deeply lodged within me. Instead of seeing this as a problem that someone else needs to fix or that will go away on its own, I want to understand my role in this through reeducation, and I want to follow that with action. I hope this for us all, so that each of us—as individuals and as the collective body of humanity—can move into health and thriving.

Whatever identities you carry that have led to marginalization or oppression can also be the places where you find agency. When harmful stories about your body have insidiously crept into your own thinking and taken root, I hope you are surrounded by people who are like you and who help you remember that your body is good. Your body does not belong to anyone else, and you have the same right as every one of us to be in spaces that welcome you—as is.

SOME THINGS TO THINK ABOUT

- Growing up, what bodies did you learn were "other"? Have you had one of the bodies that you learned was other? How do those ideas express themselves in your life?
- In what ways have you changed your posture, tone of voice, eye contact, or movement to make yourself less threatening to someone who has more social privilege than you? What did that cost you?
- What are barriers to examining the ways you have internalized messages about oppression and the body?
- If you have experienced identity-based oppression and marginalization, in which spaces have you found yourself more at ease? How can you better identify with and spend more time with your people?
- How did you respond emotionally as you read this chapter? When, if at all, did you feel fear, defensiveness, or relief?

༠ ﹀ ﹏ SOME THINGS TO TRY ﹏ ﹀ ༠

- Find books, talks, podcasts, online courses, and social media accounts from those who have experienced bodily, identity-based oppression that is unfamiliar to you.

- Educate yourself about racism, weight stigma, colonization, heterosexism, ableism, and intersectionality, learning to see what the dominant culture has made it hard to see. Try reading books by people who have experienced oppression, listening to podcasts that help you see yourself more fully, and highlighting the work of experts who represent often unheard stories and experiences that differ from yours. Try taking an online course or workshop from an expert on one of these topics, especially a program that pays the creators fairly for their expertise and for sharing their lived experience.

- Read *My Grandmother's Hands: Racialized Trauma and the Pathway to Mending Our Hearts and Bodies* by Resmaa Menakem or *Oppression and the Body: Roots, Resistance, and Resolutions*, a book with a variety of authors, edited by Christine Caldwell and Lucia Bennett Leighton.

- Notice the experiences of code-switching as they are happening, and then find some spaces to undo its effect. This might include anything from going to therapy and doing body-based trauma work, shaking all your muscles to release the stress activation, telling someone you trust about it, or engaging in free movement to regain some agency.

8

Pleasure and Enjoyment

The Sensual and Sexual Body

Several years ago, my friends and I were sitting around eating falafel before a speaking event. We started talking about the weird and wonderful things we eat and the way we eat them. I mentioned my strategy for eating sour candies long after my tongue was raw, and someone else described a childhood delicacy and comfort involving bread, milk, and sugar. There is a kind of closeness that comes with knowing your friends' oddities—the ones we aren't quick to disclose. After a certain level of vulnerability in my self-disclosure, I asked the group, "What about the rest of you? What are your guilty pleasures?" Without skipping a beat, my friend Jamie stated, in the most matter-of-fact manner, "I don't feel guilty about any of my pleasures."

Guilty pleasures. Why do we even say that? It's one of those phrases that rolls off the tongue, like a kid randomly using a swear word they learned on TV without knowing the meaning of it.

Guilt is hardwired in to help us align our actions with our values—values we have learned based on what we need to survive in our social context and what reflects our identity in the world. While the ability to feel guilt is there from the get-go, the specifics of what we feel guilty about come later. Guilt is the somatic alarm bell that goes off to help us keep our behavior in check so we don't stray too far outside the lines of what matters to us and those around us. But as we like to say in the therapy community, guilt is best for when we have done something wrong. So, where did we get the idea that pleasure itself is wrong?

In her essential essay "Uses of the Erotic: The Erotic as Power," civil rights activist and womanist writer Audre Lorde reminds us that we cannot separate our sexuality from power and that we have been trained to fear our deepest longings, what she calls the essential "yes" within ourselves.[1] Our experiences of pleasure, sensuality, and sexuality, just as much as any other aspect of being a body, are inscribed with the social, cultural, and political stories of the context in which we exist. Many of us have no idea that what we experience as pleasurable or sensual—our denial of it or our reaction to it—is a mysterious combination of what we have experienced in the past, our temperament and hardwired preferences, and what we have learned to celebrate or to fear based on our context. We have what seems to be an instinctual drive or desire (or we have a reaction, like guilt, to such desire), but we rarely stop to inquire about the factors that shape it.

To start, let's do a thought experiment. For each of the words or phrases listed below, notice the first thing that comes to your awareness or how you would finish the sentence.[2]

Sexy
Pleasure

Sensual
I want . . .
I desire . . .
I turn myself on when . . .[3]
Orgasm feels like . . .
My sexuality is . . .
My sexuality is for . . .
I access my sensuality whenever I . . .
A time I felt most aroused was . . .

What do you notice happening right now in your body? And what do you find yourself thinking about? Do you want to talk about this with a partner or friend, think about it more, or blush or turn the page?

Sexual excitement or desire, as described in chapter 5, is a part of our humanity and for the most part is hardwired into our physiology. But our physiology exists in context. And that context taught us how to police ourselves, lean into sensation, treasure curiosity and exploration, or wonder what someone else is thinking about us based on what experiences we had and what they meant for those around us.

To find a starting point for sifting through some misinformation and hurtful narratives, and to create a more embodied sexuality, sensuality, and experience of pleasure, I want to start where any faithful academic starts: with language. We need to know what the words we use mean to us and how that shapes our experiences of our sexuality.

What Is Sexuality, Really?

Sitting around in a group of women, talking about our relationships to our bodies, I heard my friend Kathy point out the seemingly incongruous sentiment she'd heard in the evangelical church growing up: "Sex is dirty, horrible, and vile, so make sure you save it for the one you love." Growing up, many of us were taught that sexuality was essentially the same as but limited to the practice of sex—specifically, heterosexual married sex. If you grew up in a community like mine, you learned that sexuality was most fully expressed through intercourse but was also budding in the intense romantic passions of the teenage years, nighttime wet dreams of adolescent boys, and sloppy first kisses. Sexuality, as many of us were told, showed up in behavior, or sometimes in thinking about behavior. In some cases, sexuality was defined by who you desired. But even then, it was still almost always related to sex.

Take a moment to recall the definition of sexuality you were given. Just as interesting, do you remember how you learned about sex? Toward the end of elementary school when we discussed sexual health in school, I remember learning to use terms such as *sexually active* to refer to engaging in sexual activity or *sexual health* to refer to practices around safe sex. Of course, many of us think of sex and sexuality as synonymous, and our language contributes to the conflation of the two.

But what happens for us when our definition of sexuality is much more expansive than sex? Somewhere in the last decade or so, I came across two similar definitions of sexuality that have powerful implications for how we understand and experience ourselves as bodies. Audre Lorde invites us to see sexuality as much more than sex. She calls sexuality "the erotic" and describes it as "the deepest life force, a force which moves us toward living in a fundamental way."[4] It is the personification of "creative power and harmony. . . . The sharing of joy, whether physical, emotional, psychic, or intellectual, forms a bridge between the sharers which can be the basis for understanding much of what is not shared between [people], and lessens the threat of their difference, . . . and [it] can give us

186

the energy to pursue genuine change within the world."[5] Decades later scholar Joseph Wittstock defined sexuality as "that physical, emotional, psychological, and spiritual energy that permeates, influences, and colors our entire being and personality in its quest for love, communion, friendship, wholeness, self-perpetuation, and self-transcendence."[6] Note that nowhere in Lorde's or Wittstock's definition do you find the words *sex* or *intercourse*.

How we define sexuality and what we believe about sexuality matters for how we understand, experience, and take responsibility for ourselves as bodies. It can also act as an antidote for a culture that seems to offer us two primary sexual narratives: shame-based repression and denial, or objectification and using the bodies of others. More expansive definitions matter for how we advocate for, set boundaries about, and form our beliefs about who is responsible for our arousal. Because unlike what most of us have been led to believe, our sexuality is not primarily about anyone else. It is about us. Sexuality may be invited to the surface of your attention by certain contexts, people, sensations, and more, but it is yours—in you, through you, and for you.

It's important to stress this because many of us have had others—partners, authorities, systems—tell us so much about our bodies that we believe sexuality is outside of us or belongs to someone else. This can lead us to unquestioningly perform our sexuality, in one way or another. It's also true that other people, systems, communities, and political landscapes act as if that is in fact the case. After all, our bodies are where sexuality and sex happen. And fear, shame, and disgust around sex and sexuality, among other experiences of the body, have been the primary rationale for instituting systemic control over the body.[7]

As we start to de-pathologize sex and sexuality, some will immediately raise concerns about rape, sexualized violence, pornography, and sex addiction. However, these behaviors involve much more than "just" sex.

First, rape and sexualized violence are about power, not sex. They are about conquest and domination of another, and they involve the assumption that one person has the right to do that to another. In the same way, when a person is stabbed, we identify the perpetration of violence as the problem, not the knife. We use knives in our daily lives to lovingly prepare food for our family without assuming that all knives result in stabbing.

Second, addiction to pornography or sex is also not really about sex or sexuality but rather about emotional dysregulation (for more information, you can refer back to chapter 5). Emotional dysregulation is managed in a variety of ways, some that predominantly hurt the individual and some that hurt others. Just as a shopping or gambling addiction is not really about shopping or gambling, the intense physiological experience of the high from pornography and sex addiction is not as much about sex as about using those avenues to regulate distress. But it is easier to point the finger at sex and sexuality, the visible and identifiable element of the hurt, than it is to explore the inner experiences and motivations that mediated a person's hurtful behavior.

Defining Sexuality

Where do we get the ideas that sex is dangerous, that sexuality is a problem, and that both must be controlled? How we have been hurt, what we have or have not been told, what we experience, and with whom we experience it are all factors that shape our sexuality. These beliefs, while held in our mind, are about our bodies and impact what we experience through our bodies.

As noted in chapter 3, the brain forms powerful associations with events of emotional intensity. When something triggers fear or shame, we tend to shut down in an effort to achieve safety. However, this simultaneously stops us from experiencing ourselves more fully.

I sometimes liken this dynamic to living in a house in which some of the doors are shut and posted with Keep Out signs. It is essential to respect closed doors if we are in someone else's home. But when it's our home, we need to be able to explore that room and understand where the signs came from in the first place. Perhaps you're thinking something like, "What if there is a wild animal in that room?" If that's the case, then it's time to call someone who can help that animal get free and help you stay safe in the process. And sometimes we find that there never was a wild animal in that room, just a Keep Out sign posted long ago that no one ever took down. I can't imagine what it would be like to live in my own home but to have to avoid the hallway that leads to that room. Instead, I'd like to imagine how great it would be to have that space back.

To thicken the definitions of sexuality mentioned above, and to help us start renegotiating our relationship with our sexuality, I want to introduce a theoretical model of sexuality I learned about while developing and researching a treatment program for postpartum sexual health. The model is called the Five Circles of Sexuality. First introduced by Dr. Dennis Dailey in 1981, it has been widely used with both youth and adults in reconstructing a holistic perspective of sexuality, and it has also been used in academic and clinical research about human sexuality.[8]

The model is represented visually as five overlapping circles around a central circle and looks like an elementary drawing of a flower (see fig. 5). The five circles are sexual identity, intimacy, sexual health and reproduction, power and sexualization, and sensuality.

Sexual identity refers to how we identify ourselves and the labels we use as sexual beings for what and who we desire. This includes what we learned about biological sex, gender roles and

Figure 5

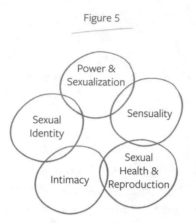

expression, and sexual orientation. Although sexual identity is central to our expression of personhood, we are rarely taught about it formally, and therefore we learn informally through cultural assumptions. Often, this informal learning leaves those who are marginalized because of sexual identity to do the most work to negotiate themselves within a social context.

Intimacy is the closeness that happens between us and others. This applies to all kinds of relationships—such as family and friends—not just romantic relationships. Intimacy is the drive behind most of our close relationships, and it empowers us to be vulnerable, take risks, and establish trust. Unlike other aspects of sexuality such as contraception and pregnancy, it is highly unlikely that we received any formal education about building intimacy.

Sexual health and reproduction identifies all the elements of our bodies and how these parts function for the purpose of sexual expression and childbearing. This is the circle about which we get the most public education, specifically about puberty, anatomy, contraception, sexually transmitted infections, pregnancy, and childbirth.

Power and sexualization describes how power is woven into our sexuality, including what and how we learn about sexuality.

190

It concerns both positive and negative aspects of power, as well as exchanges of power such as flirting, consent, abuse and rape, and the giving and receiving of pleasure. The naming of power is one reason this model is so useful: power is conferred socially, and this model identifies how sexuality is located within a socio political context.

Sensuality describes how we use our senses (sight, touch, taste, hearing, and smell) to experience pleasure. This includes our sexual response cycle and what activates that process, such as fantasy, eroticism, body image, and skin hunger. Skin hunger is an aspect of our sexuality we rarely learn about; it refers to the amount of physical contact each person wants.

The petals on the Five Circles of Sexuality overlap because they are all in relationship with one another. For example, a person's experience of *sensuality* (what feels good in their body) is directly related to *sexual identity* (the label a person uses, such as queer or straight). *Intimacy* (the ability to trust or be vulnerable in a relationship) is a lot more difficult when there was a damaging experience of *power and sexualization* (such as childhood sexual abuse). A person who struggles with an element of *sensuality* (such as body image) is likely to struggle with *sexual health and reproduction* (such as seeking out health care related to sexuality, including contraception). These examples identify how struggling in one sphere of sexuality affects other spheres.

The opposite is also true. When we have been educated about *power and sexualization* (the right to have consent and negotiate mutual pleasure), we are more likely to prioritize our *sensuality* in a relationship (asking for what we need to feel aroused). When we are aware of the normative changes to *sexual health and reproduction* across a lifespan (how sexual arousal and anatomy and physiology change with age), we are more likely to continue to experience *intimacy* over time (communicating and taking risks to self-disclose (dis)likes and finding ways to

191

adapt to changing bodies and preferences). Our awareness and confidence in our *sexual identity* (knowing who we are attracted to and our comfort with that label) is also connected to our ability to experience our *sensuality* (seeking out experiences that feel pleasurable, with confidence to articulate our needs and expect respect while doing so).

When we believe sexuality is limited to intercourse, we miss the connection between each of these circles and how that affects our quality of life. A middle-aged woman who has never experienced an orgasm may not realize that this is related to the abuse of power and sexualization of her body she experienced as a child. A man might feel so much shame about his sexual past that he is unable to enjoy pleasure without feeling guilt or disgust. A person who identifies as asexual might be misunderstood when discussing their preferences for satisfying skin hunger. A woman might find herself pregnant, unexpectedly, because she was never educated about pregnancy and contraception. The lack of understanding of power as a central element of sexuality could lead an adult to control, take, or abuse another person's body, to think it was their right and that it was solely about desire. Seeing sexuality in this rich way sheds light on the complexity of who we are as people and the various factors that intersect to create our struggles and our flourishing. Seeing sexuality in this way also allows us to be mindful with and think critically about sexuality and about what we have been told and shown about what sexuality is.

The Purity Problem

While the Five Circles of Sexuality model is robust, holistic, and phenomenologically oriented, it is a far cry from what I learned within the purity culture movement in the 1990s. For those new to the purity culture movement, here is a quick overview.

192

Following the sexual revolution in the sixties, there was increased public concern about the number of sexually transmitted infections (STIs) and pregnancies occurring outside of traditional heterosexual marriages. In some faith communities across North America, mostly white and evangelical churches, sexual impurity was conflated with spiritual impurity to dissuade teens from engaging in sexual activity outside of marriage.[9] This was effective in shaping the behavior of many within these communities, and the rhetoric such churches used stemmed from three related beliefs: bodies are dangerous and must be controlled; bodies are related to our spirituality in that what we do sexually can defile an individual's spirituality in an eternal sense; and despite having little to no training in empirically based sexual education or critical thought about the role of social power and sexuality, church leaders have the absolute authority about what others should do with their bodies.[10]

This resulted in no small number of teens and young adults learning from their faith communities that having sex or engaging in anything that could lead to sex (flirting, kissing, dating, wearing clothing others considered sexy) needed to be controlled. Research conducted in 2005 indicated that by 1995, near the height of the purity movement, over 2.2 million teenagers had signed a document promising not to have intercourse until they were in a heterosexual marriage, and they donned purity rings to prove it.[11] While this was presented as proof of spiritual purity and the way to please God—and included the promise of an attractive spouse and completely satisfying intercourse for the duration of a heterosexual marriage—it facilitated rigid sexual scripts and victim-blaming rhetoric in which women were held responsible for the sexual sins of men. To maintain sexual and spiritual purity, while also wrestling with age-appropriate sexual desire, the permeating question was, "How far can I go before I cross the purity line?" This question was evidence of an all-or-nothing way of thinking that asked the wrong questions about sexuality instead of teaching about more complex skills like negotiating power and consent, asking for touch that feels good, and understanding consequences.

The problem is not that the ideas and expression we experience are a conglomeration of all our experiences, culture, temperament, and social values. Rather, it's that a rigid, black-and-white mindset shaped the social context many of us grew up in. This creates a limited view of sexuality (i.e., sex is heterosexual intercourse) and leaves people with complex sexual sequelae that cause dysfunction and self-fragmentation.

While the purity movement appears to be losing steam, the kids who came of age at the height of the purity culture movement are now adults. What they learned in adolescence about sex and sexuality has had a lasting impact but not in the way that the pastors and youth leaders who were educating them would have guessed. When purity culture survivors show up in my clinical practice, they are often confused, angry, defeated, or riddled with shame.

Now in their thirties and forties, many are trying to reconcile what went wrong when they did everything they were told to do. They have been left wondering why they are so sexually illiterate and unsatisfied, why they married the first person they kissed, and why they feel so afraid of sexual activity, even with their trusted and loving spouse. As it turns out, refraining from sexual activity until marriage does not mean that the wedding day automatically comes with the ability to negotiate consent, pleasure, and differing sexual expectations.

Having only the handed-down set of inflexible sexual scripts meant neglected opportunities to learn to ask questions outside of the pure/impure sexual dichotomy. What many of these adults learned post–purity culture is that for all the effort of trying to do what was "right," they lacked the space to nurture a nuanced, developmentally appropriate, real-world sexual ethic with a sense of personal responsibility or agency.

Research about living through purity culture explains that the associated bodily beliefs can manifest in some surprising and not-so-surprising concerns: generalized body shame, body dysmorphia, and eating disorders; difficulty with arousal (for both men and women); low, erratic, or seemingly out-of-control sexual desire; difficulty articulating preferences and boundaries to sexual partners; challenges exploring what is satisfying sexually; genital pain (vaginismus, dyspareunia, and vulvodynia); lack of relational closeness and conflict from unrealistic expectations about frequency of sexual activity; and stress-related autoimmune disease. Not surprisingly, research outside the purity culture movement has shown that having restricted sexual scripts (scripts that tell you to follow a limited range of sexual behaviors to have a "successful" sexual encounter with a partner), especially when externally derived, is linked to decreased sexual and relationship satisfaction across the lifespan for both men and women.[12]

What our nervous system has learned is shameful can't immediately become the most pleasurable thing the next day. Our bodies are not machines that our intellect and thoughts can turn on and off. In fact, if anything is true, it is likely the other way around. Our body is the intelligence—the seat of the self that turns our thoughts on and off.

Over time, the shame that we use to suppress our sexuality lodges itself not only in our thinking but also in our nervous system. Regardless of whether we grew up learning about abstinence in church, the shame of sexuality extends far beyond youth-group walls and into classrooms through the form of abstinence-based sex education in schools. Proponents of this kind of sex education hoped that it would decrease pregnancy and STI rates. After all, as they taught, abstinence is the only form of birth control that is 100 percent effective.

However, research shows that this form of sex education made no difference in sexual behavior for most teens. This despite the hundreds of millions of dollars invested in abstinence-based education annually by the government. In 2009, the journal *Pediatrics* published an article by researcher Janet Rosenbaum that identified the effect of abstinence and purity-pledge education on teens' sexual attitudes and behavior.[13] The research team collected data from thousands of kids under age fifteen who had never had intercourse, had received abstinence-only education, and had pledged virginity until marriage. Five years later, the researchers went back to the original kids in the study to ask about their sexual activity, birth control use, and history of STIs. Here is what they found: 82 percent of the individuals who made a purity pledge denied that they had ever done so. There was no difference between those who had pledged purity and those who had not for rates of premarital sex, STIs, and other variables related to anal and oral sex. And the big kicker: compared to their peers who did not pledge purity, those who did take the pledge were less likely to use birth control or condoms in the previous year, or the last time they had intercourse.[14]

Perhaps the most ironic unintended impact of the purity culture movement is the overt hyperfocus on sexual activity and sexuality in general. For a movement about spiritual purity, it often makes girls into sexual objects. This leads many girls to experience confusion and shame about their developing bodies and how to dress. It leads many boys to sexualize girls' bodies and blame girls for boys' sexual thoughts and actions. Unfortunately, this suggests that boys have little to no responsibility for their actions, leads to an overall lack of understanding of the value of sexual consent, and supports the proliferation of rape myths in which women are blamed when they are victims of sexualized violence.

Being handed rigid and inflexible sexual scripts—without being taught to think critically about social context, rights and consent, consequences, and pleasure—can limit our ability to engage critically, mindfully, and flexibly in each of the five circles that make up our sexual selves. It is analogous to a rigid diet program: When followed for long enough, diets can train the brain to experience guilt in response to foods we used to enjoy (we label the chocolate cake as a "cheat food" and consequently experience guilt for eating it). What we missed all along was the support to eat intuitively and to trust that when we are in tune with ourselves, slow down, and think critically, we know how to feed ourselves in a healthy way and can enjoy, guilt-free, the foods we eat in moderation.

All that to say, purity culture has left a lot of devastation in its wake.

However, since I'm touting the importance of evidence-based education and scientific research about sexuality, it is important to note that reducing early adolescent sexual activity is an important public health objective. We want our kids to be kids instead of sexual objects pressured into sexual activity before they are ready; and we want them to understand the consequences of their actions (both positive and negative). Engaging in sexual activity early is linked to sexual risk-taking, pregnancy, and STIs. It is correlated with mental health issues and other risk-taking behaviors such as substance use. The earlier it occurs, the more likely it is to be connected to anxiety and depression, especially for girls.[15]

It is important to educate pre-teens, teenagers, and adults about sexual activity, consent, reproduction, and sexual health. Instead of avoiding education, we have much to benefit from education that starts early, with the understanding that autonomy over one's body is an essential right.

As someone who has done research and clinical work within the field of human sexuality, I am often asked about what kind of sexuality is the right kind. People will ask me at public events, in media interviews, and at social gatherings: "How long do I wait until I have sex with someone I am dating?" "Is abstinence good or bad?" "How frequently should I have intercourse with my partner?" "What is the right way to . . . ?"

I learned early on in my clinical training that giving a person an answer or advice about something unique to them disempowers them from making the best choices for their lives and takes away their self-responsibility and freedom. Giving blanket answers or advice related to sexual activity neglects the complexity of the Five Circles of Sexuality and how behavior intersects with things such as (lack of) intimacy, communication, and power. Instead, I would rather educate a person about the options, how to think critically, and how to make choices that feel right, safe, and honoring of themselves and whomever they are with.

I believe it is unhelpful when we create systems in which certain people in power tell other people that their sexual activity can make them morally superior or somehow exclude them from Divine love. This creates communities in which people are disconnected from their bodies, suggests that worth and love are conditional, and undermines a sense of responsibility for their own behavior. Moving the locus of control for sexuality outside of a person creates the conditions under which a person could use another person's body sexually and blame someone else instead of taking personal responsibility.

I often hear from adults who lament their parents' silence about sexuality when they were growing up. I've heard countless stories about how "the talk" happened once, in a very awkward car ride home from basketball practice. Research about sexual health conducted within a Western context has shown that for children and adolescents to become adults who make good sexual choices, they need to be educated early and regularly, in age-appropriate ways, about sexual activity, consent, body boundaries, reproduction, and sexual health. Unlike what was originally thought, this does not promote early or risky sexual behavior but is actually linked to less risky, more satisfying, and more equitable and mutually respectful sexual choices late into adulthood.[16] These findings apply across non-Western contexts, with the UNESCO global review of Comprehensive Sexuality Education showing that in countries such as Pakistan, Bangladesh, and Colombia, as well as countries across Africa, sex education is linked to measures of individual and community health (like lower rates of infection and unplanned pregnancy). Sex education more broadly impacts the liberation of girls and women: girls who receive such education stay in school longer, get better jobs, and have more sustainable sources of income. Because they're better educated, they are less likely to be in positions that would lead to their being trafficked and less likely to be involuntarily given over in child marriage.[17]

For many of us who grew up in cultures in which there was no dialogue about bodies or sexuality, such conversations are hard. We run the risk of avoiding conversations or creating miseducation that stems from our fears and misunderstandings. It can be difficult to give someone something we ourselves don't have. When we consider educating someone else about all that lies in the Five Circles of Sexuality, it reminds us that we likely have some learning and unlearning of our own left to do.

Reeducating Ourselves toward Healthy Sexuality

We can never have enough education about sexuality, especially because sexuality includes the ways our bodies naturally change as we age, how we negotiate consent, our awareness of what is pleasurable for us, and how we negotiate trust and emotional vulnerability in our relationships. Most of us never received even close to enough information about these aspects of our lives. The following six ideas or practices have been collected from my research and clinical training. They've proven especially helpful in my practice and fill gaps many of us have in our sexual education.

199

The Dual Control Model

In the 2000s, Drs. John Bancroft and Erick Janssen proposed the Dual Control Model of Sexual Response, which suggests that our sexual response is a balance of both inhibitory processes (such as the brake pedal on a car) and excitatory processes (such as the accelerator pedal on a car), both of which are located in our central nervous system.[18] Research about this model shows us two things: that these two systems seem to function independently and that the sensitivity of the pedals is unique to each person and is shaped by their physiology, personality, and lived experiences (including sexual and sociocultural).

The accelerator or excitation system is always working through the unconscious brain-body to take in contextual information about relevant sexual stimuli so it can send the message to "go" sexually. But the brake or inhibition system is also always working through the unconscious brain-body to notice contextual information, such as threats, boundaries, or reasons to send "stop" messages.

This information makes the most difference when it allows us to

- understand the reasons why partners have different sexual responses (one has a high level of desire, the other not so much) so we can choose to be curious about differences instead of blaming;
- be more compassionate to ourselves when we struggle with desire, arousal, and orgasm, and see ourselves as normal, even in our uniqueness; and
- take responsibility for understanding and negotiating with our own brake and accelerator and the contexts that affect them in order to have a sexual response system more reflective of what we want for ourselves and our relationships.

Having read this, now might be the right moment to pause and consider what influences your sexual brake and accelerator, taking note of how that connects to the list above.

Mindfulness and Sensuality

Sensuality is all about our ability to tune in to our five senses and notice what is pleasurable and which senses influence our accelerator. Mindfulness is being aware of what is happening in the present without judgment. Although some think of passionate sexual encounters as being intense, fast-moving, and mindless, mindfulness can also be an important ingredient for increasing sexual arousal and pleasure. The research now exists to prove that being mindful of our senses can both heighten our sexual experience and heal the wounds that interfere with our sexual satisfaction and functioning. Vancouver sex researcher and psychologist Dr. Lori Brotto has demonstrated that mindfulness-based interventions show significant improvements in women who have struggled with sexual interest, arousal, and pain.[19] Instead of shutting down awareness of our bodies, or trying to move fast or spontaneously, slowing down and being more present can be the answer to many sexual woes. The emerging research exploring mindfulness with men has been similarly compelling, showing that mindfulness can be a treatment for erectile difficulty, sexual anxiety and avoidance, compulsive sexual behavior, and distractibility during sex.[20]

For individuals and couples who have struggled with sexual arousal and desire or who have spent extended periods of time trying to conceive, sexual activity can become "goal oriented," where orgasm (particularly male orgasm in heterosexual relationships) can become the primary focus. Not surprisingly, this can decrease the quality of the sexual encounter, adding to the list of things that activate the sexual brake. To help, researchers Masters and Johnson developed Sensate Focus, a technique to help partners practice slowing down, focusing on the senses, removing the demand for orgasm, and practicing noticing and talking about what feels good.[21] Sensate Focus is most effective when practiced regularly, with consent, kindness, curiosity, and the desire to establish connection with self and other without the competition of contextual distractions.

Spontaneous and Responsive Desire

If you learned about the cycle of sexual response in high school, you likely learned about the four-phase model that Masters and Johnson introduced in 1966. It goes like this: excitement (arousal), plateau, orgasm, and resolution. It was a good start to understanding human sexual response, but it portrayed individual sexual response in a uniform and linear fashion without accounting for power, politics, and a person's psychological and interpersonal landscape.

Some important information is missing from this model—namely, desire and the two different ways we experience it. *Spontaneous desire*, just as it sounds, arises out of the blue to express our body's readiness to engage in sexual activity, sometimes even before our thinking brain has caught on. This is good and normal, and it is what often comes to mind when we think about sexual desire: it just happens, and it is full of anticipation and motivation. *Responsive desire* is also good and normal. This form of desire occurs after we've already begun engaging in some form of sexual activity. Once we're already in the swing of things, our brain-body system catches up and says, "This feels good. I want more." Interestingly, approximately 30 percent of women experience this as their primary form of desire.[22] Men experience responsive desire as well, and increasingly so as they age. This is not a sign of dysfunction or illness, simply something most of us don't know about.

Having this information can shift our attention to the quality (rather than quantity) of our sexual activity, and it can decrease shame and increase self-compassion when our sexual activity

202

doesn't look like what we see in the movies. It also reminds us that sexual activity is a process, not an event, in which each person has changing and unique needs that are worth discovering. For some people sexual anticipation is important, and for others the sexual activity—the skin-to-skin contact and sensations involved—is most meaningful. But the pressure or shame we carry, or the expectations about what sex should look like, can eclipse the space we need to figure out our body's sexual response. For example, we can be so overwhelmed with parenting, trying to conceive, lack of privacy, or work stress that experimenting with what feels like the best kind of sex for us takes too much energy or intimacy. This can make us confused about whether the challenges we face regarding our sexuality are really about sex or whether they are about other things.

When we consider the uniqueness of each body, what each person needs, and what it is like to experience that desire, we can move toward a more expansive sexual ethic. Otherwise, in partnership we make assumptions about another person's body, turning them into an object that we use. Sometimes we even turn our own body into an object to be used. Instead, we can ask questions such as these: What tells me I have consent? How am I continuing to be present with what is happening? What does my partner enjoy? What do I enjoy? What feels mutual? What is the quality of my sexual activity? When we are willing to be open and curious, we can begin to see sexuality as an unfolding process and an adventure that draws us toward presence and connection.

The Importance of Touch

Skin hunger is an essential element of our sexual health. We need touch in order for our bodies—even brain tissues and systems—to develop and thrive. Although sexual touch can be good when we're older, here I'm talking about nonsexual touch. In the 1990s, researchers discovered how untouched children in understaffed Romanian orphanages struggled neuro-developmentally.[23] The children had low levels of appropriate hormones for their age, and they were behind same-aged peers for growth and development. We now have evidence that lack of touch is linked to poorer nervous system functioning, decreased ability to regulate attention, increased violent behavior, lower levels of serotonin, higher rates of depression, and increased pain levels in the body.[24]

Starting from birth, touch has a central role in helping us manage stress, have satisfying relationships, and strengthen our immune systems, because it mediates levels of cortisol and oxytocin. But researcher Dr. Tiffany Field of the Touch Research Institute at the University of Miami School of Medicine has suggested that the more we are on our smartphones, the less likely we are to reach out and touch one another, hug, cuddle, nap together, or rest a hand on someone's shoulder—specifically those we trust.[25] It is likely that, more than ever, and especially in light of the global pandemic and physical distancing that began in 2020, many of us are struggling with something called touch starvation.

If we are lacking touch, we can increase our overall well-being by finding ways to get more touch in our life. Some examples include getting a massage, snuggling a pet, holding hands with a partner, exchanging a gentle back scratch with a close friend, getting a haircut and scalp massage, getting a manicure, or going dancing or taking partner dancing classes. If regular touch is a part of your life, you might try holding on to a hug with a loved one for just a bit longer. Rates of oxytocin in the bloodstream increase after twenty seconds of sustained physical contact, increasing the whole-body positive impact of the hug. You could greet people you know with a handshake or hug when appropriate and sit close to your loved ones while watching a movie. Parents can cuddle, hug, or give back scratches to kids, taking care to communicate with them how good it feels to be close. There is no downside to having more appropriate and consensual touch in our lives.

Self-Responsibility and the Sexual Body

If your sexuality belongs to you, then you are responsible for taking ownership of yourself, making mindful choices about engaging in the world, and knowing your own body. Sex and couples therapist Esther Perel encourages erotic self-responsibility by asking people to shift their language from saying, "My partner turns me on when . . ." to "I turn myself on when . . ."[26] This reminds us that we have a role in our own arousal. That includes taking responsibility for what to do with the information we have about our arousal. Knowing what is a turn-on (accelerator) and what is not (brake) and knowing how to communicate that to a romantic partner are two different skills. Knowing one's own desires does not guarantee consent from a partner, and consent requires respectful and vulnerable conversations. When we remember that sexuality is not simply genital-to-genital contact but also the interpersonal expression of longings, we can begin to understand that conversations about sexuality and *how* we have those conversations are important elements of building intimacy and expressions of sexuality in and of themselves. Notice how many of the five circles were addressed here and how they work together.

The Sacred and Sexual Body

If you grew up learning that sexuality was dirty or bad, as was everything related to the physical body, it might be new to consider sexuality as an expression of spirituality. To make the connection explicit, one of the definitions of sexuality I quoted at the beginning of the chapter identifies sexuality as the "physical, emotional, psychological, and spiritual energy that permeates, influences, and colors our entire being and personality in its quest for love, communion, friendship, wholeness, self-perpetuation, and self-transcendence."[27] This quest for wholeness, love, and self-transcendence is often what we think of when we are thinking about spirituality.

We saw in the Five Circles of Sexuality model that sexuality includes emotional intimacy, trust, and reproduction—all highly valued by communities and traditions that also seem to vilify pleasure or sexual activity. But try on this definition offered to us by psychologist Dr. Chuck MacKnee: spirituality is "a core dimension of humanity that seeks to discover meaning, purpose, and connectedness with self, others, and ultimately God."[28] Scholar and therapist Paul Giblin has said that "sexuality and spirituality spring from the same vital life source and have the same end. They are both about relationship; loving and being loved, desiring and being desired; and being vulnerable, honest, and intimate. They both require growth in self-knowledge, including awareness of one's limitations and 'shadow.'"[29] Sexuality is not at odds with spirituality but, in fact, a deep human expression of it.

In fact, MacKnee researched individuals who had profound spiritual encounters during sexual activity. They described their experiences as characterized by wonder and amazement, emotional cleansing, the presence of the Divine, intense union with the other person, euphoria, intense physical arousal, transcendence, feeling blessed, the experience of ineffable mystery, and a sense of sacredness.[30] What if we could experience our sexuality not as shameful but as sacred?

Returning to Where We Started

Near the beginning of the chapter I invited you to think about some words and sentence prompts. I invite you to return to the same set of words and to notice if something different pops up.

In light of what you have been reading and what it has stirred up for you, what do you think when you read over the list?

If you notice that you answered all or most of the questions the same way, think about what you wish you could answer or how you hope your future self might respond if you keep wondering about sexuality in a new way.

My hope for you is that your sexuality is something you continue to discover—that you will experience it as an avenue for connection with self, others, and the mystery of love, a place where you find healing, an opportunity to learn more, a way to both give and receive pleasure, and something that is always your own.

SOME THINGS TO THINK ABOUT

- How did what you learned about sex and sexuality growing up shape how you think about sex and how you interact with a partner now?
- What do you wish you could go back and tell your younger self about sexuality?
- Did you notice any emotions emerge while reading this chapter? What do they tell you about what you have been through, have been taught, or want to know more about?
- What activates your accelerator and your brake?
- What do you want?

SOME THINGS TO TRY

- Notice when you experience spontaneous desire and when you experience spontaneous arousal.

- If you haven't already done so and you have a partner, try sharing some of the things that came up for you when you were reading this chapter, particularly about your accelerator and your brake.

9

Holy Flesh

Reconciling the Spirit-Body Divide

It's Wednesday, and I am again at my authentic movement class. Along one side of the room, a set of windows looks down on to a busy street. I see people carrying bags of fresh leafy things from the produce market, drinking coffee on the café patio, and turning into the vintage bowling alley on the corner. On the other side of the room, mirrors run floor to ceiling. In their reflection, I see the sun setting across the Vancouver skyline.

I'm trying not to think about what anyone else is doing or thinking. I'm here to be with me. I have to tell myself this a hundred times over because there is so much of interest going on around me. Across from me is a man wearing some of the most spectacular flares, both glittery and tie-dyed. He appears to be in his fifties, with a round belly and soft, medium-brown hair. He looks like he could be an accountant during daylight hours. I imagine him leaving work and ripping off his nine-to-five suit and tie disguise to reveal underneath his superpower outfit of psychedelic flares.

All of this—the fact that I am in this room—started because I had fought hard to recover from an eating disorder. And although my symptoms were gone and I no longer had a diagnostic label, I still did not feel quite fully alive, not quite fully at home in myself. Through learning to inhabit myself again, in a bodily sense, I realized that my body is good, that I am good. Father Richard Rohr has said, "We do not think ourselves into new ways of living, we live ourselves into new ways of thinking."[1] The deeper I dive into the study of what it means to be connected to our bodies, the clearer it becomes: being fully connected to the body is about living; being fully connected to the body is about being fully present. But we cannot get there by just thinking differently. It helps, but it does not take us all the way. The body is not just an idea or a series of words; it is also an experience. Being fully alive, fully present, lets us know we really are *in* our lives, not just passing time on autopilot until we break a hip at eighty and wake up to the fact that we never really lived at all.

For some of us, being fully alive is difficult, an experience of complexity and tension. We may not really know how to consent to all that this aliveness holds: loss, grief, pain, aloneness, illness, the pang of hunger or fullness, the grip of fear, and death. These are all experiences we have in and through our bodies. We may be trying to live our lives so as to avoid these things. But in the process, we lose all the other things that come with life through our bodies: pleasure, joy, energy, connection, sensuality, self-expression, creativity, being held, and the sun's warmth. We try to avoid the challenging things that we experience in our bodies, but in doing so we sacrifice the good, the beautiful, the rich.

The first time I attended this authentic movement class, I was very alert. I noticed everything. I tell my patients that it is normal to feel afraid when we return to a space where there once was a trauma. The hypervigilance of our entire nervous system is wondering, "Will this be painful like it was last time?" Only for me, the site of the trauma was my own physicality. It was so hard to be there, to be me, without judgment. I cried throughout most of the class. If my tears could have spoken, they would have said, "Really? We're doing this?" and "Are you sure we're not going to get hurt?" and also "I wish I could feel as free as Gordan looks in his tie-dye flares."

The second time I went, I lay on my side for almost two hours, simply allowing myself to be there. I was trying to be less alert to what was happening around me and more alert to what was happening in me. I traced fear and grief as it skated over my skin and up my spine and then came to settle in my palms, gluing them to the floorboards.

But by the fifth class, things were different. This time, fear wasn't pinning me to the ground; it was in my back pocket, moving with me as I swirled around the room. I was hot. Not from fear but from spinning, stomping, and sometimes letting a strange primal sound bubble up from deep in my belly out through my lips. Navigating around the other moving bodies in the room, I found myself up against the long wall of mirrors, staring myself in my eyes. Staring at the self that was somehow even bigger and deeper than just eyes. Feet still keeping time with the bongo, I held my own gaze longer than I ever had before. My gaze widened and I started to watch my whole self move.

Then, two things happened.

First, I couldn't stop watching myself move. I was entranced. It felt as if I were being moved by something, some animal, some spirit in me, in a dance together through space. Somehow, I was living it and watching it all at once.

Second, after what felt like hours but was likely only minutes, I peeled myself off the mirror and kept moving, completely captivated by my hands painting shapes into the thick air as if I were weaving together threads of heaven and earth. As I looked at my hands, I felt this knowing come to my awareness: *the hands of God*. Then, down at my feet, stomping as if part tantrum, part war dance: *the feet of God*.

I had heard these words growing up in my church. As a community working to practice the ways of Jesus, we heard it said that we were the hands and feet of God, of Love itself. Thousands of times, we heard this metaphor: we were the body of Christ—someone the hands of Christ, someone the feet, the head, the heart. All of it working together. All of it good. All of it the way that the Holy comes into the world to show love, to heal, to undo our aloneness. It is through all of us acting as one body that we are reminded we are not alone, that God is among us, working through us.

But I had also heard that my body was bad, that my flesh was the enemy of the Spirit. Flesh was the place where sin happened. Flesh was where lust and death and illness happened. Flesh was the reminder that we were never quite with God but could hope to be someday. In some other place very far from here, we would experience God, and all of this was just a signpost to that which would come. Flesh was the barrier between us and what was really happening.

But in that moment, while moving to the rhythm of the music, I heard in an inner-knowing kind of way that this familiar metaphor was not just a metaphor. Perhaps God was in me. Less like a "someone" out there and more like a process happening right now. Right now—in my stomping, in my rhythm, in my tendons and fascia and spinal cord. In my digestive enzymes, my cerebrospinal fluid, and in my very beating heart.

I have a friend who went through a faith deconstruction that started when he reconsidered his views on the creation poem in Genesis. After making a list of what he thought was literal and what was metaphor in the Bible, he concluded that perhaps he was a biblical literalist after all, but that what was literal to him had changed. Inspired by his list of sorting what he understood to be literal or metaphor, I made my own list:

- A six-day creation: metaphor
- A snake in the garden: metaphor
- An apple on a tree: metaphor
- And it was good: literal
- God is love: literal
- The kingdom of God is within you: literal
- I will be with you to the end of the age: literal

When I remember the mystical encounter I'd had in the movement class, I can see that the ideas I had always had about creation and matter were shifting. Shifting to be bigger, more loving, more awe-filled. Stepping back, I realized that I had always been able to see in the obvious things that all of this, life itself, was Good. I saw God in mountains beaming from sunrays that reflected off their snow-encrusted peaks, in the doctor catching a new baby as it slipped out of its mother's vulva, and in watching a person's trauma heal through therapy. I could see all of it as the mark of a Love so wild and Good that it was even now still moving itself out through us all.

Why could I see and believe that about everything else but not about myself—my fingernails, my stretched and dimpled thighs, and my eyelashes? Why did creation get to be good, profoundly telling of love itself, except when creation was my body? When God and bodies seem antithetical, I must ask, What am I missing about God? What am I missing about love, life, and the messy, gritty, unpredictable unfolding process of faith?

A Note on My Positionality

Positionality describes the various factors that constitute a person's identity, such as race, sexuality, ability status, and more. It also describes how a person's identity both influences and potentially biases how they see the world. As we begin to discuss spirituality, it's important to me to share some of the factors that have shaped my experience and my understanding of the spiritual world.

I grew up with the teachings of Jesus. Though I was introduced to this first-century Jewish mystic, his teachings were often warped by a mixture of church culture, colonization, and oppressive politics. My evolving journey of belief and spiritual practice has left me wishing that those beautiful teachings were not so entangled in the cultural story of Christianity that they would be unrecognizable to the rabbi himself. But I was born within a tradition that shaped my worldview, my privilege, my experiences, and I believe that I was born within that tradition for a reason. It may not be right for you, but for me it feels inappropriate, and premature, to leave without walking hand in hand with it further down the road of belief and life. As I clear away the surface scum and reach my hands down deeper into the well of this tradition, I always come up with fresh water.[2]

My faith and spiritual expression look different today than they did ten years ago, and certainly than they did twenty years before that. Fortunately, my parents gifted me with the understanding that ideas and beliefs are not meant to be static. In fact, it would interrupt the natural cycle of human growth and development to expect that something that made sense at age five would mean the same for us at age fifteen or fifty. We are meant to change. In the field of psychology, we call this lifespan development—it is part of our story to be different down the road than we are today.

During my studies of embodiment, I did my best to survey the frameworks that different religious traditions have for understanding the relationship between spirituality and the body. I will speak to them sparingly during this chapter, not because they do not have value or are threatening to my views but rather because it would be naive to assume I could understand the depth and richness of other belief systems—especially their experiential impact—without having lived them or studied them extensively. So I write primarily from my experience and the teachings within my tradition, knowing I can do that with integrity. Additionally, the Western contexts within which many readers of this book live have been acquainted with some version of Christian faith for centuries. This also means that those same readers will be accompanied, perhaps unknowingly, by this faith tradition and how its practices, ideas, and texts have shaped our social fabric.

When Body and Spirit Were Separated

We did not find our way to a disembodied existence on our own: we had millennia of help. Western philosophy and Gnostic religious thought influenced a popular line of thinking that goes something like this: The soul and the mind are distinct from the body (that's Plato). The mind is where truth is, but the body has needs, desires, and limitations (that's Descartes, and some translations of the apostle Paul).[3] Around the same time as Descartes lived, the Christian Reformation happened, which emphasized our mind's ability to grasp the who and what of God; feminist and liberation theologians have written that this put the body in a straitjacket.[4]

The way that sexism and patriarchy infiltrated the prevalent understanding of the garden of Eden story did not help. I do not consider a poem about the origin story of the cosmos problematic by itself, but its interpretation across millennia has done harm. When we take poetry to be literal, we may mistake the hierarchy of man over woman to be the Word of God.

215

Feminist and critical theologians have helped us see that this line of thinking came from a patriarchal and settler-colonialist belief system imposed on Scripture.[5] Women's bodies were likened to the wild and unruly systems of nature—working in cycles, "unclean" for days out of a month, and susceptible to the unpredictable weather patterns of emotion. The same logic was used to subdue other bodies considered unruly by those conferred with power. Oppressed and marginalized groups have been trying to come out from underneath the power of these stories for centuries.

As many of us were told, men's bodies, and often white bodies, were both superior and somehow irrelevant. Men, particularly those with the most social power, had no need for the body: they could leave the body and live in the mind through the academy, the monastery, and the seminary. After all, as we were told, the mind was the bridge between our depravity and good theology, where God could be found. It was in the mind where good theology happened, Scripture was memorized, and the important problems of life were solved. And God was always somewhere else, somewhere outside of whatever was happening right here.

These hierarchies—good and bad, mind over body, man over woman, the idea that somewhere out there is closer to God than whatever is right here—all lead us back to the many injustices enacted over time because of them: white is better than Black, colonizer is better than colonized, nondisabled is better than disabled, straight is better than gay, and so on. All of these created hierarches are not true in actuality but are woven into our belief systems, often unknowingly, and then are lived out in conscious and unconscious ways. And all of these stories say that bodies are bad, but some are more or less bad than others.

One subtle but notable feature of the idea that the body is bad suggests that God—the Divine, Spirit, Creator—is independent of the material world and its laws. This is called *transcendence*.

It makes sense that people thought this way over the centuries and that we have continued to think this way. Transcendence is what we experience whenever we have a moment in which we feel connected to it all and when we feel as though we are part of something bigger than ourselves. In some ways, it is a helpful theological and psychological coping mechanism to believe that the Divine is only *out there*, especially when *right here* feels unsafe, banal, and full of suffering.

Transcendence is beautiful, but I'm not convinced it's the full picture. One of my psychology professors used to remind us that if there are only two options and one of them is bad, then we aren't seeing everything. If we think of God as only out there and certainly not here, we are not seeing everything.

As meaning-making beings, when we hold just a transcendence position (thinking God is only *out there*), it is easy to think of reasons why God is not here. Prevalent options have included that the *right here* is evil or sinful in some way (this might remind you of the Gnostic position). I mentioned above that the apostle Paul, the New Testament writer who throws down about flesh and bodies more than almost every other writer in the Christian Scriptures, has written extensively about the body, and our English translations of his writings appear particularly anti-body. For example:

> "For I know that nothing good dwells within me, that is, in my flesh." (Romans 7:18)
>
> "But you are not in the flesh; you are in the Spirit." (Romans 8:9)
>
> "Flesh and blood cannot inherit the kingdom of God, nor does the perishable inherit the imperishable." (1 Corinthians 15:50)
>
> And the real heavy hitter: "Live by the Spirit, I say, and do not gratify the desires of the flesh. For what the flesh

217

desires is opposed to the Spirit, and what the Spirit
desires is opposed to the flesh; for these are opposed to
each other, to prevent you from doing what you want."
(Galatians 5:16–17)

At first blush, and even for those who are well studied in
theology, these texts—and the original language in which these
words were written—devalue, even diabolize, the body.

God Not Just There but Here

Remember, if there are only two options and one of them is
bad, it means we are missing something. That something is *immanence*. If we raise and then lower our gaze, looking first up
at the sky and then down at our hands, we have immanence. In
other words, *immanence* means seeing the world as permeated
by the spiritual. Instead of the Divine being far away, the Divine
is right here, in this moment, moving between us, through us,
and within us as bodies.

It has been well argued that the Christian tradition is built
on this foundation. The best evidence for this is Jesus—the
incarnation of God into the human story. What I have always
loved about the story of Christianity, and a large part of why I
still follow Jesus despite how much harm has been done in the
name of Christianity, is that it is a story of people who choose to
believe that God is not so far away after all. Instead, the Divine
is right here among us and showed us through his body that our
bodies are not bad, that the Divine exists in flesh, and that the
body is part of God's way of being in the world. What better
way to know that we are not alone than to remind us that the
Divine dwells within and moves through all created things? If
creation is the expression of the Creator, if all of life is made
by and through the Divine, then that includes us too—our flesh
and our beating hearts. If God is in all of it, that means there

is nowhere we can look where God is not. Everything is sacred. Everyone, everywhere, is the dwelling place. You are the temple.

In her book *Grounded*, religious studies scholar Diana Butler Bass writes, "The biblical narrative is that of a God who comes close, compelled by a burning desire to make heaven on earth and occupy human hearts."[6] The notion of spiritual intimacy is found not only in the Abrahamic faiths but also in Hinduism, Buddhism, and other Indigenous spiritual practices through which humans experience "God with us, God in the stars and sunrise, God as the face of their neighbor, God in the act of justice, or God as the wonder of love."[7]

This challenges the systems within which we live—systems that need to be challenged. If everything is sacred, if matter is valuable to God, then we have to start treating the earth differently. Believing that spirituality is about transcendence alone allows us to excuse ourselves from intervening in the ongoing oppression and marginalization of certain bodies. If bodies are not sacred, then there is no need to ensure that certain bodies are not devalued and erased. We have to wake up to see how our systems reinforce the lie that some places are not sacred: those bodies, those places, that country, that person.

Bass suggests we need a spiritual revolution to do this, one in which we expand our conventional ideas of a Divine being who exists "outside of space and time, a being beyond imagining, who lived in heaven, unaffected by the boundaries of human life."[8] She suggests we do this by shifting our language away from the *omni*s (God as omnipotent, omnipresent, and omniscient) to God as *inter*, *intra*, and *infra*. The God of the here and now "is a God in relationship with space and time as the love that connects and creates all things, known in and with the world. The *omni*s fail to describe this. Instead, we might think of God as *inter*, the spiritual thread between space and time; *intra*, within space and time; and *infra*, that which holds space and time. This God is not above or beyond, but integral to the whole of creation, entwined with the sacred ecology of the universe."[9]

Although leaning into immanence is part of the healing work of remembering our wholeness, transcendence is not at odds with immanence. In fact, our wholeness comes by reintegrating everything we thought was separate. This includes holding together matter and mystery, the self and the other, the known and the unknown—all are inextricably woven together.

For me, the deep spiritual work has come through trusting the lesson of my teacher Jesus, that every time I believe there is a place that the Holy is *not*—and believing that somehow sounds a lot like my privilege or pride, or the oppressive systems I benefit from—I'm missing something. There is nowhere we can go to get away from the Sacred: it is both in the right here and in the pull to expand into whatever lies beyond the edge of our understanding.

Spirit, Body, Flesh

This is all well and good, but we are still left with dichotomies and confusing language in the Christian Scriptures, which has been used to widen the perceived chasm between spirit and body. I became interested in the language we use in our faith traditions a few years ago, not surprisingly while on a massage table.

In 2016, during a massage therapy appointment, the therapist asked about some of my research findings, specifically about the role of spirituality in body-image resilience. She asked me to define the words *spirit* and *spirituality*. I learned early on in my doctoral program that you shouldn't use a word you cannot define—and bonus points for having a long list of citations for that definition. In that moment I encountered my unknowing. I wrangled my way through to something like this: "Spirituality is the pursuit and practice of things of a spiritual nature—that is, things that are bigger than ourselves and outside of ourselves but that connect us all." She smirked and made me promise I'd look up the word.

As it turns out, the word *spirit* comes from the Greek word *pneuma*. In Greek, *pneuma* means "breath" or "breathed" or "to be breathed." Like this breath. Like the breath you just took right now. What shocked me about this was that the word *spirit* was not about anything far away but about the most human thing we all do—breathing.

Breath keeps our body alive, our brain working, our blood pumping. It's constantly happening, unconsciously; our bodies are keeping themselves alive, animated, from moment to moment. I immediately started to reread some of the Scriptures I had read a thousand times before. I found passages that used phrases such as "Spirit of God," "spirit instead of flesh," "Spirit of Christ," and "the Holy Spirit." I read the words aloud, but instead of reading the word *spirit*, I said "breath." "Spirit of God" became "Breath of God," and "Spirit of Christ" became "Breath of Christ." That led to some very confusing texts, such as, "Live by the breath, I say, and do not gratify the desires of the flesh. For what the flesh desires is opposed to the breath" (Galatians 5:16–17, adapted). Obviously more was going on here. Where is the breath if not in the body? Where is the breath if not in the here and now?

I began to wonder if this text hinted at something more mystical and nuanced than a dichotomy between actual flesh and supposedly superior spiritual things. Over the years of listening to sermons and lectures and reading books and articles, I kept being led back to the word Yʜwʜ, a Hebrew name for God that Christians pronounce as *Yahweh*.

In the Jewish sacred texts, which are the first part of the Christian Bible, we meet a man named Moses. He is a member of a people who are living under the thumb of a brutal empire, and he ends up living off the grid after he murders a man in defense of one of the Israelites. There, he comes across an ignited bush, in which a voice calls to him by name. God tells Moses that he is standing on holy ground and then asks him to go back to the land from which he fled in order to lead his own people out of slavery and oppression.

God and Moses go back and forth because Moses lacks the confidence to do such a thing. God nudges him toward it, reminding Moses that he won't have to do any of it alone. In one of the most fascinating elements of the story, Moses asks God what he should say when the empire asks who he's working for. In other words, "Who are you?" Personally, I'm confused about what took Moses so long to ask this question. The first thing out of my mouth would have been, "What is going on here? Who are you? And why are you asking me to do this right now?" Then, in a kind of mic-drop way, God responds by saying, "I AM who I AM." God tells Moses to let everyone know that "I AM," or being itself, sent him. Bold move, God. God responds by saying that God *is*.

"I AM" is the English translation of the Hebrew letters YHWH (or YHVH), which is called the Tetragrammaton, the sacred name of God. In Hebrew, the original language in which this passage was written, the four letters YHWH are pronounced *Yod, Hay, Vav, Hay*. Growing up, I'd learned that this holy word was written as such because it was unspeakable. But the writings of some rabbis, in particular Rabbi Arthur Waskow, provided clarity.[10] Rabbi Waskow suggests that while it is true that YHWH is unpronounceable, it is not because we are forbidden to pronounce it, but rather that in order to pronounce these letters—part vowel, part consonant, labeled by linguists as aspirate consonants—without any vowels between them, one has to do so simply by breathing. Try it for yourself: say each letter and its corresponding sound, without adding any vowels, and you find yourself making some breaths that sound a lot like exhales.[11]

The Jewish prayer book, the Siddur, says of this embodied spirituality, "Every breath praises the breath of life." Rabbi Waskow says it is the breathing of all life that *is* the name of God. He goes on to say that this invites us to see God in all breathing beings—there is no language, no culture, no "those people" or "that person" who does not breathe. What we breathe in is air that is mixed with the breath of all others—or what Waskow calls "interbreathing."[12] What we put into the world with our bodies is taken up by other bodies and living beings. He suggest that our interconnectedness to all living things through breath, the way we breathe life into one another, is somehow the sound of the name of God.

This name of God is meant to evoke intimacy and interconnectedness between us and the Divine, and between all things that breathe, including the natural world. After all, what is closer to us than our breath? When I read about this and think about Spirit as breath, and the name of God as the sound of breath, I cannot help thinking about bodies. Bodies alive are bodies breathed: when we come into this world, inhaling is the first thing babies do earth-side, and exhaling is the last thing that bodies do before death.

The exploration into language took me to the Christian Scriptures in which the words of Paul seem to exacerbate the flesh-body divide. If spirit seems to be all about life, breath, and being, how could the Spirit be separate from our physicality?

Stephanie Paulsell, theologian and professor at Harvard Divinity School, suggests that honoring the sacredness of the body is not outside the Christian tradition but rather lies at the heart of it. This is evidenced in two ways. The first is the scriptural understanding that God "judges creation as good, and so everything God created, including bodies of all sorts, is good. . . . The body reflects God's own goodness."[13] And the second is the belief that God becomes a flesh-and-blood human being, incarnate, in the person of Jesus. He "drank, slept and woke, touched and received touch. . . . Whatever else it means [this] suggests that bodies matter to God. And, they ought to matter to us, too."[14] If this is true, as I believe it is, then what do we do about the writings in the New Testament that seem to suggest otherwise?

The New Testament writers use two Greek words in these passages. The Greek word translated as "body" is *soma*, and the Greek word translated as "flesh" is *sarx*. *Sarx* is more often used to refer to meat, in a kind of disembodied way, whereas *soma* often refers to the living, breathing, subjective experience of being a person or to a system such as a family or a community. Feminist theologians Lisa Isherwood and Elizabeth Stuart write, "In the letters of Paul, we find a complex approach to the body. Paul was not a dualist: nowhere in his letters do we find a contrast between body (*soma*) and soul or spirit."[15] If that is true, how did we arrive at such a problematic view of the body in our faith communities, and why do we believe we learned this from the writings of Paul?

In researching this I came across something called a "semantic field," which is the range any given word can have for how it is used while still remaining within its ascribed meaning. Here's how I ended up grasping the concept: The word *broccoli* has a fairly narrow semantic field—most of us will be thinking about little else but a green vegetable when we hear or read the word. But words such as *love* or *grow* have a wide semantic field because they can mean so many things and can communicate so many different ideas.

The texts that compose the New Testament were written in Greek. And just as all native speakers of a language do, the Greeks knew how to play games with words. For example, in English, phrases such as "hit the road" or "keep your eye on the prize" are not about smacking the ground with your hand or staring at a treasure; they are sayings that use metaphors to convey a principle. So, when we come to how the New Testament writers used *soma* and *sarx*, we have to understand that these words have a broad semantic field. They are used in many ways in Scripture—sometimes to describe actual flesh and blood, other times to talk about community, and other times to describe the experiences of being human, enduring pain and suffering, or feeling alive in our personhood.

I consulted other scholars with expertise in this area as well. One of them even created a spreadsheet for every time the words *sarx* and *soma* appear in the Bible, with columns for their various locations, uses, and so on. A labor of love, and one of the most well-studied Excel spreadsheets on my computer. These scholars shared their research and directed me to volumes of additional resources, all of which led me to two conclusions.

First, it seems no one can really know with precision what an author was thinking when they wrote something. We can get close and sometimes we can make educated guesses, but we can never remove our biased, personal meaning-making lens.

Reading some expert analyses of the New Testament, I noticed how some scholars used different angles to interpret the same word or phrase, using the same text in Greek but each person drawing an entirely different meaning out of it— hermeneutics and phenomenology in a semantic dance. I imagine this by drawing a flowchart backward: the interpretation of the texts is shaped by a person's theology, their theology is shaped by their life experience and social power, and all of it is informed by their place in history.

With this in mind, I knew that there was no one way to interpret the passages that use *sarx* and *soma*. But I could choose to do so in light of what I believe to be true about God and the Bible, owning that my interpretation comes out of my positionality.

My second conclusion is that a lot more is going on in the supposed flesh-spirit dichotomy than is obvious or than is communicated when these passages are used to condone self-hatred.[16] The words for "body" and "flesh," *soma* and *sarx*, are both used to describe important, sustaining, holistic principles: what it means to be human, the struggles of existing, and the importance of coming together in community. These words are often about the whole of humanity, not just an individual person. In some cases, the words are used in a negative sense to represent our way of being in the world that is not loving or that moves us away from wholeness. This way of being (often conveyed by *sarx*) is not our true nature—it is fragmentation, when the body becomes an object to itself, when the unit of humanity segments off from itself and chooses hierarchies and oppressive systems that make someone an "other" instead of seeing them as part of our body.

What I learned about these words reminded me of something we often talk about in therapy: our "parts."[17] We all have different parts of ourselves that make up the whole of who we are. You could think of them as ways of being in the world. For example, just think about the kind of language you use with a partner while flirting in contrast to how you talk to your boss or your mom. Most of the time, we switch effortlessly between our parts. Sometimes when I'm scared, I feel more like a child and call my mom for reassurance, and then, within hours, I'm an expert teaching my class of graduate students. These parts of us develop to play a role or meet a need, and they often protect our vulnerability or fear.

I understand the distinction New Testament writers make between flesh and spirit this way. We all have access to these two primary ways of being. One part of us, the flesh, is trying to manage other people's opinions of us, get approval, keep us from being hurt, and keep us blind to how we hurt others and ourselves. The other part of us, the spirit, sees that something bigger is going on in this human story, knows we are loved, wants to love others, and knows we are all saying the name of God every time we breathe.

We could simplify that and use language often found in other spiritual contexts by talking about the contrast between the ego and the true self. The ego is the part that convinces us we are separate from everything and considers our agenda to be the most important one. The true self, or spirit, is the part that knows we are loved and connected with God and everything and everyone around us. New Testament scholar Richard J. Erickson states that Paul's metaphor of the flesh can be interpreted as our "dependence upon human value systems and institutions for securing power and position."[18] The word *flesh* has been taken literally and used as a scapegoat, an interpretation less symbolic of the text's meaning and more a sign of our existing conflict with physicality. Instead, this metaphor was meant to remind us that we are living in our true nature when we are undoing oppressive systems, choosing connection over conquest, and paying attention to the miracle of our existence.

Seeing Paul's New Testament writings in this light can help us recover what has been lost through our misinterpretations, and it can help us see what Paul was likely trying to say: the body is central to God's plan for being in the world. When Paul uses the word *soma*, the image we are given repeatedly is of the collective body of humans as the body of Christ. That is us in our togetherness, working as one living system to release and reveal and re-experience Christ in the world to and through one another. Some of my favorite words on this are attributed to Saint Teresa of Avila, who was deemed a Doctor of the Church: "Christ has no body now but yours. No hands, no feet on earth but yours. Yours are the eyes through which [Christ] looks with compassion on this world. Yours are the feet with which [Christ] walks to do good. Yours are the hands through which [Christ] blesses all the world. Yours are the hands, yours are the feet, yours are the eyes, you are his body. Christ has no body now on earth but yours."[19]

When I put together the words of Paul and of Teresa of Avila, there is no body in which I cannot find the Holy. God is both inside these bodies and inside the body of humanity. There is no body outside the interconnected web of incarnation we are part of.

This has implications for how we relate to bodies, our own and others. If Christ has no body now but yours and mine and ours, it makes it very hard for us to live in a culture that keeps asking us to forget the bodies of the poor, the bodies with disabilities, Indigenous bodies, Black bodies, bodies with addiction, bodies that are elderly, nonbinary bodies, and every body that does not seem to fit within our rigid cultural system of what is ideal. This is disruptive, and it is meant to be. Remembering that we are bodies, and that bodies are Holy, is meant to stir in us the need to craft a social structure that protects and celebrates all bodies. Our human bodily system is meant to fold like an arm around a torso to protect precious organs; we as the body are collectively meant to act in service and protection of whoever is in need, as they are vital to our collective flourishing and liberation. This is how our bodies become central again to our spirituality.

The Spiritual Practice

If bodies are not bad but are instead the seat of our spirituality, then this has implications for justice work—where we recognize the institutional and political disappearance and marginalization of certain bodies, and attune compassionately to our bodily selves. It means that, as the first-century mystics wrote about, we have to take care of ourselves as dwelling places of the Divine and work against systems that erase and oppress other temples of the Divine. It means becoming aware of the parts of ourselves that have enjoyed power and that feel the need to defend it for fear of losing it. It means working to transform those parts within us so they can join in the work to equalize the power imbalances that we have benefited from as a body.

Although it might seem most natural to find a conversation about beauty in the chapter about body image and appearance, to me beauty belongs right here, in the chapter about spirituality. When we conflate beauty with a set of appearance structures, we can worship beauty itself and miss how beauty acts as a doorway to the sacred. While beauty is about whatever we are encountering—the person, landscape, quality, or object—it is also about the awe it stirs in us and how it woos us into deeper engagement with our world. For this reason, I define beauty as whatever I am drawn to, whatever holds me in the place where I want to linger, whatever celebrates something numinous and ineffable. Sometimes that is an unusual color on a building at sunset, affection between a father and his son, the melody in a song a friend wrote about love, or the colorful iris circling a pupil. In a research interview once, a participant shared with me about how she could marvel at the curve of her hips, which reminded her of the long line of women she had come from. As she described this beauty in her body, I saw the beauty in her sense of interconnectedness through her hips. To turn this into a practice, you might try going on a treasure hunt for beauty, looking for it in unexpected places, noticing the bodily reactions that happen in you when you experience it, and lingering for a moment in wonder.

The In and Out of Breath

Those are important big-picture ideas, but there are also moment-to-moment practices that can take this from out there to right here. One of my favorite therapeutic practices is to remember the immediacy of the breath. We can make time to breathe together, to synchronize our breaths, teaching others how to breathe to manage stress and anxiety. Breath is the source of so much healing and connectedness, to ourselves and to others.

Remember the staircase of stress response from chapter 3? The neurophysiology of trauma has revealed that breath can be a powerful tool to shift us from going down the staircase to moving back up the staircase toward connection and rest. When we breathe in a specific way, it signals to our nervous system that we are okay. To do this, we breathe in through our nose, down into our belly until our bottom ribs in the front, back, and sides expand, instead of our breath just going into the top of our chest. When we're in danger, we don't breathe deeply and slowly, so deep breathing can signal, through communication between nerves running between our belly and brain, that we are safe.

Intentional breathing can also remind us that we are in the present. Our breath is never anywhere else but right here. When we feel stuck—somewhere real or imagined, past or future—we can invite ourselves into our breath. The in-and-out rhythm reminds us that we are always taking in and letting go. When we do notice that we are breathing, we could consider that as we breathe in we are either saying the name of God or sharing in the life force that moves through every living thing around us.

Another option is to place our hands on our belly or chest and breathe deeply and slowly. Through breath we can begin making peace with our physicality. We are invited to notice and thank our breath for carrying us all the way from life to death, from one moment to the next, across an unbroken chain of holy and mundane ins and outs.

Remembering the Body of the Earth

Just as we have sometimes treated our bodies as objects to use, we have also treated the earth as an object to use. Diminishing our living, breathing earth from "mother" to "thing" has allowed us to justify our abuse of her. I use the pronoun *her* for the same reason I use the pronoun *her* for my body, using language to help me remember matter as being and to remember that my physicality deserves the same reverence that I offer other forms of creation.

Our Indigenous brothers and sisters have been urging us settlers to see all life as a unified whole since first contact. Remembering the body of the earth as a living thing is a spiritual practice like any other. To remember the earth as a loving mother, whose body we need in order to survive, just as an infant needs the mother's breast, is to remember our bodies in a disembodied world. It means taking the elements of life that are central to our thriving but have painfully been diminished and relegated to an inferior position and recentering them as foundational for both our continued existence and our thriving. We have disregarded the earth as we have disregarded our bodies, but remembering our bodies helps us remember the earth and the connection we have to all life. The Franciscan tradition has long held that creation is the first incarnation.[20] To remember the earth as alive is to experience the Divine written into all life.

The Way Home

Not long ago, I met with seventeen other women in a remote retreat center in the middle of a rainforest. We gathered to heal spiritual wounds and trauma and to practice living into what whole and healthy spiritual practice looked like for us. Madison, Varvara, and I facilitated the gathering, and we called it The Way Home.

Like me, most of the women there had some sort of conflicted relationship with their physicality, and it was bound up in stories about sin, death, and seduction. As we were planning the retreat, Varvara, a minister and therapist, told us that The Way Home was the name of a service she used to hold for folks in her community. It was the perfect name, we thought, as we planned a time for women to come together to heal, reclaim their spirituality, rewrite the stories of their bodies, and find the Holy right here. The way home we were all seeking would be not in spite of our bodies but through them. As the rain exhaled onto the roof above us, we told the truth, and we did it in a way that didn't require disappearing in order to belong.

On the last night of the retreat, I led the movement practice I described at the beginning of this chapter. Two years since I started practicing authentic movement, I danced with these women whom I had grown to love and admire over our five days together. Their movements portrayed victory as well as sorrow. Arms telling the story of freedom wove around the feet of others, hair swinging from grief into vibrancy. Bodies and stories being reclaimed by their rightful owners. The room grew hot; all these spectacular bodies moving around one another, in time with the rhythm and with their own beating hearts. And when the music slowed, I remember saying to the room, "Ever wanted to see God? Open your eyes"—as if to say that God is right here, living and moving and dancing within and through us right now.

The next morning, we ended our retreat with a ceremony, an impromptu reimagining of Communion. As we all stood in a circle, shoulder to shoulder, Varvara held in her hands a holy hamburger bun—the only available bread option in our remote retreat location, yet also a very suitable representation of the body we would distribute among us. In this case, what was common and a symbol of everyday life was sufficient to communicate the message: *God is here, among us, and you might remember God from such places as that barbeque you had last summer, and your kid's birthday party at the fast-food chain, and the bakery counter, where you were handed bread made by someone who was up early that morning.* Varvara told us that the representation of God's body as bread often brings up different imagery for each person. Sometimes it is the murder of a first-century prophet who led with love, not violence, and who gave power away to those society had disregarded. Or it might remind us of the five loaves that fed thousands, where there was enough food for all who were hungry and no one who wanted went without.

Then Varvara invited us to think about another image. This bread was the work of thousands, beginning with those who readied the soil, planted the wheat, and harvested the wheat. Someone ground the wheat into flour. Yet another put the flour into bags, and someone else transported bags to a bakery. There, someone made the flour into the bread, which was transported to a store, purchased by someone else, and then placed in the hands of the woman in front of us. This bread was the work of many, each adding something so that we could be fed. None of our nourishment comes to us from isolation. Varvara then began to tear the bread apart. This bread, like the breath, reminded us that our bodies are woven together. After all the connection we forged during the week, we had become a body in our own way. We were a body of Christ as Paul talks about in the New Testament—moving, breathing, dynamic—each of us necessary parts of something new and very much alive.

Varvara invited us to pass the pieces of bread around to each other and say something true or offer a blessing. After the bread had been passed, we were reminded that there would be moments when we might feel lost in our daily lives. At those moments, we could mentally return to this moment when she pulled the bread apart, remembering how she traced the path from the bun in her hands back to the person who first planted the wheat. Just as the bread in our stomachs was the product of many parts coming together, so we had come together from different parts of the world to make one body during the retreat. And as the bread was pulled apart, so we would soon be sent into the world to nourish others as we had been nourished.

In moments when we felt lost, we could recall that no matter where we are, whatever is ours or is right in front of us is the work of many and is part of a bigger story. All of it invited us to remember our place in the family of life.

If you grew up in the Christian tradition, during Communion or the Eucharist, you might have heard the phrase "This is my body" when taking the bread. When I think of those words now, I do not picture God as an old white man in the sky. I think about every body, each and every one of us. Eucharist is an invitation to look at all bodies everywhere, including our own, and feel the voice of God whispering through us, "This is my body."

For many years, I tried to disappear, to take up less space, and to say with my body that I did not want to exist. But realizing that Spirit and body are not so different invited me back into wholeness with myself and into the desire for wholeness around me. I am learning that it is hard to envision a connected world when I cannot hold connection within myself. Healing my relationship with my bodily self changed the way I move, eat, feel, connect, rest, and create. It made me come alive and start paying attention to what kinds of bodies our dominant culture has tried to make disappear. Not one of us lives without breath in our lungs. Not one of us is less mysterious and wildly beautiful than the mountains or trees or ocean. All inhales and exhales are doorways for the Divine.

SOME THINGS TO THINK ABOUT

- Take a moment to remember a time you felt most alive. I can guess based on some good hard science that you were probably in your body, experiencing something, not just sitting on the couch scrolling through social media. Think about that time and make a plan for the future when you can do that again or when you can do something else that makes you feel alive.

- What would it mean for you to believe that Sacred breath is in you from the moment you are born to the moment you will die? How might this change the way you think about yourself and others?

- Bring to mind your body or your last meal or the piece of paper in front of you. Try to think about all the things that had to happen for that to be there. If you are thinking about your body, think about your parents, and their parents, and their parents, and so on. If you are thinking about your meal, think of each ingredient, where it came from, who picked it, and so on. Pick a focal point and zoom out, so to speak.

SOME THINGS TO TRY

- Practice authentic movement or dance in your home, preferably when no one is around. Try moving to music in ways you never would if you were being judged. See if you can hang in there long enough to quiet the inner critic and let your movement tell the story of what you are experiencing, what it is like to be you. If this is new to you, try going to a 5Rhythms class.

- Take a few deep breaths with your hands on your belly or chest, and feel yourself breathing. While you do that, take a moment to consider that all living beings are breathing.

- Right now, get really slow and quiet, just for a moment. Close your eyes if you need to. Try to sense a pulsing, vibrating, or heat in your hands. Think of that as life itself, and stay with the sensation in your hands to help you feel your aliveness.

10

Living as a Body

Embodiment Practices to Return to Ourselves

Gabriel looked tense, hands wringing in his lap and knee bouncing at a racing speed. He had his head down, and his brow was puckered—as if he were working hard on something. He wondered out loud, "I don't know how to exercise if it's not to beat my body into submission. I don't know how to feel myself as a body. I can control myself better than anyone else, but then I eat until I'm in a food coma. But be present to my body? I don't really think I understand what that means."

His story echoes so many of ours—an oscillation between over-fixating on appearance or bodily control and completely forgetting the experience of being a body. To Gabriel, his physicality was an object to control, by which to measure worth, and over which to exercise discipline—especially when other areas of life seemed chaotic.

Rachel represents another common aspect of feeling stuck and unable to experience embodiment. A woman in her late forties, she has been a researcher her whole life. Unlike Gabriel, Rachel's challenge with embodiment is the "why" of it all. In a profession that has rewarded her for forgetting about her bodily needs and limits, she has been celebrated for her exquisite cognitive command and has learned to relegate her body to a meat-taxi that transports her thinking brain around a laboratory. When the stressors of her profession left her with autoimmune diseases made visible in her skin, digestion, and energy levels, she felt at war with herself—her body was communicating that something was not working, but her value system was saying that changing anything would mean forgoing her way of finding worth and control in the world.

These are just two examples of the kinds of stories I hear regularly. If we go back to the house-and-front-lawn metaphor, for people like Gabriel and Rachel—who are used to living on the lawn and doing constant renovations—the thought of living peacefully within their house can feel impossible.

When our old ways of relating to our bodily selves no longer work, what does it mean to leave them behind and practice embodiment instead?

Embodiment is difficult to talk about because the very definition of it is experiential. Dr. Daniel Stern, a psychiatrist specializing in psychological development and mindfulness, says that to be in the body, "*presentness* is key. The present moment that I am after is the moment of subjective experience as it is occurring—not as it is later reshaped by words."[1] An important part of embodiment is what is happening right now, not the story we will tell about it later.

To reiterate what Richard Rohr voices so well, *we do not think ourselves into new ways of living; we have to live ourselves into new ways of thinking.*[2] Having new experiences of ourselves over time helps our thinking to be more creative, flexible, and curious. Living the way we always have comes with the comfort of familiarity, so the risk and adventure of something new requires rigorous accompaniment and patience. Yet when we dare to live into the new, we will experience the widening and ever-expanding process of growth and freedom.

Movement Matters

If you think of your body as a house, movement is the large front door swinging wide open to allow your awareness, your thinking, to enter back inside where you have always belonged. Notice here that I have used the word *movement* rather than *exercise*. Exercise is a particular use of movement, but it often gets embroiled in diet culture, shame, rigidity, insecurity, or fear of failure. So back up and think about movement as something you did long before you learned about changing your body or competing in sports. Think about one of the first things a mother gets excited about when pregnant—when the baby first moves. The care providers ask about how the baby is moving, and a mother's heart skips a beat when feeling that first kick.

I recently asked Jerome Lubbe, a functional neurologist, about movement and why it matters. He said this: "Simply put, movement is the single greatest resource in our human experience. Movement not only turns the brain on in pediatric development; it also informs, integrates, and sustains every aspect of what it means to be alive in our bodies. We have assumed our five senses are how we experience the world around us. However, truth be told, all of those senses are secondary survival systems. We could lose one or all five and our brain will survive. Yet, if we lose our relationship with gravity and/or our capacity for movement, our brain suffers. Movement is paramount for our physical, mental, emotional and relational health."[3] His words echo this description of movement by neuroscientists Wolpert, Ghahramani, and Flanagan: "The entire purpose of the human brain is to produce movement. Movement is the only way we have of interacting with the world."[4]

You have probably heard statements such as "Go for a walk, you'll feel better" or "Shake it off" after a failure or receiving tough feedback. You may have seen a person who just finished a run express an optimistic outlook, or you may have felt refreshed and a little high after a dance party. Movement makes us feel better. In fact, we now know that muscular contractions (movement) release something called "myokines." Myokines are peptides (peptides are short chains of amino acids, which are building blocks that create certain proteins) that are released when muscle fibers contract. These myokines are then dumped into the bloodstream and can travel all the way up to the brain where they can impact mood and cognition. Myokines have been shown to make us more collaborative, better at teamwork, and more hopeful or resilient in the face of stressors.[5] More broadly, myokines are thought to be the bridge between movement and health, linked to preventing and regulating many non-communicable diseases.[6] In her book *The Joy of Movement*, Dr. Kelly McGonigal says this about movement: "The psychological effects of movement cannot be reduced to an endorphin rush. . . . [Movement] remodels the physical structure of your brain to make you more receptive to joy and social connection. These neurological changes rival those observed in the most cutting-edge treatments for both depression and addiction."[7]

Even so, it's hard to think of movement without thinking of exercise. While there is nothing wrong with exercise, for many of us the word carries assumptions about appearance management and rigidity in behavior and thinking, such as, "I need to do it this way or not at all." We have specific gear, plans, or coaches, someone on the outside telling us the "right way" to move our body. Sometimes we don't even realize that another person's control of our bodies is ensconced in our ideas about exercise. And that is often linked with the idea that we have to control or change the appearance or size of our body in order to be more desirable or conquer our "unruly" body. Appearance, you might remember, is one of the ways we have learned to leave the experience of being a body. In a way, exercise can become a pathway out of our bodies and into the world of ideal-based bodily control. However, while exercise is often a means to an end, movement is for joy alone.

When we think about movement this way, we discover that movement is a human right because it is a human need. It is also a pathway to health, an expression and discovery of identity, an invitation into satisfaction, and a doorway to play. If there is a tension in our relationship with our body, looking for pleasure in movement is a way to bridge the gap.

Start by asking, "How do I like to move?" The movement you are drawn to can reveal the edges of your identity. You might like to take risks, be on your own, feel a part of something, practice the same thing over and over, do something new, be inside or outside, or move to music in the privacy of your own home. This can be hard to negotiate if you are unfamiliar with what delight feels like. It can also be hard if you were told that movement needed to look a certain way. To make movement as meaningful as possible and as beneficial to your whole person, the right kind of movement is what works best for you.

If you feel stuck when you think about exploring movement, try looking at it backward. Start by thinking about times when you felt most alive; maybe even pause here and make a list. As you are thinking about when you felt most alive, notice the emotions that move through your body. What were you doing in those moments? And what about what you were doing had the most meaning? What is it like to remember that?

Meaning and Movement

Movement is one of the best opportunities to experience ourselves as good bodies. While movement creates well-being in our future selves (such as euphoria or a sense of accomplishment

241

after a run), it offers just as many opportunities to feel good in the present. When we move, we feel our aliveness—the rush of blood and increase in body temperature, the experience of motion and action in the world, the expression of freedom, mastery, and agency.

We can move in ways that help us practice new ways of being. If feeling free is something you are drawn to developing in your life, or feel you are lacking, what might it be like to use movement as an experiment with more freedom? What form of movement might you choose if freedom were your goal?

Maybe what you're after isn't freedom but rather interconnectedness, community, and shared experience. What might it be like to choose movement that allows you to experience more of that? Movement is a place we can practice new ways of thinking or being. It can be a healing or therapeutic space, our dress rehearsal for other parts of our life in which we long to be more truly ourselves.

Meaning is a powerful motivator and guide. It allows us to reorient ourselves and begin again when we find ourselves disoriented, distracted, or using movement associated with shame and body control. Whatever movement you try, start by reminding yourself that whatever you are about to do has a purpose.

My friend Karly does this so well. She started something called the Public Run Club, a running club for runners at all levels that connects mostly online. Instead of running for distance, time, calories burned, or intensity, Karly encourages people to structure their runs around what they value or what evokes delight. So for the joy of it, she'll run past a stretch of blooming flowers near her house. Another woman in the club who loves cappuccinos plans runs around some of the best coffee shops in town. Stories such as these show us that movement does not have to be a means to an end, but it can unlock even more of the experiences that make life so pleasurable.

The Goodness of Feeding Ourselves

For most people who want to talk about their bodies, food comes up in some way. While eating and nutrition come up in my clinical work, most of the time it has less to do with specific foods we eat and more to do with the process of eating. People come in to work on their disordered relationship with food, their eating disorder diagnosis, or their appearance frustrations.

Our relationship with food speaks volumes about our ability or inability to see our bodies as good and to trust the body's wisdom. Remember, the senses are bodily. Many of us have learned to mistrust, disregard, or suppress our body for that reason. After all, our senses got us in trouble; our sensuality made our body impure, or at least that was what we were taught. You might be surprised or amused to learn that Sylvester Graham—creator of an essential component of the summertime s'more favorite, the graham cracker—was a minister during the temperance movement in the United States. In the early 1800s, he proposed a diet oriented around bland food, based on the belief that bland food did not excite the senses and thus suppressed sexual urges.[8]

Graham's idea sounds outrageous, but it is not too different from things we overhear and say today about the pleasures of eating: "I was 'bad' last night; I ate so many carbs" or "It's my cheat day." We have moralized food, making it good or bad, "clean" or "dirty." When we have learned to see our body as bad, as a "thing" to manipulate, or when we have come to believe our appearance makes us valuable, we can point the finger at food—the ingredient responsible for it all.

The devaluation of the body, together with unrealistic appearance ideals and lack of information about the ineffectiveness of dieting,[9] can land us in a cycle of shame, control, and further disconnection. And all of this can easily leave us feeling betrayed: we can do everything as instructed by an industry only to turn up empty and think it's our fault. Even for people who do not find themselves in this dance, it is normal to feel shame, self-judgment, and criticism from others for opting out of trying to change their body or feeling like a failure for not being able to do so. The hateful, violent, and shaming social media comments received by body-positive activists show us that our culture still needs to heal from a diet mentality disguised as health and moral superiority.

We can begin to reclaim our agency and whole-person health by changing our relationship with food. The best, most evidence-based way to do this is through intuitive eating. The main idea behind intuitive eating is to pay attention to your interoceptive cues (what your body is telling you from the inside out) to break the cycle of dieting or binge eating, heal your relationship with bodily signals, and get back in touch with yourself as a whole person. While dieting seems to be about shutting down the body's voice, intuitive eating is about learning to listen again.

Doing anything from a place of attunement and connection with ourselves can help us experience health in a more holistic way. Here are just a few of the Ten Intuitive Eating Principles:[10]

- Honor your hunger (keep your body fed with adequate energy).
- Make peace with food (give yourself permission to eat, without "shoulds" or labels about foods that are forbidden or bad).
- Discover the satisfaction factor (pay attention to what is satisfying, including quantity, taste, and texture).
- Feel your fullness (honor your body's cue of fullness).
- Honor your health (there is no such thing as perfectly healthy, but you can notice what you need as a body and what makes you feel good).

Ways to Practice Feeding Yourself

Too many people have told us how we should eat, wooing us away from building a trusting relationship with our body through interoceptive skills. So if reading my words about eating feels uncomfortable, first note that reaction and get curious about what that means for you, and second, remind yourself that you do not have to do anything described here.

If you are new to the idea of listening to internal messages in order to feed yourself, you might start with doing your best to notice when you feel hungry or full. More than ever, we are eating during a commute or while we are distracted in some way. Scientists have proved that eating while distracted negatively impacts our ability to pay attention to our hunger cues; we eat differently when we are focused on something other than what our bellies are saying.[11]

Even if it is just once, try eating a meal without any obvious distractions, sitting down in a quiet place and trying to notice when you feel full. When you feel full, what is it like? Without judgment, imagine trying to describe the sensation to someone who has never felt it. What sensory language, imagery, and metaphors would you use? I sometimes use the words *pressure*, *tightness*, and *satisfaction*. I also notice that the speed at which I'm eating slows down when I do this.

The same can be done with hunger. What does hunger feel like? Without judging it, how does it show up? How do you know? How would you describe hunger to someone who has never felt it before? What metaphors or images would you use, and what sensory language? For me, the sensations of hunger are a little harder to put my finger on. Sometimes they feel like a pulling or stretching, or like my organs are twisting or dancing. Other times, I notice hunger because I'm preoccupied with food, I feel irritable, or I hear my stomach growl. The same questions apply to thirst.

Just as we feel emotions across a continuum, we experience our hunger, thirst, and fullness cues as interoceptive markers for what our body needs. Hunger might be present, but to a lesser degree. Or thirst might be present at the highest degree, a ten out of ten. On this one-to-ten scale, try asking yourself how hungry or full you are when you sit down to eat, partway through a meal, and again at the end.

Building a Trusting Relationship with Our Bodily Selves

I was sitting with a client who had come to therapy to work on her relationship with her body after years of chronic dieting and feeling self-hatred due to the associated weight fluctuations. We had been talking about movement, eating, and noticing sensory cues when she got quiet and said, "I just don't believe I could ever get to the place of really trusting myself as a body; it seems so different from how I live now." I could feel her hesitation and the fear and sadness underneath. She had been struggling for so long that anything different seemed impossible, and the fear of starting something new with the risk that it too could fail, like all the diets had, was exhausting.

Because she was in a healthy long-term relationship, I used that to paint a picture of how embodiment might look for her. As with any long-term partnership characterized by trust, deep connection, and mutual support, developing our ability to trust ourselves as a body does not happen overnight. There are misunderstandings, repairs of those misunderstandings, adventures, discoveries, and the bliss of finding a rhythm. Developing a trusting relationship with our body is a lot like building a relationship with another person—it requires a million little choices and tiny experiments to help us know we are in good hands with ourselves.

There is no one right way to begin and build a relationship. How each of us learns to connect with our body will differ. If our body has been a place of trauma, injury, illness, disorder, pain, emotional dysregulation, or shame, it can take time to even build up the courage to approach a relationship with our body. In that case, we need lots of undoing and renegotiating. Just as you wouldn't expect to fall in love with an enemy overnight, being connected to yourself as a body will take time and reparation to get to the point of peace.

By the time I began clinical training in couples therapy, I was surprised to learn that many of the skills I was learning for marriage and partnership I had already employed within myself. First is the language of repair. When there has been a fracture in the trust or connection within a relational system, there needs to be special attention to creating closeness, teamwork, or safety again. Often that means taking responsibility and acknowledging what was wrong and hurtful. For me, this meant getting comfortable with saying sorry to my body, including apologizing for how my socialized thinking brain had participated in the disruption. I wrote this in the form of a letter to my body, included at the end of this book for you to read.

In addition to using the language of repair, we engage the process of repair by doing what was missing all along: we learn to listen. When there is conflict or hurt with a partner, we can easily become defensive and stop trying to hear the other person. To avoid replicating this pattern, we need to regulate our emotions, check our assumptions and reactivity, and spend time trying to understand the other person. This is true of reconciling with our bodies as well. Slowing down to listen, instead of getting angry at the messages our bodies are communicating, can move us from body shame or body fear to body trust. We might need to ask questions, getting to know the language with which our body speaks, and we might need to slow down to sort through the layers of communication. It is through this nuanced and intimate kind of listening that we can discern our bodily messages—like when that thing I think is hunger is actually a feeling of loneliness, or when I feel a drive to finish a project to feel peace, but what I actually need is to rest and reset.

Trust is a process, not an event. It takes time to build a trust-based relationship with ourselves. We always have the chance to rebuild trust after it has been disrupted. Doing so within ourselves is no one's responsibility but our own. But if we feel stuck, we can ask a skilled guide to help us, like an intuitive eating coach, a somatic therapist, or a psychologist or counselor who specializes in embodiment or interoceptive work. Or you might make it a practice to get curious—pausing throughout the day to ask, "What's up with me right now?" Having a helper is especially important if we have a history of trauma: re-entering the body after trauma can reactivate old memories and sensations, and it is important to have a skilled guide present.

When we are able to be in relationship with our *full* bodily self beyond our appearance—in a way that is present, non-judgmental, and supportive—we can become our best resource through the challenges of life. We can deal with stressors as if we are our own best companion and most loyal and protective friend, building trust with ourselves that no matter what happens around us or to us, "I will always be for and with myself."

Christine Caldwell has called this state "bodyfulness." The creative subversion of "mindfulness" reminds us that our experience of the present is not just in our minds but in our bodies. Caldwell describes it this way: "Bodyfulness begins when the embodied self is held in a conscious, contemplative environment, coupled with a non-judgmental engagement with bodily processes, an acceptance and appreciation of one's bodily nature, and an ethical and aesthetic orientation toward taking right actions so that a lessening of suffering and an increase in human potential may emerge."[12] In other words, kind attunement to our bodily selves goes beyond mindfulness to help us both heal and thrive.

Additional Practices to Get You Started or to Take You Further

Here are some suggestions for how you might begin to deepen your relationship with your bodily self. As with any new skill or project, doing too much too soon can be unsustainable. I recommend trying a few that stick out to you and noticing your response without judgment.

Dance. There is something deeply nourishing—spiritually, culturally, and psychosocially—about dancing. If we are uncomfortable with dancing, it often comes from fear that others are judging us. We can even internalize others' judgment to the point that we are afraid of what we look like, even when no one is around. This is a result of objectifying our bodies from the outside, instead of experiencing ourselves from the inside.

Dance, whether choreographed or spontaneous, in solitude or with others, has been shown to have significant physical and psychosocial health benefits. Find ways to dance spontaneously as often as possible in ways that make sense for you and your physical ability. This might mean putting on music while cooking, feeling the rhythm move through you as you stir a pot. Or you might use high-energy music to help you shake off the stressors of the day or celebrate a significant event. Before big speaking events, I often get nervous, and I find myself more present and confident when I discharge some of the extra fear energy by dancing it all out before it's my turn to speak. I have danced wildly in a lot of hotel rooms and backstage green rooms all over the world for this reason.

Touch yourself daily. Start the day by placing your hands on your chest, neck, or cheeks, and think of something kind to say to yourself. Initiate intimacy with yourself just as you might with your lover in bed next to you or when waking a child—a smile and a kind word can be profoundly orienting. Before I get out of bed, I often put my hand on my chest and say to myself, "Good morning. I'm glad we get to spend the day together." Trying this at the end of the day can also be a way to settle yourself after being out in the world. Review everything you did through the day—starting from the moment your feet hit the ground in the morning—and whisper a word of thanks to all the parts of your body: your feet, legs, genitals and pelvis and hips, organs and belly, chest and lungs, shoulders and neck, arms and hands, face, scalp, eyes, and brain.

Say "I'm sorry" to parts that receive criticism. When you catch yourself having a critical internal dialogue about your body, or even beating yourself up about how you beat yourself up, try noticing that dialogue, pausing for a moment, and placing your hands on the part of your body about which you have felt shame or judgment. Then, instead of focusing on how that part needs to be different, say, "I'm so sorry I have done that to you. I'm so sorry we live in a context where anyone said you were bad. You don't need to change, but how I think about and talk to you does." Sometimes when we are feeling out of control in an area of our lives, experiencing pain or illness, or longing for connection with someone, it is easy to attack our bodies without realizing that our response is a defense against feeling something else that is painful.

Use touch meditation. If you are feeling particularly disconnected, try placing your hands on different parts of your body and stating to yourself, out loud or in your head, "This is my body." If that feels like enough to start, feel free to leave it there. But if you are up for it, try feeling both sides of the touch, what you are feeling through your hand and what you are feeling in your body through the touch of your hand. For example, you might squeeze your left shoulder with your right hand. As you do so, try to be aware of all the sensation that is

250

in your right hand, all the way down your right forearm and into your right shoulder. Then, try to be aware of the sensation in your left shoulder, what it feels like in your muscles to receive that squeeze. To build an experience of connection, notice the invisible internal line (or all the specific systems, if physiology is your strong suit) that connects your left shoulder to your right hand. You can do this with any part of your body. This practice is especially useful if you have been told that your body belongs to someone else.

Practice sensation-based mindfulness. You might struggle to notice what a specific part of your body feels like unless you create sensation in that part of your body. Think about this as a kind of sensory or interoceptive thawing out.

You can easily start doing this by using a practice you already do several times a day: hand washing. When your hands are under the water, notice the temperature on your hands, and notice if that affects the experience of energy within your hands. If you change the pressure or temperature of the water, notice if that makes you feel more or less sensation or satisfaction. Other ways of doing this with specific parts of your body are to use a showerhead to direct water and pressure to different parts of your body and notice what that feels like. Sometimes, you might even notice an emotional response—such as fear or calmness, which, again, is something worth being curious about. If possible, you can try using a showerhead with different pressures or pulsing rhythms. This also works with a heating pad, weighted pillow, or small beanbag.

Scan your body. Try scanning your body, starting either at the top of your head or at the bottom of your feet, on the left side with your leftmost finger or on the right side with the rightmost finger. As you work your way through your body, try sensing into that part of your body: What does it feel like? What is the temperature? Is there tightness or a sense of openness? Is there pain? How is energy moving? Taking time as regularly

251

as possible to check in with and scan our body helps us know what our baselines feel like, whether we need anything in the moment, and when something is off or there is a bodily message we need to pay attention to.

When you find something worth noting, you have some options. You can ask yourself, *Can I accept this? Can I tolerate it?* You can also ask yourself if that sensation is telling you something such as "I'm angry" or "I'm tired" or "I need to take a deep breath." Other times, you might imagine drawing warmth, kindness, or ease into that part of your body with each breath. Or allow the sensation to expand and take up more space in your body with each breath.

Notice yourself in space. Embodiment is the experience of being a body, not just in isolation but also in the world. If we are used to being unaware of ourselves in space, or have become skilled at shrinking down, it can be especially useful to be aware of our experience of ourselves in space and practice noticing our expansion and contraction.

Try this standing, seated on the floor, or lying down on a bed: First, notice if you can get as small as possible. While doing this, be curious about your emotional reaction to this change: What is it like? When have you felt this way before? What spaces does it remind you of? What are the sensations that emerge in and through your body? When you're ready, get as big as you possibly can. What is that like? When have you felt that way before? What spaces does it remind you of, and what sensations and emotions emerge in you as you do this? When you are ready, return to a neutral posture and notice how that feels—physically, emotionally, socially—compared to the small and the big version of yourself. Listen for what this encounter tells you about what it is like for you to be a body in the world and what things are uncomfortable for you.

Experiment with all the extras. Here are a few more things to experiment with based on your health and comfort level, all of which you can research further if you are not familiar with them:

Eye gaze with yourself in a mirror

Play with a child

Remember a time you felt a specific emotion

Shake your whole body

Stay as still as possible for a set amount of time

Freewrite about what came up in this chapter

Attend an authentic movement class

Take a warm bath or a cold shower

Make a meal with different textures (crispy, watery, chewy, creamy, etc.)

Attend an improv class

Go on a waterslide or to an amusement park

Attend a group meditation

Write letters to your body

Try something you have never tried before

As you go through this list, notice what jumps out to you or if something is missing that you wish I had included.

May this book be just the beginning, an invitation into fully inhabiting yourself as a body in a way that helps you carry safety and wisdom within yourself, fully alive to the mystery of being human and connected to all life. And may our individual *re*-membering ignite a common remembering, necessitating the dismantling of systems that fragment our collective body.

For your journey, I hope for feet both light and firmly planted, hands that easily give and receive, eyes open to see the beauty around and within, and steady breaths filling your lungs, re-minding you of your voice in the choir of all living things.

SOME THINGS TO THINK ABOUT

- What kind of movement feels fun, joyful, or meaningful? Why is that?
- What kinds of movement have you never allowed yourself to experience? Are those barriers real or perceived?
- What other reasons might you have for choosing to move your body, other than changing your appearance?
- How do you think about your body? What is the quality of your relationship with your body?
- What would you like to believe about your body? What are some steps you could take to get there?

Epilogue: A Letter to My Body

Dear Body, I'm Sorry, I Love You

Dear Body,

I'm sorry for telling so many lies about you. I called you ugly, a waste of space, just this and just that. I reduced you and used words with you I would never use with others. I told myself and others stories about you that were not true and did not honor how sacred you are.

I'm sorry for all the times I've hurt you, both on the outside and on the inside. I have starved you, scraped you, plucked, pulled, cut, and burned you. I scrubbed you too hard in the shower. I filled you with food, then made you empty yourself. I have celebrated when there was less of you and screamed at you when I thought there was even just a quarter-inch more of you where there used to be less. You never asked for this. You never deserved this.

I'm sorry for the ways I have neglected and ignored you. You told me so many times, "This isn't safe" or "This feels good," or you screamed, "LISTEN TO ME." But I silenced you. I covered up your voice with distractions and the promise that

255

maybe I would love you, that maybe I would love me, if you just stopped telling me things.

I'm sorry for how I've kept you stuck and small when you wanted to expand and be free and wild. I sat there, trying to be "good," but it cost you. I told you we couldn't climb the tree; instead, we would sit still with our legs crossed. I made you think you were better if you behaved and didn't challenge anyone's ideas of what it means to be a woman.

I'm sorry for how I believed what other people said about you. They said you were so many things. They called the beautiful, life-giving parts of you bad and horrible names. I let them. I said nothing; sometimes I laughed.

I'm sorry for blaming you for holding all the feelings I didn't know how to feel. You have been so good at telling me when I'm in danger, when I am alive or full of joy. But the hard things were too scary. Just to get away from feelings, I tried to make you go away, to be invisible, to shut up.

I'm sorry for making you an object to use and be used. I am sorry I felt better for a while when I let people use you. I really thought I would be more lovable. And when you told me you didn't like it, I didn't listen.

I'm sorry I didn't know how to protect you from a world that told us both that you were for someone else's pleasure, not quite enough of that, too this, bad, ugly, broken, a thing, a puppet, not wearing enough, the best thing about me, and dangerous.

I'm sorry for hating you when you did nothing wrong.

I love you for staying with me, for never leaving me even though I have tried to leave you. You are there, always. As long as I am here, you will be here. We cannot be apart and never will be.

I love you for the ways you let me experience life. Through adventure, through taste and smell and sound. Without you, I would not know joy. Without you, I would not even be alive.

I used to think my mind was safe and you were unsafe. Now I know that my thoughts told me lies, but you never have.

I love you because you allow me to love others. To hold close my dear ones, to make love, to grasp a hand, to wipe away the tear from another's cheek. It is through you that I can show and feel love and know what being connected really means.

I love you for helping me move. Taking me from here to there, fast and slow, with intention and sometimes without even knowing it. Together, we have traveled the world and seen it all. We move differently than anyone else, and it reminds me that we are constantly in a mystical dance, moving through the world like the breath of God.

I love you for introducing me to time. No one else will take the journey of life with me, all the way from beginning to end. As you change, I will remember what we have been through together. When you show lines and marks, it will be the storybook of what I have lived, reminding me daily of all the times I have laughed, chopped apples carelessly, fallen from the swing set, and squinted to see the beautiful day under a bright sky. Skin, you tell me about what it means to become wise, and joints, you remind me that we are not permanent. But I refuse to shame you because you cannot do what you used to.

I love you for teaching me how to rest. You remind me to care for myself and have deepened my understanding of what it means to be present and still. In teaching me how to rest, you have taught me how to need, and in needing, I have allowed others to love me and give me parts of themselves. Through rest, I understand the rhythms of life. I understand that humility is a spiritual discipline, and I do not have to do it all to be loved.

I love you for carrying life inside. You have always had life within you, even before you were born. Each month, I am reminded of this. I plan my week, what I will wear, what activities I do or do not do because of this life-reminder that you bring to my awareness. Oh, how this reminds me that we are

257

connected to those who come before us and after us. And you remind me, always, that I am not alone; even when I am alone, we are together.

I love you for being a miracle on the inside. There is so much to you that I will never understand, such as why you and I wrestle sometimes about when to begin the day in the morning or when to end it at night. Why you make a clicking noise sometimes and not other times. Why you seem to like it when I feed you some things and not others. You are a mystery to me. And instead of frustration, now I feel full of wonder and appreciation.

I love you, just as you are.

Now, I am sometimes surprised to find myself in this in-between place of not hating anymore, not quite where I used to be but not certain that love *is the right word for how I feel about you. While these words are true, some days they feel absolute and other days they feel more tentative, hopeful, and aspirational. But because you have done nothing wrong, I want to keep reminding us both that I am sorry, and that I do love you.*

———— ♥ ————

Now that you have read my letter, I invite you to write your own. If this is your first time writing to yourself in this way, I'm so thrilled for you to join this practice. If you have done this before, it is always worthwhile to do it again. I engage in this exercise regularly as a reminder to slow down, connect all the parts of me, and do the important things that make relationships work, such as saying, "I'm sorry," "I appreciate you," and "I love you." There is no right way to begin your letter, but a simple "Dear Body" is often a good way to start. What comes next is an unfolding story, and it is yours alone to tell.

Notes

An Invitation to Begin

1. Quoted in Christine Caldwell, "Mindfulness and Bodyfulness: A New Paradigm," *Journal of Contemplative Inquiry* 1, no. 1 (2014): 90.

Chapter 1 Fully Alive

1. C. D. Runfola et al., "Body Dissatisfaction in Women across the Lifespan: Results of the UNC-SELF and Gender and Body Image (GABI) Studies," *European Eating Disorders Review* 21, no. 1 (2013): 52–59; D. Frederick, L. Peplau, and J. Lever, "The Swimsuit Issue: Correlates of Body Image in a Sample of 52,677 Heterosexual Adults," *Body Image: An International Journal of Research* 4 (2006): 413–19; D. A. Frederick et al., "Desiring the Muscular Ideal: Men's Body Satisfaction in the United States, Ukraine, and Ghana," *Psychology of Men and Masculinity* 8 (2007): 103.

2. J. Rodin, L. Silberstein, and R. Striegel-Moore, "Women and Weight: A Normative Discontent," *Nebraska Symposium on Motivation* 32 (1984): 267–307; and S. Tantleff-Dunn, R. D. Barnes, and J. G. Larose, "It's Not Just a 'Woman Thing': The Current State of Normative Discontent," *Eating Disorders* 19, no. 5 (2011): 392–402.

3. Philip Shepherd, *New Self, New World: Recovering Our Senses in the Twenty-First Century* (Berkeley: North Atlantic Books, 2010), 147.

4. Barbara Weber, "From Having a Body, to Being a Body: Phenomenological Theories on Embodiment," in *Embodiment and Eating Disorders: Theory, Research, Prevention, and Treatment*, ed. Hillary L. McBride and Janelle L. Kwee (New York: Routledge, 2015), 53–75.

5. The vagus nerve is a multibranched nerve that acts as the information superhighway between the brain and the body. Ninety percent of the neuronal messages passed through this nerve flow from body to brain, while only 10 percent flow from brain to body. The ratio of these neuronal messages highlights

the emergent scientific findings that our bodies are not just brain suitcases and are more important for our personhood than our culture has led us to believe.

6. Tada Hozumi, "Open Letter to Mark Walsh and the Embodiment Conference," Tada Hozumi, October 18, 2020, https://tadahozumi.medium.com/public -letter-to-mark-walsh-and-the-embodiment-conference-ab9319ee4b69.

7. David Foster Wallace, "2005 Kenyon Commencement Address," Kenyon College, May 21, 2005, https://web.ics.purdue.edu/~drkelly/DFWKenyonAddress 2005.pdf, 1.

8. Maurice Merleau-Ponty, quoted in H. T. Allan, "Gender and Embodiment in Nursing: The Role of the Female Chaperone in the Infertility Clinic," *Nursing Inquiry* 12, no. 3 (September 2005): 175.

Chapter 2 How We Become Disembodied

1. For people without training in developmental neuroscience, it can seem strange that social context shapes the organ of the brain—but many structures, functions, and interconnectedness within the actual tissues of our brain are experientially dependent in their development. In short, the interpersonal and social-contextual experiences we have actually shape the development of our neuroanatomical tissue.

2. To learn more, see these resources: Christine Caldwell and Lucia Bennett Leighton, eds., *Oppression and the Body: Roots, Resistance, and Resolutions* (Berkeley: North Atlantic Books, 2018); Alan Fogel, *Body Sense: The Science and Practice of Embodied Self-Awareness* (New York: Norton, 2009); Amanda Blake, *Your Body Is Your Brain: Leverage Your Somatic Intelligence to Find Purpose, Build Resilience, Deepen Relationships and Lead More Powerfully* (Truckee, CA: Trokay, 2018); Antonio Damasio, *Descartes' Error: Emotion, Reason and the Human Brain* (New York: Penguin, 1994); Antonio Damasio, *The Feeling of What Happens: Body and Emotion in the Making of Consciousness* (New York: Harcourt, 1999); Resmaa Menakem, *My Grandmothers' Hands: Racialized Trauma and the Pathway to Mending Our Hearts and Bodies* (New York: Penguin, 2021); and Niva Piran, *Journeys of Embodiment at the Intersection of Body and Culture: The Developmental Theory of Embodiment* (Cambridge, MA: Elsevier, 2017).

3. Some resources to read more about this are as follows: Alice Miller, *The Body Never Lies: The Lingering Effects of Hurtful Parenting*, trans. Andrew Jenkins (New York: Norton, 2005); Peter A. Levine, *Waking the Tiger: Healing Trauma* (Berkeley: North Atlantic Books, 1997); Peter A. Levine, *In an Unspoken Voice: How the Body Releases Trauma and Restores Goodness* (Berkeley: North Atlantic Books, 2010); Sonya Renee Taylor, *The Body Is Not an Apology: The Power of Radical Self-Love* (Oakland, CA: Brett-Koehler, 2018); Babette Rothschild, *The Body Remembers: The Psychophysiology of Trauma and Trauma Treatment* (New York: Norton, 2000); Bessel van der Kolk, *The Body Keeps the Score: Brain, Mind, and Body in the Healing of Trauma* (New York: Penguin, 2014); and Christine Caldwell, *Bodyfulness: Somatic Practices for Presence, Empowerment, and Waking Up in This Life* (Boulder, CO: Shambhala, 2018).

4. To learn more about these ideas, read adrienne maree brown, *Pleasure Activism: The Politics of Feeling Good* (Chico, CA: AK Press, 2019); Audre Lorde, *Sister*

Outsider: Essays and Speeches (New York: Penguin, 1984); Rebekah Taussig, *Sitting Pretty: The View from My Ordinary Resilient Disabled Body* (San Francisco: HarperOne, 2020); Sabrina Strings, *Fearing the Black Body: The Racial Origins of Fat Phobia* (New York: New York University Press, 2019); and Leah Lakshmi Piepzna-Samarasinha, *Care Work: Dreaming Disability Justice* (Vancouver, BC: Arsenal Pulp, 2018).

5. To learn more about this, read some of these books: Rosalind Barnett and Caryl Rivers, *Same Difference: How Gender Myths Are Hurting Our Relationships, Our Children, and Our Jobs* (New York: Basic Books, 2004); Cordelia Fine, *Delusions of Gender: How Our Minds, Society, and Neurosexism Create Difference* (New York: Norton, 2010); Judith Butler, *Gender Trouble: Feminism and the Subversion of Identity* (New York: Routledge, 1990); bell hooks, *The Will to Change: Men, Masculinity, and Love* (New York: Atria Books, 2004); Anne Fausto-Sterling, *Myths of Gender: Biological Theories about Women and Men*, 2nd ed. (New York: Basic Books, 1985); Susan Faludi, *Backlash: The Undeclared War against Women* (New York: Random House, 2010); and Susan Faludi, *Stiffed: The Betrayal of the American Man* (New York: HarperCollins, 1999).

6. To learn more about these ideas, read the following books: Naomi Wolf, *The Beauty Myth: How Images of Beauty Are Used against Women* (New York: Harper Perennial, 2002); Mary Pipher, *Women Rowing North: Navigating Life's Currents and Flourishing As We Age* (New York: Bloomsbury, 2019); Simone de Beauvoir, *The Second Sex* (New York: Vintage Books, 2011); bell hooks, *Feminist Theory: From Margin to Center* (London: Pluto, 2000); Germaine Greer, *The Female Eunuch* (New York: Harper Perennial, 2008); and Germaine Greer, *The Change* (New York: Bloomsbury, 1991).

7. For more on this, read Emily Nagoski, *Come As You Are: The Surprising New Science That Will Transform Your Sex Life* (New York: Simon & Schuster, 2015); Judith C. Daniluk, *Women's Sexuality across the Lifespan: Challenging Myths, Creating Meanings* (New York: Guilford, 1998); Peggy Orenstein, *Boys & Sex: Young Men on Hookups, Love, Porn, Consent, and Navigating the New Masculinity* (New York: Harper, 2020); Peggy Orenstein, *Girls & Sex: Navigating the Complicated New Landscape* (New York: Harper, 2016); Barry McCarthy and Emily McCarthy, *Sexual Awareness* (New York: Routledge, 2012); Matthias Roberts, *Beyond Shame: Creating a Healthy Sex Life on Your Own Terms* (Minneapolis: Fortress, 2020); Rob Bell, *Sex God: Exploring the Endless Connections between Sexuality and Spirituality* (Grand Rapids: Zondervan, 2007); Jan Phillips, *Divining the Body: Reclaim the Holiness of Your Physical Self* (Woodstock, VT: Skylight Paths, 2005); and Tara M. Owens, *Embracing the Body: Finding God in Our Flesh and Bone* (Downers Grove, IL: InterVarsity, 2015).

8. If you are interested in these ideas, you might like these resources: Marc Brackett, *Permission to Feel: Unlocking the Power of Emotions to Help Our Kids, Ourselves, and Our Society Thrive* (New York: Celadon Books, 2019); Lexie Kite and Lindsay Kite, *More Than a Body: Your Body Is an Instrument, Not an Ornament* (New York: Houghton Mifflin Harcourt, 2021); Ophira Edut, *Body Outlaws: Rewriting the Rules of Beauty and Body Image* (New York: Basic Books, 2004); Joan Jacobs Brumberg, *The Body Project: An Intimate History of American Girls* (New York: Vintage Books, 1997); Caldwell, *Bodyfulness*; and Geneen Roth,

Women, Food, and God: An Unexpected Path to Almost Everything (New York: Simon & Schuster, 2010).

9. T. Mann et al., "Medicare's Search for Effective Obesity Treatments: Diets Are Not the Answer," *American Psychologist* 62 (2007): 220–33; see also Daniel Engber, "Unexpected Clues Emerge about Why Diets Fail," *Scientific American*, January 13, 2020, https://www.scientificamerican.com/article/unexpected-clues -emerge-about-why-diets-fail; and Harriet Brown, "The Weight of the Evidence," *Slate*, March 24, 2015, https://slate.com/technology/2015/03/diets-do-not-work -the-thin-evidence-that-losing-weight-makes-you-healthier.html.

10. If these ideas are new to you, or you are looking to learn more, try reading these: Victoria Emanuela and Caitlin Metz, *My Body, My Home: A Radical Guide to Resilience and Belonging* (New York: Clarkson Potter, 2020); David I. Rome, *Your Body Knows the Answer: Using Your Felt Sense to Solve Problems, Effect Change, and Liberate Creativity* (Boston: Shambhala, 2014); Kelly McGonigal, *The Joy of Movement: How Exercise Helps Us Find Happiness, Hope, Connection, and Courage* (New York: Penguin Random House, 2019); and Emily Sandoz and Troy DuFrene, *Living with your Body and Other Things You Hate: How to Let Go of Your Struggle with Body Image Using Acceptance and Commitment Therapy* (Oakland, CA: New Harbinger, 2013).

11. Strings, *Fearing the Black Body*.

12. Kathryn Ratcliff, *The Social Determinants of Health: Looking Upstream* (Cambridge: Polity, 2017); M. Boullier and M. Blair, "Adverse Childhood Experiences," *Paediatrics and Child Health* 28, no. 3 (2018): 132–37; W. H. Foege, "Adverse Childhood Experiences: A Public Health Perspective," *American Journal of Preventative Medicine* 14, no. 4 (1998): 354–55; J. H. Geiger, "Race and Health Care—an American Dilemma?," *New England Journal of Medicine* 335, no. 11 (1996): 815–16.

13. To learn more about these ideas, consider the following: Christy Harrison, *Anti-Diet: Reclaim Your Time, Money, Well-Being, and Happiness through Intuitive Eating* (New York: Hachette, 2019); Joy Cox, *Fat Girls in Black Bodies: Creating Communities of Our Own* (Berkeley: North Atlantic Books, 2020); Linda Bacon, *Health at Every Size* (Dallas: BenBella Books, 2008); Strings, *Fearing the Black Body*; and Evelyn Tribole and Elyse Resch, *Intuitive Eating: A Revolutionary Anti-Diet Approach*, 4th ed. (New York: St. Martin's Essentials, 2020).

14. To learn more about the distinction between the body-for-self and the body-for-others, investigate the work of Jean-Paul Sartre, particularly *Being and Nothingness*, trans. Hazel E. Barnes (1943; repr., New York: Washington Square, 1992). You can also look into resources related to bodily integrity, bodily autonomy, consent, and boundaries.

15. For more resources on these ideas, see the following books: Esau McCaulley, *Reading While Black: African American Biblical Interpretation as an Exercise in Hope* (Downers Grove, IL: IVP Academic, 2020); George Lakoff and Mark Johnson, *Philosophy in the Flesh: The Embodied Mind and Its Challenge to Western Thought* (New York: Basic Books, 1999); Jaak Panskepp, *Affective Neuroscience: The Foundations of Human and Animal Emotion* (New York: Oxford University Press, 1998); Elisabeth Moltmann-Wendel, *I Am My Body:*

A Theology of Embodiment (New York: Bloomsbury, 1995); Stephan Paulsell, *Honoring the Body: Meditations on a Christian Practice* (Minneapolis: Fortress, 2019); Mitzi J. Smith, ed., *I Found God in Me: A Womanist Biblical Hermeneutics Reader* (Eugene, OR: Cascade Books, 2015); and Philip Shepherd, *New Self, New World: Recovering Our Senses in the Twenty-First Century* (Berkeley: North Atlantic Books, 2010).

16. Piran, *Journeys of Embodiment.*

17. Piran, *Journeys of Embodiment.*

18. Piran has published extensively about the Developmental Theory of Embodiment. If you'd like to read more about these ideas or the research that formulated them, the most comprehensive overview is found in Piran, *Journeys of Embodiment.*

19. Barbara L. Fredrickson and Tomi-Ann Roberts, "Objectification Theory: Toward Understanding Women's Lived Experiences and Mental Health Risks," *Psychology of Women Quarterly* 21, no. 2 (June 1997): 193.

20. To think that change happens mostly by encountering new information is to reinforce the mind-body divide and to prop up the narrative that intellect and insight are superior to the lowlier, feet-on-the-ground parts of life. I understand the irony.

21. See Robyn Henderson-Espinoza, *Activist Theology* (Minneapolis: Fortress, 2019); and Tricia Hersey, *The Nap Ministry* (blog), https://thenapministry.wordpress.com.

Chapter 3 The Body Overwhelmed

1. This is called the Stress Mindset Theory. The theory asks us to rethink what we've heard about stress by identifying that positive beliefs about stress actually have more positive than negative outcomes on our physiology, cognitive performance, sense of meaning, and overall thriving. There are so many research studies, books, and TED talks out there if you want to learn more. Start with the TED talk by Dr. Kelly McGonigal, "How to Make Stress Your Friend," TED, June 2013, https://www.ted.com/talks/kelly_mcgonigal_how_to_make_stress_your_friend, and her book *The Upside of Stress: Why Stress Is Good for You, and How to Get Good at It* (New York: Penguin, 2015). For the original theoretical and academic work, see A. J. Crum, P. Salovey, and S. Achor, "Rethinking Stress: The Role of Mindsets in Determining the Stress Response," *Journal of Personality and Social Psychology* 104, no. 4 (2013): 716–33, https://psycnet.apa.org/doi/10.1037/a0031201.

2. Rick Bradshaw, course lecture, Trauma and Sexual Abuse Counselling, Trinity Western University, 2013.

3. The information summarized here comes from Dr. Stephen Porges's Polyvagal Theory. You will find more in Porges's original text *The Polyvagal Theory: Neurophysiological Foundations of Emotions, Attachment, Communication, and Self-Regulation* (New York: Norton, 2011), or his more accessible version *The Pocket Guide to the Polyvagal Theory: The Transformative Power of Feeling Safe* (New York: Norton, 2017). If you search "polyvagal theory" in a podcast

app, you will find many podcasts relating this theory to parenting, relationships, and therapy.

4. The vagus nerve is the tenth cranial nerve, also known as CNX or the pneumogastric nerve. It runs from the medulla oblongata (a deep brain structure) all the way to the colon, passing through organs, including the heart and lungs, along the way. It is often referred to in the singular, but the nerve has multiple branches, which is why the related theory is referred to as the Polyvagal Theory.

5. Knowing that people can skip a step on the staircase is extremely important, particularly for understanding responses to sexual violence. Myths around sexual violence that reinforce victim-blaming often point to a shutdown response—silence, freezing, or flopping on the part of a survivor—as an indication that the survivor was giving consent. As the rape myth goes, "If she didn't want it, she would have said no or fought back." However, the neuroscientific evidence suggests just the opposite. Far from indications of consent, silence, freezing, and flopping are proof of traumatic overwhelm in which the nervous system determined that a shutdown response was the victim's best chance for survival.

6. If you're curious about how animal trauma response applies to therapy and humans healing from trauma, you may be interested in the work of Peter Levine, specifically *Waking the Tiger: Healing Trauma* (Berkeley: North Atlantic Books, 1997) and *In an Unspoken Voice: How the Body Releases Trauma and Restores Goodness* (Berkeley: North Atlantic Books, 2010).

7. Rape myths are a series of false but deeply held prejudicial beliefs within a culture that shift the blame for sexual assault to the survivor while excusing the perpetrator. They have been shown to have wide-ranging impact both informally and in the judicial system.

8. Robert Scaer, *The Body Bears the Burden: Trauma, Dissociation, and Disease*, 3rd ed. (New York: Routledge, 2014), 19.

9. The information stored in this memory package even includes something called *ocular proprioception*, which refers to the position of the muscles around our eyes.

10. Lorimer Moseley, "Why Things Hurt," TED Ed, November 22, 2011, https://ed.ted.com/on/Li50Ci7S.

11. V. M. Sales, A. C. Ferguson-Smith, and M. E. Patti, "Epigenetic Mechanisms of Transmission of Metabolic Disease across Generations," *Cell Metabolism* 25, no. 3 (2017): 559–71; C. Ling and L. Groop, "Epigenetics: A Molecular Link between Environmental Factors and Type 2 Diabetes," *Diabetes* 58, no. 12 (2009): 2718–25.

12. B. G. Dias and K. J. Ressler, "Parental Olfactory Experience Influences Behavior and Neural Structure in Subsequent Generations," *Nature Neuroscience* 17, no. 1 (2014): 89–96; R. Yehuda, N. P. Daskalakis, A. Lehrner, F. Desarnaud, H. N. Bader, et al., "Influences of Maternal and Paternal PTSD on Epigenetic Regulation of the Glucocorticoid Receptor Gene in Holocaust Survivor Offspring," *American Journal of Psychiatry* 171, no. 8 (2014): 872–80; R. Yehuda and A. Lehrner, "Intergenerational Transmission of Trauma Effects: Putative Role of Epigenetic Mechanisms," *World Psychiatry* 17, no. 3 (2018): 243–57; and A. Lehrner and R. Yehuda, "Cultural Trauma and Epigenetic Inheritance," *Development and Psychopathology* 30, no. 5 (2018): 1763–77.

13. An attuned other is someone who is sensing and tracking with physical, emotional, and cognitive changes as they are happening in another person. This person is tuning in to another, going beyond empathy to create a sense of unbroken connectedness as demonstrated through their affect or resonating responses.

14. Judith Herman, *Trauma and Recovery: The Aftermath of Violence—from Domestic Abuse to Political Terror* (New York: Basic Books, 1997).

15. Alia J. Crum, Modupe Akinola, Ashley Martin, and Sean Fath, "The Role of Stress Mindset in Shaping Cognitive, Emotional, and Physiological Responses to Challenging and Threatening Stress," *Anxiety, Stress, and Coping* 30, no. 4 (July 2017): 379–95; McGonigal, *Upside of Stress*; Daeun Park, Alisa Yu, Sarah E. Metz, Eli Tsukayama, Alia J. Crum, and Angela L. Duckworth, "Beliefs about Stress Attenuate the Relation among Adverse Life Events, Perceived Distress, and Self-Control," *Child Development* 89, no. 6 (November/December 2018): 2059–69.

16. Even though I specialize in trauma therapies, I too need help. I tell you this for three reasons: (1) I want you to know that I would never ask you to do something I would not do; (2) there is no shame in going to therapy or asking for help; (3) you never have to "arrive" somewhere where you no longer need people. In fact, the healthier I become as an adult, the easier it is for me to know when I can do things on my own and when I need someone to do them with me because that would just be more fun for us all.

17. EMDR, or Eye Movement Desensitization and Reprocessing, is a kind of therapy that uses our eyes (or sometimes tapping, buzzing, or noise) to help our brains resume normal memory processing and integration, which can often get stuck or blocked during and after a trauma. Of all kinds of therapies, it is one of the most effective forms of trauma treatment for processing a single traumatic event.

Chapter 4 Appearance and Image

1. Paul Schilder, *The Image and Appearance of the Human Body* (New York: Routledge, 1950), 11.

2. E. Stice, "Review of the Evidence for a Sociocultural Model of Bulimia Nervosa and an Exploration of the Mechanisms of Action," *Clinical Psychology Review* 14, no. 7 (1994): 633–61.

3. N. McKinley and L. Lyon, "Menopausal Attitudes, Objectified Body Consciousness, Aging Anxiety, and Body Esteem: European American Women's Body Experiences in Midlife," *Body Image* 5, no. 4 (2008): 375–80; G. Pearce, C. Thøgersen-Ntoumani, and J. Duda, "Body Image during the Menopausal Transition: A Systematic Scoping Review," *Health Psychology Review* 8, no. 4 (2014): 473–89; H. R. Rubinstein, and J. L. H. Foster, "'I Don't Know Whether It Is to Do with Age . . .': Making Sense of Menopause and the Body," *Journal of Health Psychology* 18, no. 2 (2013): 292.

4. S. L. Zaitsoff, R. Pullmer, and J. S. Coelho, "A Longitudinal Examination of Body-Checking Behaviors and Eating Disorder Pathology in a Community Sample of Adolescent Males and Females," *International Journal of Eating Disorders* 53, no. 11 (2020): 1836–43; D. C. Walker, D. A. Anderson, and T. Hildebrandt, "Body

Checking Behaviors in Men," *Body Image* 6, no. 3 (2009): 164–70; G. Waller, H. Cordery, E. Corstorphine, H. Hinrichsen, R. Lawson, V. Mountford, and K. Russell, *Cognitive Behavioral Therapy for Eating Disorders: A Comprehensive Treatment Guide* (Cambridge: Cambridge University Press, 2007); H. B. Murray, N. Tabri, J. J. Thomas, D. B. Herzog, D. L. Franko, and T. K. Eddy, "Will I Get Fat? 22-Year Weight Trajectories of Individuals with Eating Disorders," *International Journal of Eating Disorders* 50, no. 7 (2017): 739–47; J. D. Latner, "Body Checking and Avoidance among Behavioral Weight-Loss Participants," *Body Image* 5, no. 1 (2008): 91–98; J. M. Liechty and M. Lee, "Longitudinal Predictors of Dieting and Disordered Eating among Young Adults in the U.S.," *International Journal of Eating Disorders* 46, no. 8 (2013): 790–800.

5. B. L. Fredrickson and T. A. Roberts, "Objectification Theory: Towards Understanding Women's Lived Experience and Mental Health Risks," *Psychology of Women Quarterly* 21 (1997): 173–206.

6. Michael Levine and Niva Piran, "The Role of Body Image in the Prevention of Eating Disorders," *Body Image* 1, no. 1 (2004): 57–70; Jessie Menzel and Michael Levine, "Embodying Experiences and the Promotion of Positive Body Image: The Example of Competitive Athletics," in *Self-Objectification in Women: Causes, Consequences, and Counteractions*, ed. Rachel Calogero, Stacey Tantleff-Dunn, and J. Kevin Thompson (Washington, DC: American Psychological Association, 2011): 163–86.

7. Carol Gilligan, *In a Different Voice: Psychological Theory and Women's Development* (Cambridge, MA: Harvard University Press, 1982). See also Jill McLean Taylor, Carol Gilligan, and Amy M. Sullivan, *Between Voice and Silence: Women and Girls, Race and Relationship* (Cambridge, MA: Harvard University Press, 1995); and Lyn Brown and Carol Gilligan, *Meeting at the Crossroads: Women's Psychology and Girls' Development* (New York: Ballantine Books, 1992).

8. Gilligan, *In a Different Voice*, 24–63.

9. Mimi Nichter, *Fat Talk: What Girls and Their Parents Say about Dieting* (Cambridge, MA: Harvard University Press, 2000); and Lauren E. Britton et al., "Fat Talk and Self-Presentation of Body Image: Is There a Social Norm for Women to Self-Degrade?," *Body Image* 3, no. 3 (2006): 247–54.

10. Body positivity is a social movement developed in response to the overwhelming negative sociocultural messages about bodies and appearance, and it challenges restrictive and harmful body ideals. Instead of changing one's appearance to develop a positive body image, those within this movement suggest that a body needn't change for someone's body image to be positive. Broader social scripts about acceptable bodies (including through the development of the body positive movement itself) are a meaningful part of making that possible.

11. Sonya Renee Taylor, *The Body Is Not an Apology: The Power of Radical Self-Love* (Oakland, CA: Barrett-Koehler, 2018), 4.

12. Debora Badoud and Manos Tsakiris, "From the Body's Viscera to the Body's Image: Is There a Link between Interoception and Body Image Concerns?," *Neuroscience and Biobehavioral Reviews* 77 (June 2017): 237–46.

13. Rainer Schandry, "Heart Beat Perception and Emotional Experience," *Psychophysiology* 18, no. 4 (July 1981): 483–88.

14. Barnaby B. Dunn, Tim Dalgleish, Andrew D. Lawrence, and Alan D. Ogilvie, "The Accuracy of Self-Monitoring and Its Relationship to Self-Focused Attention in Dysphoria and Clinical Depression," *Journal of Abnormal Psychology* 116, no. 1 (February 2007): 1–15; Secondo Fassino, Andrea Pierò, Carla Gramaglia, and Giovanni Abbate-Daga, "Clinical, Psychopathological and Personality Correlates of Interoceptive Awareness in Anorexia Nervosa, Bulimia Nervosa and Obesity," *Psychopathology* 37, no. 4 (July/August 2004): 168–74; Olga Pollatos and Eleana Georgiou, "Normal Interoceptive Accuracy in Women with Bulimia Nervosa," *Psychiatry Research* 240 (June 2016): 328–32; Olga Pollatos, Anne-Lene Kurz, Jessica Albrecht, Tatjana Schreder, Anna Maria Kleemann, Veronika Schöpf, Rainer Kopietz, Martin Wiesmann, and Rainer Schandry, "Reduced Perception of Bodily Signals in Anorexia Nervosa," *Eating Behaviors* 9, no. 4 (December 2008): 381–88.

15. Rachel F. Rodgers, Siân A. McLean, and Susan J. Paxton, "When Seeing Is Not Believing: An Examination of the Mechanisms Accounting for the Protective Effect of Media Literacy on Body Image," *Sex Roles* 81, nos. 1–2 (2019): 87–96; Siân A. McLean, Susan J. Paxton, and Eleanor H. Wertheim, "Does Media Literacy Mitigate Risk for Reduced Body Satisfaction Following Exposure to Thin-Ideal Media?," *Journal of Youth and Adolescence* 45, no. 8 (2016): 1678–95; and Simon Wilksch, Niva Piran, and Tracy L. Tylka, *Media Literacy Interventions to Facilitate Positive Body Image and Embodiment* (Oxford: Oxford University Press, 2019).

Chapter 5 Feeling Feelings

1. Jaak Panksepp, "Brain Emotional Systems and Qualities of Mental Life," in *The Healing Power of Emotion: Effective Neuroscience, Development, and Clinical Practice*, ed. Diana Fosha, Daniel J. Siegel, and Marion F. Solomon (New York: Norton, 2009), 4.

2. Kenneth L. Davis and Jaak Panksepp, *The Emotional Foundations of Personality: A Neurobiological and Evolutionary Approach* (New York: Norton, 2018); Jaak Panksepp and Lucy Biven, *The Archaeology of Mind: Neuroevolutionary Origins of Human Emotions* (New York: Norton, 2012); Jaak Panksepp, *Affective Neuroscience: The Foundations of Human and Animal Emotions* (New York: Oxford University Press, 1998).

3. Hilary Jacobs Hendel, *It's Not Always Depression: A New Theory of Listening to Your Body, Discovering Core Emotions, and Reconnecting with Your Authentic Self* (New York: Penguin, 2018), 231.

4. Diana Fosha, *The Transforming Power of Affect: A Model for Accelerated Change* (New York: Basic Books, 2000); and Diana Fosha, "The Activation of Affective Change Processes in Accelerated Experiential-Dynamic Psychotherapy (AEDP)," *Comprehensive Handbook of Psychotherapy* 1 (2002): 309–44.

5. Brian Heilman, Gary Barker, and Alexander Harrison, *The Man Box: A Study on Being a Young Man in the US, UK, and Mexico* (Washington, DC: Promundo-US, 2017). Make time to read this report. It is published online and is both free and relatively free of dense academic language. The random and representative sample consisted of 3,673 men between the ages of eighteen and thirty

who were ethnically, sexually, and financially diverse and who resided in the US, the UK, and Mexico.

6. Heilman, Barker, and Harrison, *Man Box*, 21–22.

7. Heilman, Barker, and Harrison, *Man Box*, 32–53.

8. Heilman, Barker, and Harrison, *Man Box*, 32–53.

9. Heilman, Barker, and Harrison, *Man Box*, 36–45.

10. Heilman, Barker, and Harrison, *Man Box*, 36–45.

11. Diana Fosha, Daniel Siegel, and Marion Solomon, *The Healing Power of Emotion: Affective Neuroscience, Development, and Clinical Practice* (New York: Norton, 2009), 177 (see also 172–203).

12. If you're interested in learning more about this process, see Jaak Panksepp and Jules Panksepp, "Toward a Cross-Species Understanding of Empathy," *Trends in Neuroscience* 36, no. 8 (2013): 489–96; Marco Iacoboni and Gian Lenzi, "Mirror Neurons, the Insula, and Empathy," *Behavioral and Brain Sciences* 25, no. 1 (2002): 39–40; and Tania Singer and Claus Lamm, "The Social Neuroscience of Empathy," *Annals of the New York Academy of Sciences* 1156, no. 1 (2009): 81–96.

Chapter 6 You Are Not Broken

1. I have learned from friends who are disability rights activists that I too have a variety of disabilities—some of which I have had since birth and others which I've had for a limited time—but my ableism prevented me from labeling them as such. This is due to believing that disability looks only one way. We believe that a person is either disabled or not, causing us to miss the ability of those with disabilities. However, I am not the authority on disability. No one person is. This chapter represents what I know to this point, but my hope is that as I engage ableist ideas around and within me, my thinking will evolve. And so I write not from the position of one who knows the full picture but from the place where my lived experience intersects with my training and expertise.

To learn more, there are many great disability activists who have written and spoken extensively based on their expertise and lived experience, and no one voice is the authority when it comes to the body. For a start, see Rebekah Tausig, *Sitting Pretty: The View from My Ordinary Resilient Disabled Body* (New York: HarperOne, 2020); Alice Wong, ed., *Disability Visibility: First-Person Stories from the Twenty-First Century* (New York: Vintage, 2020); and Sonia Renee Taylor, *The Body Is Not an Apology: The Power of Radical Self-Love* (New York: Berrett-Koehler, 2018).

If you are disabled, have a disability, or are differently abled, I invite you to take from this chapter what works for you and to leave the rest behind.

2. G. Lorimer Moseley and Arnoud Arntz, "The Context of a Noxious Stimulus Affects the Pain It Evokes," *Pain* 133, nos. 1–3 (December 15, 2007): 64–71.

3. Ron Siegel, *The Mindfulness Solution: Everyday Practices for Everyday Problems* (New York: Guilford, 2009); Tami Simon, "Ron Siegel: The Psychophysiological Component in Healing," *Insights at the Edge*, 1:10, https://podcasts .apple.com/il/podcast/ronald-siegel-psychophysiological-component-in-healing /id307934313?i=1000422846354.

4. Richard A. Sternbach, "Psychophysiology of Pain," *International Journal of Psychiatry in Medicine* 6, nos. 1–2 (1975): 63–73; Gisèle Pickering and Stephen Gibson, eds., *Pain, Emotion and Cognition: A Complex Nexus* (New York: Springer, 2015); Juliane Traxler et al., "General versus Pain-Specific Cognitions: Pain Catastrophizing but Not Optimism Influences Conditioned Pain Modulation," *European Journal of Pain* 23, no. 1 (2019): 150–59; and Ronald D. Siegel, "Mindfulness in the Treatment of Trauma-Related Chronic Pain," in *Mindfulness-Oriented Interventions for Trauma: Integrating Contemplative Practices*, ed. Victoria M. Follette, John Briere, Deborah Rozelle, James W. Hopper, and David I. Rome (New York: Guilford, 2015), 257–72.

5. For more sophisticated and clinical versions of the process of pain, check out the following book: Ronald Siegel, Michael Urdang, and Douglas Johnson, *Back Sense: A Revolutionary Approach to Halting the Cycle of Chronic Back Pain* (New York: Harmony, 2013).

6. If you are suffering from pain, injury, or illness and have not seen a medical professional, please do so. Especially when the pain first comes on, it is important that we listen to rather than ignore what our bodies are telling us about what might not be going as planned in our system.

7. The research on using mindfulness as it pertains to stress-related diseases, pain, illness, and injury has historically been fairly fringe. But the research is now mainstream and is well validated scientifically for its effectiveness in treating, and in some cases eradicating, pain. See Siegel, Urdang, and Johnson, *Back Sense*; John Sarno, *The Mindbody Prescription: Healing the Body, Healing Pain* (New York: Little, Brown, 2007); Nicole Sachs, host, *The Cure for Chronic Pain*, podcast, https://podcasts.apple.com/us/podcast/the-cure-for-chronic-pain-with-nicole-sachs-lcsw/id1439580309; see also Curable, an app for pain relief (https://www.curablehealth.com/).

8. Flavia Mancini et al., "Pain Relief by Touch: A Quantitative Approach," *Pain* (Amsterdam) 155, no. 3 (2014): 635–42; Danielle Gentile et al., "Cancer Pain Relief after Healing Touch and Massage," *Journal of Alternative and Complementary Medicine* 24, nos. 9–10 (2018): 968–73; Flavia Mancini et al., "Touch Inhibits Subcortical and Cortical Nociceptive Responses," *Pain* (Amsterdam) 156, no. 10 (2015): 1936–44; and Carolyn M. Monroe, "The Effects of Therapeutic Touch on Pain," *Journal of Holistic Nursing* 27, no. 2 (2009): 85–92.

9. For additional information, see Laura Polloni, Emilia Ferruzza, Lucia Ranconi, Francesca Lazarotto, Alice Toniolo, Roberta Bonaguro, and Antonella Muraro, "Perinatal Stress and Food Allergy: A Preliminary Study on Maternal Reports," *Psychology, Health, and Medicine* 20, no. 6 (2015): 732–41.

10. Barbara Wróblewska et al., "Increased Prevalence of Eating Disorders as a Biopsychosocial Implication of Food Allergy," *PloS One* 13, no. 6 (2018): e0198607; Lilly Shanahan et al., "Are Children and Adolescents with Food Allergies at Increased Risk for Psychopathology?," *Journal of Psychosomatic Research* 77, no. 6 (2014): 468–73; and Angela M. Haas, "Feeding Disorders in Food Allergic Children," *Current Allergy and Asthma Reports* 10, no. 4 (2010): 258–64.

Chapter 7 The Body and Oppression

1. For an exceptional article on all this, especially from a clinical perspective, see Rae Johnson, Lucia Leighton, and Christine Caldwell, "The Embodied Experience of Microaggressions: Implications for Clinical Practice," *Journal of Multicultural Counseling and Development* 46, no. 3 (July 2018): 156–70.

2. Naomi I. Eisenberger, Matthew D. Lieberman, and Kipling D. Williams, "Does Rejection Hurt? An fMRI Study of Social Exclusion," *Science* 302, no. 5643 (October 2003): 290–92; Naomi I. Eisenberger and Matthew D. Lieberman, "Why Rejection Hurts: A Common Neural Alarm System for Physical and Social Pain," *Trends in Cognitive Sciences* 8, no. 7 (July 2004): 294–300.

3. For more on this, see Ibrahim A. Kira, Jeffrey S. Ashby, Linda Lewandowski, Abdul Wahhab Nasser Alawneh, Jamal Mohanesh, and Lydia Odenat, "Advances in Continuous Traumatic Stress Theory: Traumatogenic Dynamics and Consequences of Intergroup Conflict," *Psychology* 4, no. 4 (April 2013): 396–409.

4. Michael J. Scott and Stephen G. Stradling, "Post-Traumatic Stress Disorder without the Trauma," *British Journal of Clinical Psychology* 33, no. 1 (February 1994): 71–74.

5. Christine Caldwell, *Bodyfulness: Somatic Practices for Presence, Empowerment, and Waking Up in this Life* (Boulder, CO: Shambala, 2018), xxvii.

6. Because of these specific people in my life and what I have learned from those who do justice and advocacy work, I've learned that asking people who are different from us to educate us about themselves requires a significant social and emotional act of generosity from them. It can be a way we objectify another person and "use them" for ourselves and our gain, making them do the hard work of teaching when they are already doing the hard work of navigating systems built to ignore or outright oppress them. For that reason, I believe it's critical to note that these conversations took place with the consent of the person with whom I am in relationship and are not the result of approaching a person I don't know, without context, and asking them to tell me about their experiences of oppression. For that reason, these four people are also giving us a gift. By allowing us to read their stories and learn from them, they help us understand the ways we are like them, and so we feel our aloneness undone through their offering of themselves.

7. As I encounter Melaney's words again while writing this, I am struck by the similarity to what Ta-Nehisi Coates writes: "Disembodiment is a kind of terrorism, and the threat of it alters the orbit of all our lives and, like terrorism, this distortion is intentional." Ta-Nehisi Coates, *Between the World and Me* (New York: Spiegel & Grau, 2015), 114.

8. Heather uses they/them pronouns instead of the he/him or she/her pronouns with which we are culturally more familiar.

9. Robert M. Sellers and J. Nicole Shelton, "The Role of Racial Identity in Perceived Racial Discrimination," *Journal of Personality and Social Psychology* 84, no. 5 (2003): 1079–92; Lucia Bennett Leighton, "Trauma and the Body: Somatic Practices for Everyday Resiliency," in *Oppression and the Body: Roots, Resistance, and Resolutions*, ed. Christine Caldwell and Lucia Bennett Leighton (Berkeley: North Atlantic Books, 2018), 205–16.

Chapter 8 Pleasure and Enjoyment

1. Audre Lorde, *Sister Outsider: Essays and Speeches* (Berkeley: Ten Speed, 1984).

2. A fun adaptation is to finish the sentences or write the word association in a journal or secure document that you can revisit to see how your responses change over time. Another option is to draw three or more columns on the page to represent different points in time—such as puberty, when you first became sexually active, and the present.

3. This question comes from the work of psychotherapist Esther Perel in her book *Mating in Captivity: Unlocking Erotic Intelligence* (New York: Harper, 2007).

4. Audre Lorde, *Conversations with Audre Lorde*, ed. Joan Wylie Hall (Jackson: University Press of Mississippi, 2004), 99.

5. Lorde, *Sister Outsider*, 55–57.

6. Joseph Wittstock, "Further Validation of the Sexual-Spiritual Integration Scale: Factor Structure and Relations to Spirituality and Psychological Integration" (PhD diss., Loyola College, 2009), 27.

7. If you are interested in reading and learning more about power, control, and the body from a philosophical perspective, in addition to reading Audre Lorde's work, I recommend reading Michel Foucault. His writing is helpful for understanding how we come to internalize the systemic and political views of the body that end up impacting our sense of self. You might like to start with *The History of Sexuality* (New York: Pantheon, 1978) or *Discipline and Punish: The Birth of the Prison* (New York: Vintage Books, 1977), 311–30.

8. Dennis Dailey, "Sexual Expression and Ageing," in *The Dynamics of Ageing: Original Essays on the Processes and Experiences of Growing Old*, ed. D. Berghorn and D. Schafer (Boulder, CO: Westview, 1981), 311–30.

9. Sarah Moslener, *Virgin Nation: Sexual Purity and American Adolescence* (New York: Oxford University Press, 2015).

10. Antoinette Landor and Leslie Gordon Simons, "Why Virginity Pledges Succeed or Fail: The Moderating Effect of Religious Commitment versus Religious Participation," *Journal of Child and Family Studies* 26, no. 3 (2014): 1102–13; Linda Kay Klein, *Pure: Inside the Evangelical Movement That Shamed a Generation of Young Women and How I Broke Free* (New York: Touchstone, 2018); R. Mark Regnerus, *Forbidden Fruit: Sex and Religion in the Lives of American Teenagers* (New York: Oxford University Press, 2007).

11. Hannah Brückner and Peter Bearman, "After the Promise: The STD Consequences of Adolescent Virginity Pledges," *Journal of Adolescent Health* 36, no. 4 (2005): 271–78.

12. Michael Metz and Barry McCarthy, "The 'Good-Enough Sex' Model for Couple Sexual Satisfaction," *Sexual and Relationship Therapy* 22, no. 3 (2007): 351–62; Chyng Sun, Ana Bridges, Jennifer A. Johnson, and Matt Ezzell, "Pornography and the Male Sexual Script: An Analysis of Consumption and Sexual Relations," *Archives of Sexual Behavior* 45, no. 4 (2016): 983–94; Stephanie Gauvin and Caroline Pukall, "The SexFlex Scale: A Measure of Sexual Script

Flexibility When Approaching Sexual Problems in a Relationship," *Journal of Sex and Marital Therapy* 44, no. 4 (2018): 382–97.

13. Janet Rosenbaum, "Patient Teenagers? A Comparison of the Sexual Behavior of Virginity Pledgers and Matched Nonpledgers," *Pediatrics* 123, no. 1 (October 2009): 110–20.

14. Rosenbaum, "Patient Teenagers?," 113–15.

15. Argyro Caminis, Christopher Henrich, Vladislav Ruchkin, Mary Schwab-Stone, and Andrés Martin, "Psychosocial Predictors of Sexual Initiation and High-Risk Sexual Behaviors in Early Adolescence," *Child and Adolescent Psychiatry and Mental Health* 1, no. 14 (November 2007): 1–14; Lisa J. Crockett, C. Raymond Bingham, Joanne S. Chopak, and Judith Vicary, "Timing of First Sexual Intercourse: The Role of Social Control, Social Learning, and Problem Behavior," *Journal of Youth and Adolescence* 25, no. 1 (February 1996): 89–111; John S. Santelli, Javaid Kaiser, Lesley Hirsch, Alice Radosh, Linda Simkin, and Susan Middlestadt, "Initiation of Sexual Intercourse among Middle School Adolescents: The Influence of Psychosocial Factors," *Journal of Adolescent Health* 34, no. 3 (March 2004): 200–208.

16. Laura D. Lindberg and Isaac Maddow-Zimet, "Consequences of Sex Education on Teen and Young Adult Sexual Behaviors and Outcomes," *Journal of Adolescent Health* 51, no. 4 (2012): 332–38; Chelsea N. Proulx et al., "Associations of Lesbian, Gay, Bisexual, Transgender, and Questioning—Inclusive Sex Education with Mental Health Outcomes and School-Based Victimization in U.S. High School Students," *Journal of Adolescent Health* 64, no. 5 (2019): 608–14; Ashling Bourke et al., "Sex Education, First Sex and Sexual Health Outcomes in Adulthood: Findings from a Nationally Representative Sexual Health Survey," *Sex Education* 14, no. 3 (2014): 299–309; and Molly Secor-Turner et al., "Associations between Sexually Experienced Adolescents' Sources of Information about Sex and Sexual Risk Outcomes," *Sex Education* 11, no. 4 (2011): 489–500.

17. UNESCO, *Emerging Evidence, Lessons and Practice in Comprehensive Sexuality Education: A Global Review* (Paris: UNESCO, 2015); "Facing the Challenge of Adolescent Pregnancy in Zimbabwe," UNFPA, https://tinyurl.com/ncpfd4wt; "Child Marriage," UNICEF, April 2020, https://data.unicef.org/topic/child-protection/child-marriage; "Sexual and Reproductive Health Education Key to Tackle Child Marriage in Bangladesh," Girls Not Brides, March 13, 2013, https://tinyurl.com/35jsb58e.

18. John Bancroft et al., "The Dual Control Model: Current Status and Future Directions," *Journal of Sex Research* 46, nos. 2–3 (2009): 121–42.

19. Lori Brotto, *Better Sex through Mindfulness* (Vancouver: Greystone Books, 2018).

20. Asimina Lazaridou and Christina Kalogianni, "Mindfulness and Sexuality," *Sexual and Relationship Therapy* 28, nos. 1–2 (2013): 29–38; Frank G. Sommers, "Mindfulness in Love and Love Making: A Way of Life," *Sexual and Relationship Therapy* 28, nos. 1–2 (2013): 84–91; Jennifer A. Bossio et al., "Mindfulness-Based Group Therapy for Men with Situational Erectile Dysfunction: A Mixed-Methods Feasibility Analysis and Pilot Study," *Journal of Sexual Medicine* 15, no. 10 (2018): 1478–90; and Kyle R. Stephenson and John P. Welch, "Statistical Mediators of the Association between Mindfulness and Sexual Experiences

in Men with Impaired Sexual Function," *Archives of Sexual Behavior* 49, no. 5 (2020): 1545–57.

21. William H. Masters and Virginia E. Johnson, *Human Sexual Inadequacy* (Boston: Little, Brown, 1970); see also Linda Weiner and Constance Avery-Clark, *Sensate Focus in Sex Therapy: The Illustrated Manual* (New York: Routledge, 2017).

22. Emily Nagoski, "Pleasure Is the Measure," Medium, August 19, 2015, https://enagoski.medium.com/pleasure-is-the-measure-d8c5a2dff33f; see also Emily Nagoski, *Come As You Are: The Surprising New Science That Will Transform Your Sex Life* (New York: Simon & Schuster, 2015).

23. Mary Carlson and Felton Earls, "Psychological and Neuroendocrinological Sequelae of Early Social Deprivation in Institutionalized Children in Romania," *Annals of the New York Academy of Sciences* 807, no. 1 (1997): 419–28; Celia Beckett et al., "Do the Effects of Early Severe Deprivation on Cognition Persist into Early Adolescence? Findings from the English and Romanian Adoptees Study," *Child Development* 77, no. 3 (2006): 696–711; Patricia L. Blackwell, "The Influence of Touch on Child Development: Implications for Intervention," *Infants and Young Children* 13, no. 1 (2000): 25–39.

24. Tiffany Field, "Touch for Socioemotional and Physical Well-Being: A Review," *Developmental Review* 30, no. 4 (December 2010): 367–83.

25. Tiffany Field, *Touch* (Cambridge, MA: MIT, 2014).

26. Esther Perel, "Why Eroticism Should Be Part of Your Self-Care Plan," *Esther Perel* (blog), https://estherperel.com/blog/eroticism-self-care-plan.

27. Wittstock, "Further Validation of the Sexual-Spiritual Integration Scale," 27.

28. Chuck MacKnee, "Profound Sexual Encounters among Practicing Christians: A Phenomenological Analysis," *Journal of Psychology and Theology* 30, no. 3 (2002): 234.

29. Paul Giblin, "Men Reconnecting Spirituality and Sexuality," *Journal of Spirituality in Mental Health* 16, no. 2 (2014): 79.

30. MacKnee, "Profound Sexual Encounters," 234.

Chapter 9 Holy Flesh

1. Richard Rohr, "Journey to the Center," Center for Action and Contemplation, December 28, 2015, https://cac.org/journey-to-the-center-2015-12-28.

2. I am neither a theologian nor a historian, but I have read scholars whose works span thousands of years and who write about these themes with more depth and nuance than I could hope to. I have done my best to summarize some of their ideas, but if you want more, there is much out there for you to discover. Start now, especially with the work of liberation theologians, womanist and Black theologians, and feminist theologians. Their work poignantly describes how the social and economic positionality of an individual or a group is directly correlated with how they interpret Christian Scripture, and how interpretations by those with the most social power often miss the heart of the gospel. You might start with one of these: Gustavo Gutiérrez and Gerhard Ludwig Müller, *On the Side of the Poor: The Theology of Liberation* (New York: Orbis Books, 2015); James Cone,

A Black Theology of Liberation (New York: Orbis Books, 2010); Mitzi Smith, ed., *I Found God in Me: A Womanist Biblical Hermeneutics Reader* (Eugene, OR: Cascade Books, 2015); Wil Gafney, *Womanist Midrash: A Reintroduction to the Women of the Torah and the Throne* (Louisville: Westminster John Knox, 2017); or Rosemary Radford Reuther, *Sexism and God-Talk: Toward a Feminist Theology* (Boston: Beacon, 1993).

3. René Descartes, *Meditations on First Philosophy*, trans. J. Cottingham (Cambridge: Cambridge University Press, 1996); Plato, *Alcibiades I*, trans. Benjamin Jowett, https://www.gutenberg.org/files/1676/1676-h/1676-h.htm; Plato, *The Republic*, trans. Benjamin Jowett, https://www.gutenberg.org/files/1497 /1497-h/1497-h.htm; and Lisa Isherwood and Elizabeth Stuart, *Introducing Body Theology* (Sheffield: Sheffield Academic Press, 1998).

4. Marcella Althaus-Reid, "Doing a Theology from Disappeared Bodies: Theology, Sexuality, and the Excluded Bodies of the Discourses of Latin American Liberation Theology," in *The Oxford Handbook of Feminist Theology*, ed. Sheila Briggs and Mary McClintock Fulkerson (New York: Oxford University Press, 2011); and Isherwood and Stuart, *Introducing Body Theology*.

5. Mark Charles and Soong-Chan Rah, *Unsettling Truths: The Ongoing, Dehumanizing Legacy of the Doctrine of Discovery* (Downers Grove, IL: InterVarsity, 2019); Rosemary Radford Ruether, *Feminist Theologies: Legacy and Prospect* (Minneapolis: Fortress, 2007); Rosemary Radford Ruether, *Gaia and God: An Ecofeminist Theology of Earth Healing* (San Francisco: HarperSanFrancisco, 1992); Emily L. Silverman et al., *Voices of Feminist Liberation: Writings in Celebration of Rosemary Radford Ruether* (Bristol, CT: Equinox, 2012); and Marilú R. Salazar, "Experiences and Reflections on a Latin American Feminist Theology of Liberation Using an Ecofeminist Key Toward an Indigenous Women's Perspective: Experiences and Reflections on a Latin American Feminist Theology of Liberation," *Ecumenical Review* 62, no. 4 (2010): 411–22.

6. Diana Butler Bass, *Grounded: Finding God in the World—A Spiritual Revolution* (San Francisco: HarperOne, 2015), 13.

7. Bass, *Grounded*, 14.

8. Bass, *Grounded*, 25.

9. Bass, *Grounded*, 25.

10. Rabbi Arthur Waskow, "Why YAH/YHWH," The Shalom Center, April 14, 2004, https://theshalomcenter.org/content/why-yahyhwh.

11. If you have ever taken a Kundalini yoga class, this also sounds a lot like the Breath of Fire.

12. Arthur Waskow, *Prayer as if Earth Really Matters*, ed. John Hart (Chichester, UK: Wiley & Sons, 2017), 389.

13. Stephanie Paulsell, *Honoring the Body: Meditations on a Christian Practice* (Minneapolis: Fortress, 2019), 6.

14. Paulsell, *Honoring the Body*, 7.

15. Isherwood and Stuart, *Introducing Body Theology*, 62.

16. My summary of these comments is drawn from *Dictionary of Paul and His Letters*, ed. Gerald F. Hawthorne, Ralph P. Martin, and Daniel G. Reid (Downers Grove, IL: IVP Academic, 1993), a resource that academics with PhDs specializing in New Testament studies and Paul's Letters have told me is the most balanced

and useful dictionary for supporting interpretation of these passages. This is also supported by the work of Isherwood and Stuart in their book *Introducing Body Theology*.

17. To learn more about parts, I recommend exploring the work of Richard Schwartz and Internal Family Systems Theory, from which I first learned about the parts we all carry inside us. Some resources to get you started include Richard Schwartz, *Greater Than the Sum of Our Parts: Discovering Your True Self through Internal Family Systems Therapy* (audiobook, Sounds True, 2018), and *No Bad Parts: Healing Trauma and Restoring Wholeness with the Internal Family Systems Model* (audiobook, Sounds True, 2021).

18. Richard J. Erickson, "Flesh," in Hawthorne, Martin, and Reid, *Dictionary of Paul and His Letters*, 303–6.

19. "Christ for Others," Together at One Altar, https://www.togetheratone altar.catholic.edu.au/live/christ-for-others.

20. Richard Rohr, "The First Incarnation," Center for Action and Contemplation, February 21, 2019, https://cac.org/the-first-incarnation-2019-02-21; see also Richard Rohr, *The Universal Christ: How a Forgotten Reality Can Change Everything We See, Hope for, and Believe* (Colorado Springs: Convergent Books, 2019).

Chapter 10 Living as a Body

1. Daniel N. Stern, *The Present Moment in Psychotherapy and Everyday Life* (New York: Norton, 2004), xiii.

2. Richard Rohr, "Journey to the Center," Center for Action and Contemplation, December 28, 2015, https://cac.org/journey-to-the-center-2015-12-28.

3. Jerome Lubbe, personal e-mail communication, March 11, 2020. See also Jerome Lubbe, *The Brain-Based Enneagram: You Are Not a Number* (self-pub., 2020), which is based on his development of a model by the same name. He is the founder of Thrive Neuro, a medical practice specializing in unresolved and complex cases.

4. Daniel M. Wolpert, Zoubin Ghahramani, and J. Randall Flanagan, "Perspectives and Problems in Motor Learning," *Trends in Cognitive Sciences* 5, no. 11 (November 2001): 487.

5. Kelly McGonigal, *The Joy of Movement: How Exercise Helps Us Find Happiness, Hope, Connection, and Courage* (New York: Avery, 2019), 5, 191–94.

6. Luana G. Leal, Magno A. Lopes, and Miguel L. Batista Jr., "Physical Exercise-Induced Myokines and Muscle-Adipose Tissue Crosstalk: A Review of Current Knowledge and the Implications for Health and Metabolic Diseases," *Frontiers in Physiology* 9, no. 1307 (September 2018), https://www.frontiersin .org/articles/10.3389/fphys.2018.01307/full.

7. McGonigal, *Joy of Movement*, 4–5.

8. Adee Braun, "Looking to Quell Sexual Urges? Consider the Graham Cracker," *The Atlantic*, January 15, 2014, https://www.theatlantic.com/health /archive/2014/01/looking-to-quell-sexual-urges-consider-the-graham-cracker /282769.

9. What the diet industry doesn't tell us, the scientific literature about dieting has known for a long time: dieting does not work. Not only do most people regain

the weight they lost during a diet, in some cases one- to two-thirds of dieters regain more weight than they lost on the diet. A diet puts the body into starvation mode. When the body is starving, the survival process of retaining nutrients begins. Because of the survival response related to restricted food intake, it's more likely we will binge eat to try to make up for the calories we had previously restricted. But the diet industry blames individuals for not working hard enough at their diets (be more rigorous, have fewer cheat days, deprive ourselves more), without us ever knowing that it's false advertising. Traci Mann et al., "Medicare's Search for Effective Obesity Treatments: Diets Are Not the Answer," *American Psychologist* 62, no. 3 (2007): 220–33; A. J. Tomiyama et al., "Low Calorie Dieting Increases Cortisol, *Psychosomatic Medicine* 72, no. 4 (2010): 357–64; Priya Sumithran et al., "Long-Term Persistence of Hormonal Adaptations to Weight Loss," *New England Journal of Medicine* 365, no. 17 (2011): 1597–604; Rachel Larder and Stephen O'Rahilly, "Guts over Glory—Why Diets Fail," *Nature Medicine* 18, no. 5 (2012): 666; Yoni Freedhoff, "No, 95 Percent of People Don't Fail Their Diets," *U.S. News*, November 17, 2014, https://health.usnews.com/health-news/blogs/eat -run/2014/11/17/no-95-percent-of-people-dont-fail-their-diets; Christy Harrison, *Anti-Diet: Reclaim Your Time, Well-Being and Happiness with Intuitive Eating* (New York: Little, Brown, 2019).

10. Evelyn Tribole and Elyse Resch, "Ten Principles of Intuitive Eating," The Original Intuitive Eating Pros, https://www.intuitiveeating.org/10-principles-of -intuitive-eating.

11. Andrew Ward and Traci Mann, "Don't Mind If I Do: Disinhibited Eating under Cognitive Load," *Journal of Personality and Social Psychology* 78, no. 4 (April 2000): 753–63.

12. Christine Caldwell, "Mindfulness and Bodyfulness: A New Paradigm," *Journal of Contemplative Inquiry* 1, no. 1 (2014): 82.

With Gratitude

A book is a kind of body, and like each of us, it is raised into being through and for community.

To the Sḵwx̱wú7mesh (Squamish), X^wməθkʷəy̓əm (Musqueam), and Səl̓ilwətaʔɬ (Tsleil-Waututh) people on whose unceded traditional territories I live and wrote this book: Thank you for your stewardship of the land and for teaching me about my connection to all life.

To my soul sisters Alexandra, Kelsey, and Lisa: It is because of you I am certain that God exists and that we have found Her in the right here and in all the places I would have been too afraid to go alone. I don't want to discover any of the magical things, new and ancient, without you by my side in this life. Thank you for loving me, and this book, into being through our friendship.

To my beloved friends: I am so glad I don't have to do life without each of you. I have won the lottery with our friendship. The specific ways you care for me, encourage me to unfold, witness my growth and pain, support from near and far, and have patience with my delayed replies to emails and texts—thank you for all of it.

To Mike: You have offered me a kind of kinship most people doubt exists. Thank you for buying a ticket when you heard I was in an accident, for connecting me to my agent, and most importantly, for letting me in close. In so many ways, this book is here because of you.

To my family: Thank you for supporting me in all the quiet, invisible ways you do so that I can do what I love to do in the world. I love you.

To my clients: Because of you, I know true courage, have hope for healing, and know myself more fully.

To early readers and shapers of the book Stephanie, Heather, Kurt, Kelsey, Melaney, and Kathy: Your encouragement, additions, editorial insight, attention to what was missing and what was already there, and friendship through it has made me richer.

To the community of The Liturgists: Thank you for listening, for using your voices, and for building a community within which I can learn, grow, know, and unknow.

To everyone who gave their stories for this book: Your generosity is unmatched. I'm so humbled to know you.

To Katelyn and Melisa: thank you for believing in me and in this book.

To my agent, Angela: Your wise and kind presence has been a gift. Thanks for believing in me and this book, even in its earlier phases that looked much different than this.

To Kevin, my love: You are both my home and the constant reminder to return lovingly to the home within myself. Because of who you are and how you love me, I can move forward into all the things that make me more fully me, knowing no matter what happens I am completely loved by you already, just as I am.

About the Author

Hillary L. McBride (PhD, University of British Columbia) is a licensed therapist, an award-winning researcher, and a sought-after speaker who specializes in embodiment. She formerly co-hosted *The Liturgists* podcast (averages four million downloads per year), hosts the *Other People's Problems* podcast, and has appeared on other popular podcasts. McBride's clinical and academic work has been recognized by the American Psychological Association and the Canadian Psychological Association. She teaches in the department of counseling psychology at the University of British Columbia and has a private counseling practice in Vancouver. McBride is the author of *Mothers, Daughters, and Body Image* and coeditor of *Embodiment and Eating Disorders*. Visit her website at hillarylmcbride.com.